CLASSIC
RACING
ENGINES

Praise for Karl Ludvigsen's *Classic Racing Engines*

"This book is everything you would expect it to be. . . . Ludvigsen clearly cares a great deal about his subject and makes the technical information engaging and enlightening. He manages to provide just enough colour about the people and races to prevent the technical information from becoming too heavy for all but experts to read."

—*Formula One Magazine*

"Ludvigsen's engineering background and longstanding interest in engines really come through in the way he unerringly focuses on the main details and innovations of each powerplant, along with the technical shortcomings that were obstacles to the engine's success."

—Csaba Csere, *Car and Driver*

"The book pulls no punches and wastes no time on inconsequentials. Like the engines it describes, space is not for wasting. All 50 chapters are tightly presented with riveting text, informative photographs and specification tables."

—Richard Gunn, *Classic Car Weekly*

CLASSIC
RACING
ENGINES

Expert technical analysis of fifty of
the greatest motorsport power units

KARL LUDVIGSEN

Foreword by Eiji Taguchi

Bentley Publishers, a division of Robert Bentley, Inc.
1734 Massachusetts Avenue
Cambridge, MA 02138 USA
800-423-4595 / 617-547-4170

Information that makes
the difference®

BentleyPublishers®
.com

ISBN 978-0-8376-1734-3
Job code: H635-02

Library of Congress Cataloging-in-Publication Data

Names: Ludvigsen, Karl E., author.
Title: Classic racing engines : expert technical analysis of fifty of the
    greatest motorsport power units / by Karl Ludvigsen ; foreword by Eiji
    Taguchi.
Description: Cambridge, Massachusetts : Bentley Publishers, [2017] | Includes
    index.
Identifiers: LCCN 2017026471 | ISBN 9780837617343 (hardcover)
Subjects: LCSH: Automobiles--Motors--History. | Automobiles,
    Racing--Motors--Design and construction--History.
Classification: LCC TL210 .L813 2017 | DDC 629.25/04--dc23
LC record available at https://lccn.loc.gov/2017026471

Front cover photo by Neill Bruce

The paper used in this publication is acid free and meets the requirements of the National Standard for Information Sciences-Permanence of Paper for Printed Library Materials. ∞

Manufactured in the United States of America.

*In memory of my wonderfully creative son
Miles Elliot Ludvigsen*

CONTENTS

INTRODUCTION

I may as well admit it. If I were selected for a landing party to another planet my first request on arriving would be, 'Take me to your racing-engine builders.' I love racing engines and I love visiting and talking to the people who make them.

In the country of my birth, the United States, few trips to Los Angeles failed to include a stop at Meyer-Drake, where I gossiped about racing engines with Leo Goossen, great and generous designer of Millers and Offys, and Dale and John Drake. I've been to Paxton where the Granatellis developed the fabulous Novi V8s. Down the coast at All-American Racers, John Miller made big power for Dan Gurney.

Travers and Coon at Traco in Los Angeles did for Chevrolets what Keith Black did for Chryslers; I visited both. At Reventlow Automobiles I saw the desmodromic Scarab Formula 1 engine that both Goossen and Traco helped design and make. Back in Indianapolis, Louie and Sonny Meyer were building and developing the four-cam Ford Indy engine.

In Detroit I visited the 'skunk works' of the big companies where Zora Arkus-Duntov invented new engines for Chevrolet, and Ford made pushrod Fairlanes for Indianapolis Lotuses. GM, believe it or not, built special overhead-cam Buick V8s for Mickey Thompson's 1962 Indy effort, although Mickey never used them. In Livonia was McLaren Engines, where Gary Knutson showed me his blown Offys capable of more than 1,000 horsepower. His data appears in this book.

Italy, of course, is horsepower country. When Ferrari racing director Eugenio Dragoni told me about an engine in which he was interested, I asked him where his dynamometer was. 'In my garage,' he said. Naturally. Isn't everyone's?

I've seen exotic Lancia and BMW engines at Nardi, tiny high-revving V8s at Giannini near Rome, potent Fiat-based twin-cam engines at Stanguellini, modified straight-eight 1½-litre Talbot engines at Platé in Milan and brilliant small-displacement screamers at OSCA and Abarth. At Autodelta Carlo Chiti showed me the stunning flat-12s that powered the successful Alfa Romeo 33-series sports-racers and Formula 1 Brabhams; they're in this book.

My Maserati racing-engine visits were first in the 250F days and later in the V8 and V12 era. At Ferrari I've poked and prodded the V6, V12 and flat-12 racing engines. In fact I managed to get on the wrong side of Enzo Ferrari (fairly easy to do, apparently) not for taking pictures of the dismantled boxer 312B, but for publishing them! Some appear in the following pages.

In France I called on Moteur Moderne in Paris (remember their racing V6?) and on Amédée Gordini and Bugatti in the twilight of their great years. I visited Matra at Vélizy, there to see some of the finest racing V12s ever made.

Renault Gordini was carrying on the great

name with racing V6s for Formula 2 and Le Mans, both at Alpine in Dieppe and at the Gordini works near Paris. There I was introduced to the natal stages of the turbocharged Renault that was to revolutionise Formula 1 racing, an engine described in this book.

My visits to Germany were early enough to include Bremen in the heyday of the fuel-injected 16-valve Borgward four (I later owned and raced a Borgward 1500RS). In Ingolstadt I met Richard Küchen and his magnificent four-cam Formula 2 V8. In Munich I became friends with Alex von Falkenhausen and studied his own engine projects as well as his highly successful BMW racing fours.

At Mercedes-Benz I saw the 300SL six on the test bench and learned more of the secrets of the 1954–55 Silver Arrows. Rudy Uhlenhaut showed me where the rotary engines for the C111s were made. And at AMG I peered inside the special V6s of the Mercedes-Benz C-Class racers in the German Touring Car Championship, and the V12s and V8s of the CLK sports-racing cars.

Many Porsche visits included the original four-cam Carrera workshop, the creation of the 1½-litre flat-8 for Formula 1 in 1962, the 917's Type 912 engine and the later turbocharged flat-6s and flat-12s.

At Zakspeed near Cologne, Erich Zakowski explained the high-pressure Ford-based engines of his racing Capris, two of which I raced at Hockenheim. He was co-operating with our Ford Motorsport projects, as was Dr Schrick with the development of our RS1700T rally car engine.

In Liechtenstein, Max Heidegger built some of the hottest BMW engines. On my visit I saw the

Opposite: In the drafting room above Drake Engineering in Los Angeles, Karl Ludvigsen discusses racing engine design with Miller, Novi and Offy engineering wizard Leo Goossen.

Above right: During a 1978 visit to Mugen, the company founded by Hirotoshi Honda, the author photographed the son of the founder of the Honda Motor Company.

Mugen subsequently became a leading Formula 1 engine builder.

Right: The first author to reveal the secrets of the remarkable pushrod V8 that won Indianapolis for Mercedes-Benz and the Penske team in 1994, Ludvigsen pictured the engine's creators during a visit to Ilmor: Paul Morgan, left, and Mario Illien.

turbocharged in-line 1½-litre six he hoped McLaren would race in Formula 1. In both Switzerland and Germany Michael May revealed the turbocharging advances he had imparted to BMW and Toyota.

Tony Rudd and Aubrey Woods at BRM at Bourne in Britain explained their 3-litre Formula 1 V12 development. I later saw Tony at Lotus where he was developing that company's inclined four for both production and racing. Brian Hart showed me the versatile two-litre four with which he first made his reputation as an independent engine builder.

I missed the salad days of Coventry Climax, although with Wally Hassan and Harry Mundy I discussed their designs as well as some new concepts, such as a broad-arrow W12, that Harry was pursuing. I still have the outline of the book on racing engines that Harry and I intended to write together. I think we each thought that the other was writing it!

My Cosworth visits began in the years of the DFV and BDA and continued through the 3.9-litre Group C DFL V8 of the early 1980s, which I encouraged Ford to support financially. Paul Morgan and Mario Illien left Cosworth to set up Ilmor Engineering, which I called upon in its very provisional first months. They now have a wonderful plant for making Mercedes-Benz racing engines.

In Japan in the late 1970s I paid a call on Hirotoshi Honda, who then was preparing engines for Japan's Formula 2 series. In a back room he showed me the disembowelled engines of Honda Formula 1 cars. They were stored there awaiting restoration and rebirth to strut their stuff at classic-racing events.

This was the background when Darryl Reach of Haynes suggested the idea of a book about racing engines. He left it largely to me to propose a list for coverage. I tried to range widely over eras and types of racing in coming up with the highly personal selection in these pages. I hope everyone will find at least some of their favourites discussed, as well as some unusual engines from the past.

Where helpful I have not hesitated to draw on engine descriptions I have written for such as *Car and Driver* and *Road & Track*. Many thanks to them and to others for encouraging my work in this field. Some descriptions are also adapted from my books on Mercedes-Benz, Porsche and Ilmor; from the last-named the first part of this Introduction is derived. I couldn't think of anything more appropriate.

At the Ludvigsen Library I appreciated the help of my colleagues Paul Parker and Miranda Carpenter. I owe warm thanks as well to Tony Merrick, racing-car restorer extraordinaire, who consented to look over the text to help catch the inevitable glaring gaffes. I am most grateful, Tony. Needless to say, all remaining errors of fact and interpretation are mine.

Many thanks are owed to all those who assisted me with information for this book. Ermanno Cozza of Maserati resolved some details of Maserati specifications, and Riccardo Andreoni did likewise at Ferrari. Tony Rudd helped with information on the BRM V8, and Ted Cutting checked and improved my copy on the racing Aston Martin engine. Elvira Ruocco of Alfa Romeo found photos of the 33TT12 and its engine. Yoshihiko Aoyama, general manager of the Honda Collection Hall at Twin Ring Motegi, helped with data on the Honda GP engines. Thanks to him this book contains the first detailed description of the remarkable 1965 Honda V12.

Speaking of Honda, I am very pleased to be able to open the book with a thoughtful contribution by Eiji Taguchi, who is not only a great car enthusiast but also an expert racing engine designer. Born in Tokyo in 1938, Taguchi-san joined Honda in 1961 after completing his university studies. In 1964 he moved to Honda's Research and Development Company to design engines for both production and racing cars.

Among designs led by Eiji Taguchi are Honda's first-generation Accord with its stratified-charge CVCC engine and, in 1966–67, the racing RA273E engine and gearbox. From 1982 to 1998 he designed Honda's turbocharged 1½-litre V6, the 3½-litre V10 and V12 GP engines and a 3-litre V8 for Formula 3000. Taguchi-san was also responsible for the 3½- and 3-litre V10 Formula 1 engines built by the Mugen company. He retired from Honda in 1998. In 1999 he joined Sauber Petronas Engineering AG to lead engine design. He is with Ricardo in the UK at the time of writing. Thus his views on the present and future of racing-engine design carry special authority.

Karl Ludvigsen
Islington
London
2001

FOREWORD
by Eiji Taguchi

Racing Engines Past and Future

When we unfold the pages of history and look back to the circumstances of the era in which the automobile was created, we are reminded that the first race took place in 1895. It was a race on public roads, as there were as yet no special circuits for the exclusive use of racing cars. The winning Panhard-Levassor, a two-cylinder car of 4 horsepower at 800rpm, completed a round trip of 732 miles (1,171km) from Paris to Bordeaux at an average speed of 24km/h.

Since then motor racing has been evolving continuously for more than a century, except for the periods during the two world wars. What kinds of goals spurred the engineers of the past to try to make highly competitive engines? The goal was 'to win', which is simple and clear enough, but their opponents also had the same idea. Thus they had to assume that their opposition had made similar efforts in their research and development, hoping to take a step forward – or even half a step.

In my view the essential elements that can be considered as the key racing-engine technologies from the perspective of history are the following:

1. The reduction of losses due to mechanical friction

Engineers made much use of ball and roller bearings, and sought to optimise the ratio of the stroke to the bore. Also, the displacement per single cylinder evolved toward a range between 180 and 400cc. There is a unique exception in the success of the light and compact Coventry Climax 2½-litre 4-cylinder engine, with its 625cc cylinder. In this instance the chassis built by Cooper with its mid-engined layout – plus the expert abilities of Jack Brabham – played a major part.

2. The improvement of charging efficiency

Reintroducing the 4-valve combustion chamber improved charging or volumetric efficiency. Also, the design of the inlet port was altered to achieve the major objective of exploitation of the best use of the inertia of the incoming gas to improve aspiration.

3. Efficiency in reducing weight

Weight was reduced by, for example, employing water jackets made of thin sheet metal, and the introduction of high-strength materials following new developments.

Actor James Garner, left, is among the onlookers as Richie Ginther drives a 1966 Honda Grand Prix car into the paddock at Monza. Its shrieks cause some nearby to protect their eardrums.

4. The development of the fuelling system
Progress from carburettors to fuel injection has improved performance.

5. The use of electronics
In the modern era the development, rapid introduction and expansion of the application of electronics have all greatly improved overall engine performance, especially as regards fuel consumption, an increasingly important parameter.

All the above are key technologies. An engine can never prevail when only one of them is excellent. Achieving a balance among all of them at a high level is absolutely essential.

As is well known, until very recently many technologies that have been used in racing have already been running on the roads as well, as if they were quite banal. Lately, however, production vehicles have been subject to retrograde development. Engine management is a good example. In order to pass the increasingly strict regulations that control exhaust emissions, engine-management progress has been remarkable. But it has not been able to contribute to specific engine performance.

What role has Honda played in this story? Based on the evidence of the results achieved, it may be said that its role was as a leader in the use of high-speed engines in all of these periods. As the essential elements of its technology one could mention, of course, the use of multiple cylinders, the shaping of an inlet port that can draw in a lot of air, and the enlargement of the effective aperture area of the inlet and exhaust valves.

The engineering of the support provided for the roller bearings used in the bottom end has been an essential element of Honda technology. Honda can take pride in the invention of the control technique by which an engine can achieve its optimum performance, including a fuel-injection system which was an in-house design. Of course, research into materials is another important element. In particular the development of materials with high strength has been carried out continuously by Honda since the 1960s.

In recent years development has been dedicated to durability and reliability. For each new engine, long-distance circuit testing has become commonplace from the outset. With other engine makers following Honda's example in this respect, it is evident that the frequency of blown-up engines in F1 racing has been greatly reduced.

Above all, the marriage of science with enthusiasm is the driving force. Success depends on how you weigh their degree of importance.

It is quite a tricky matter to forecast the direction that racing-engine technology may take in the future, but it is difficult to envisage that there will be a sudden leap. If there is, what kind of factors may be considered? I will suggest a few.

1. The question of whether rapid combustion can be achieved by creating a really compact combustion chamber offering an improvement in combustion
Generally, the present shape of the four-valve-type combustion chamber is the pent-roof type or a modification thereof. Around the mid-1960s, BMW experimentally employed a radial four-valve head for the four-cylinder engine that it used in Formula 2 at that time, the 'Apfelbeck' engine described in this book. In this system the four valves are positioned in a radial formation, producing a semi-spherical combustion chamber.

In the world of motorcycling, the 250cc single-cylinder Honda was produced on a commercial scale, with an engine fitted with a similar radial-valve head. Elaborate design techniques and

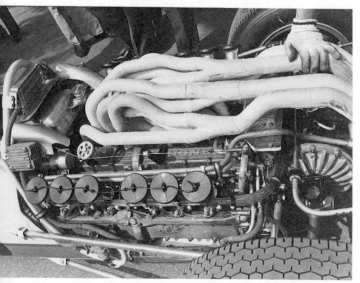

Designed by Eiji Taguchi, the engine of the 1966 Honda RA273E was a V12 with its cylinder banks set at 90°. It produced 400bhp at 10,500rpm.

difficulties are involved in creating an ideal combustion chamber of multi-cylinder semi-spherical type, but it is thought that this will be one of the chosen techniques.

2. Further evolution of control technology

Peak engine revolutions have reached the present level by exploiting the changes that have already been mentioned. From this point on, proceeding on the assumption of 10 cylinders, we are now being catapulted into the world of 18,000rpm and, when shifting up, 500rpm higher.

Drivers demand not only top-end performance but also medium-speed torque at one and the same time. Therefore the designer should invent something to provide that. Among the systems that may facilitate this, a technology that achieves a more variable control than at present will be necessary. Also, in order to help the engine operate at its optimum level whatever the conditions may be, it may become necessary to be able to control the water cooling, the temperature and/or the pressure of the oil and/or fuel.

3. It might be possible to make a much more optimal design

In today's world of design and development, the drawings that were used in former years are nowhere to be seen. Everything is done by computer design. Functionally, both two-dimensional drawings and three-dimensional sketches can easily be drawn on the screen.

A number of other techniques are available to support engineering in the course of the design process. Among these are the forecasting of horsepower, the formation and the nature of the mixture of fuel and air after they are ejected from the injector, and the flow condition of the coolant in the interior passages of a complex engine. In addition the calculation of the degree of strength of all components will become feasible. These are among the techniques which will make it possible to produce a racing engine of high efficiency which also has high reliability and power.

So far we have been considering engines from a number of different angles. However, needless to say you do not have the winning car just by virtue of its engine. This book provides ample examples of that.

I think it is important to harmonise the essential elements of the total 'package' at a higher level: namely the engine, the chassis, the special aerodynamic features, the tyres and the skill of the driver. When each of the above is focused upon, it is seen as having its own strong individual character. I believe that results will surely follow. A magnificent symphony will be heard, harmonised by the skills and abilities of the conductor who combines these essential elements.

Taguchi's RA273E was further developed for the 1967 season, during which it was photographed at Zandvoort by Ted Eves.

1913

PEUGEOT L3 3-LITRE FOUR

New designs from Peugeot just before the outbreak of the Great War transformed the technology of the racing engine. Formerly a backward provincial car maker, Peugeot regained momentum in 1910 when two formerly-separate branches of the family firm were reunited to create SA des Automobiles and Cycles Peugeot – the forebear of the Peugeot company we know today. Peugeot became France's second-largest motor company after the fast-growing Renault.

Robert Peugeot, a son of the company's co-founder, was responsible for the implementation of Peugeot's racing programme. He set up a separate dedicated unit on the west side of Paris at Suresnes to produce racing cars. The racing Peugeots were assembled there from parts made by skilled subcontractors throughout the Paris periphery. This was a new idea, as *The Automobile Engineer* explained in 1914: 'The Peugeot Company determined that it would make a great name in racing regardless of cost, and consequently the special racing factory was set up and the problem of racing car building dealt with as an entirely separate and complete business.'

Robert Peugeot had strong support from racing drivers Jules Goux and Georges Boillot, as well as from Paolo Zuccarelli who had just come over from the successful Hispano-Suiza team. Their radical ideas about engine design were interpreted by a 26-year-old Swiss engineer, Ernest Henry. Geneva-born Henry had contributed to the advanced Swiss Picker engines that powered racing hydroplanes.

This team created two new racers for the 1912 season: a 7.6-litre Grand Prix car and a smaller 3-litre model, the L3, to suit the *Voiturette* category, which since 1911 was for cars of that engine size. In its first embodiment the 1912 Peugeot 3-litre was unsuccessful, but when revised for 1913, as the L3 bis (referred to here as the L3 for simplicity's sake), it was a fine performer out of all proportion to its size.

These Peugeots were the first cars of any kind to combine a vee-inclined overhead-valve cylinder head with four valves per cylinder and twin overhead camshafts – the hallmarks of many later high-performance engines. To these characteristics the L3 added a train of gears to drive the camshafts, another ingredient that was to be common to most purebred racing engines for decades to come. In 1912 the Peugeot engines had been equipped with vertical shaft drives to their camshafts.

Its achievements on the track testified to the excellence of Peugeot's new conception of a racing car. One L3 won the 1913 *Coupe de l'Auto* race for *Voiturettes* at Boulogne, defeating a strong field over a 387-mile distance, while a sister car placed second. A lone L3 at Indianapolis in 1914 placed second among cars with engines almost twice as large, and averaged 81mph for the 500 miles. With its normal two-seater body the L3 was timed at 94mph and with a narrower body it set new Class E records at Brooklands at better than 105mph and touched 107mph on some runs.

The engine that powered this exceptional Peugeot may fairly be regarded as the most advanced to be built before the Great War. This can be said although its cylinder dimensions were in the tradition of the time at 78 x 156mm (3.07 x 6.14in), with the stroke exactly twice the bore. Displacement was 2,982cc and the compression ratio was 5.6:1. Two main elements comprised the in-line four: a thin-wall cast-iron block with an integral cylinder head, and a cast-aluminium crankcase with integral bearers at front and rear that tied it to a sub-frame carried between the Peugeot's frame rails.

As viewed from the front of the engine, the block was offset 20mm to the right in the *désaxe* position which was thought to minimise piston side thrust and maximise leverage on the crankshaft during the expansion stroke. A groove on the left side of the bottom of each cylinder gave the required clearance for the connecting rod. The small bore left ample spaces between the cylinders for studs and nuts on both sides of each such space to attach the block to the crankcase.

New in the 1913 design, the crankcase was a one-piece barrel, utterly circular in cross-section and, as a result, rigid and smooth to swirling lubricant. Detachable covers at the front and rear of the crankcase admitted the crankshaft and carried a ball bearing, two of the three bearings supporting

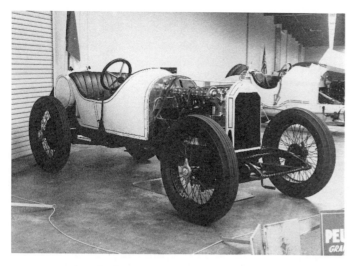

the shaft. Machined in two parts of BND steel, alloyed with chrome and nickel, the crankshaft was joined together at its centre by a tapered section secured by a bolt within a third ball bearing. This bearing's outer race was carried by a bronze diaphragm which was inserted with the crank from the rear of a heated crankcase. When cold the diaphragm was an interference fit. It was retained securely by five large bolts, radially disposed.

Ernest Henry's use of ball bearings for the crankshaft on 50mm journals made an important contribution to higher crankshaft speeds. He kept plain white-metal bearings on 50mm journals for the connecting-rod big ends, which were lubricated by oil thrown from the mains and caught by slinger rings. The I-section rod was 261mm long and had a two-bolt big end. Its small end was split so that it could be clamped around the 13mm gudgeon pin. Machined from a steel billet, the full-skirted piston carried two compression rings of 4mm width.

The crankcase was equipped with generous breathers on its left-hand side. Slots in its bottom delivered oil to a shallow sump and a unique lubrication system. The crankshaft nose powered a short cross-shaft which drove a reciprocating pump with a steel ringed piston in a bronze housing. Oil was contained in a reservoir under the driver's seat which was supplied by this pump. The latter's large capacity meant that it maintained, through a regulator, pressure in the reservoir which delivered oil back to the engine. It did so through six feed tubes incorporating sight-glasses on the dashboard which allowed driver and mechanic to verify the flow. Thus Henry contrived to provide a

dry-sump lubrication system that needed only a single oil pump.

At the front of the engine a two-piece aluminium case, attached to the block by eight studs, carried the spur-gear drive to the camshafts. The narrow gears, drilled for lightness, ran on roller bearings. From the right side of this train a half-speed gear drove a Mea high-tension magneto, towards the rear and mounted on the crankcase, and the water pump to the front. The pump delivered coolant to the bottom of the left, exhaust, side of the block's integral water jacket. The magneto sparked a single plug at the centre of the four valves.

At the top of the block, each hollow camshaft was supported by three inserted white-metal bearings in a split aluminium housing which was mounted above the head on rows of paired pylons. Guides in the base of each housing carried the stems of 'L-shaped' tappets, each of which contacted its valve through a clearance-adjusting cap screw. Each tappet had its own small shrouded coil spring to hold it against the cam lobe. Additional guidance was given to the tappet by a hollow vertical shaft integral with its end, sliding in a bushing in the cam cover. Each valve was closed by a pair of coil springs exposed to the cooling breezes.

The four valves per cylinder were equally inclined at an included angle of 60°. This moderate angle, in combination with the removable valve guides, allowed the valves to be extracted from the closed-end cylinder. Sized identically for inlets and exhausts, the valves were generously dimensioned at 40mm. Valve lift was 9mm and the timing was as follows:

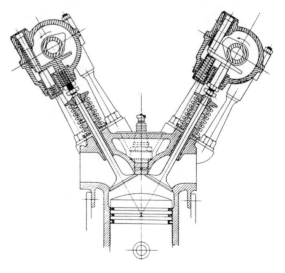

Inlet opens   3°ATDC   Exhaust opens   56°BBDC
Inlet closes   40°ABDC   Exhaust closes   12°ATDC

Thus there was a small amount of overlap past top dead centre, at that time a novel idea. The exhaust cam lobes imposed higher accelerations and a longer peak opening period than the inlet cams.

Around the valves the water jacketing was minimal, being principally designed to ensure that the spark plug was surrounded by coolant. Within the block the inlet ports for the front and rear cylinder pairs were siamesed to create a long oval opening. To these two ovals the inlet manifold was attached. Suspended from its centre was a single updraught Claudel carburettor with a rotating-barrel throttle that left no obstruction when it was fully open.

These were the characteristics of an engine which produced 92bhp at 2,900rpm, a high speed for the period. Only a year or two earlier it was customary for racing-car engines to be satisfied with 2,000rpm. It also produced better than 30 horsepower per litre; the best Grand Prix engines before the war managed no better than 25bhp per litre – even those from the same team of designers that had produced the L3. In addition to being innovative, the Peugeot L3 was also an inspired creation.

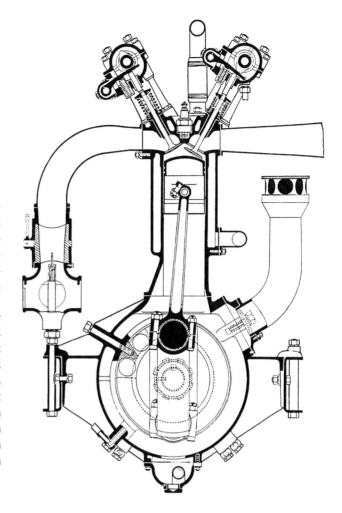

Opposite above: *Seen later in the Briggs Cunningham Collection with inappropriately large-section tyres, the 1913 Peugeot* voiturette *showed her stuff at Indianapolis in 1914 by finishing second with only 3 litres against rivals with engines as large as 7 litres. It is now in the Collier Collection.*

Opposite below: *As drawn by Jim Toensing from inspection of the Cunningham car, the valve gear of the 1913 Peugeot L3 shows its 'L-shaped' tappets. Each tappet has a vertical guide at one side, sliding in a bushing in the cam cover. A coil spring provides a separate return force for the tappet. Main valve-return coils are exposed.*

Above: *A transverse section of a 3-litre Peugeot engine shows the characteristic architecture of these pioneering fours, including one of the bolts retaining the bronze diaphragm carrying the centre roller main bearing. The gudgeon pin was pinched by the small end of the connecting rod. Valve gear shown, of finger-follower type, was an alternative design prepared by Ernest Henry.*

SPECIFICATIONS	
Cylinders	I4
Bore	78.0mm
Stroke	156.0mm
Stroke/bore ratio	2.0:1
Capacity	2,982cc
Compression ratio	5.6:1
Connecting rod length	261.0mm
Rod/crank radius ratio	3.3:1
Main bearing journal diameter	50.0mm
Rod journal diameter	50.0mm
Inlet valve diameter (2 valves)	40.0mm
Exhaust valve diameter (2 valves)	40.0mm
Inlet pressure	1.0Atm
Peak power	92bhp @ 2,900rpm
Piston speed (corrected)	2,099ft/min (10.7m/s)
Engine bhp per litre	30.9bhp per litre

1914

MERCEDES 18/100 4.5-LITRE FOUR

Early in September 1913 the rules were settled for the 1914 French Grand Prix on 4 July at Lyons. Engine size would be limited to 4,500cc – the first such capacity limit in Grand Prix racing. Lyons would have a full entry of five Daimler-built Mercedes cars, the most allowed, and there was little time to design and build them.

Daimler chief engineer Paul Daimler and his team soon realised that to stand a chance of success they would have to use much higher crankshaft speeds than their previous racing engines had attempted. New four-cylinder engines to meet this challenge were designed by Daimler's automotive staff and manufactured and tested by its aero-engine staff, which was well acquainted with the construction methods used. Preoccupation with the challenge of high engine speeds, up to 3,500rpm, shows in every detail of the engine's design.

The crankshaft was carried in five main bearings, 46mm in diameter and white-metal-lined. Integral with the bottom half of the aluminium crankcase, the main bearing caps were pulled tight by long studs through the upper half of the crankcase to the top surface, where the individual cylinders were attached.

With symmetrical cheeks on each throw and small circular weight masses opposite the rod journals, the one-piece crankshaft showed close attention to counterbalancing, a completely new art. Nevertheless the crankshafts weren't reliable at 3,500rpm until they were made from a special Aquila steel supplied by the Austrian firm of Danner. Carrying white-metal bearings cast into removable bronze shells, the big ends of the I-section connecting rods were held together by four bolts each, a novelty at Daimler. They ran on 48mm journals.

Like those then used in aero engines, the pistons were cast iron. One firm had entered an engine with aluminium pistons in the 1913 Kaiserpreis aero-engine competition but was refused entry on the ground that a metal with such a low melting point couldn't possibly stand up to an engine's combustion temperature! Nevertheless Mercedes built aluminium pistons for this Grand Prix engine (works type M93654) and tested them with complete satisfaction. The final decision as to whether to use them was left to the drivers – three

of whom doubled as master mechanics. They elected to stay with the proven iron design.

Driver option may also have accounted for the apparent presence in some engines of pistons with one bronze ring below the gudgeon pin, in others pistons with two rings below. The iron rings were above the pin, which floated in a bushing lubricated by an oil pipe running the length of the rod shank.

Lubrication was provided by a battery of piston-type oil pumps driven by a transverse shaft at the back of the sump. These served the bottom end of the engine. One of them delivered oil to the main and rod bearings at more than 30psi. Another scavenged oil from the front part of the sump to the main basin at the rear; the total capacity within the engine was four litres. A third pump metered fresh oil into the engine, at the pressure pump, from a reserve tank in the cockpit with an 11-litre capacity.

To minimise the effects of torsional resonances, Paul Daimler placed the vertical shaft drive to the overhead camshaft at the rear or output end of the engine. Only the centrifugal water pump, its shaft vertical, was driven by the nose of the crank. This set a pattern for accessory drives on Mercedes racing engines that endured for decades.

A subtlety on this 1914 engine was a pattern of bevel gearing that caused the vertical shaft to turn at faster than engine speed, thereby reducing the torque it had to transmit. An additional set of bevels drove a brace of magnetos, placed to the right and left of the shaft.

Previously, Daimler had made its engine cylinders in pairs. Individual steel cylinders for the M93654 were easier to make in small quantities (a fault in one cylinder scrapped only one, not two) and better suited to the even cylinder spacing of the five-main bearing engine. Each cylinder was fully machined from a steel forging and taper-threaded into a thin-wall cylinder-head casting. The water jacketing was welded around this assembly. The cylinders were symmetrical with individual 39mm ports serving 43mm valves – two inlets and two exhausts per cylinder.

Opposite above: Equipped with front-wheel brakes, the 1914 Mercedes 18/100 was still capable of winning in 1922 when Count Masetti drove it to victory in Sicily's Targa Florio.

Opposite below: A deep aluminium crankcase and individual fabricated steel cylinders were design characteristics of the 1914 18/100 engine. Twin magnetos were driven by the gearing at the rear of the engine.

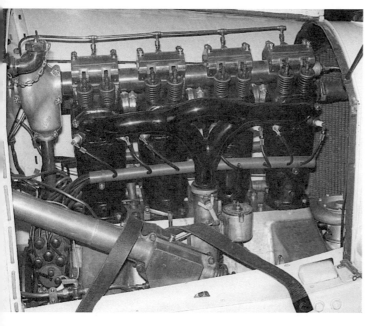

This first four-valve Mercedes cylinder head was clearly responsive to the racing successes of the contemporary French Peugeots. No four-valve aircraft engine had yet been made by the new Daimler factory that was then being built for that purpose at Sindelfingen. German as well as French four-valve aero precedents existed, including the impressive engines built by Benz for the 1910 Prince Heinrich Trials.

Each valve on the Mercedes was closed by a single coil spring, retained by a collar with threaded keepers. From the single central camshaft a forked rocker arm operated both inlet valves from one lobe. Individual lobes and rockers opened the exhaust valves. Timing was as follows:

Inlet opens TDC   Exhaust opens 50°BBDC
Inlet closes 35°ABDC Exhaust closes   9°ATDC

The hollow camshaft was carried rigidly in five long bronze bushings, supported within the cast-brass housing that tied the heads of the cylinders together. The housing also provided enclosures for the cams and rocker pivots.

An independent total-loss system catered to the oiling needs of the top end. With his foot the riding mechanic manipulated a plunger pump that delivered dollops of oil through a labyrinth of pipes to the rocker chambers, the cam drive shaft and – through fittings in the bases of the cylinders – the thrust face of each piston. Oil delivery was meticulously apportioned by calibrated flow restrictors in the system's manifolding.

A cockpit valve could be turned to direct the foot pump's oil delivery to critical chassis points, including the worm-and-nut steering gear and the rear axle. But when the pressure was on during a race both driver and mechanic relied on oil and yet more oil to the engine to stave off high-speed seizures. The 1914 Mercedes puffed smoke frequently around the Lyons circuit and in the last laps, in a battle with Peugeot, the leading Mercedes left an uninterrupted blue-white cloud behind it. Daimler would not allow a little oil to stand between it and success in the single Grand Prix in which these cars competed.

Fortunately for continued ignition under these conditions each cylinder was amply endowed with spark plugs. Two were on the inlet side of each chamber and a single one was on the exhaust side, where there was a boss for a fourth if needed. Between them the two magnetos generated enough sparks to fire two plugs simultaneously, and to deliver a double spark to the third one. Testing in Germany on a steep upgrade confirmed that the first plugs fitted weren't up to the job at high engine speeds. The Eisemann firm produced a new type of mica-insulated plug with platinum electrodes that gave satisfaction.

Induction was by a single updraught carburettor on the right side, with a barrel throttle. It fed a Y-shaped copper manifold with a large balance pipe between the cylinders. A small gearbox-driven air pump pressurised the fuel tank after a mechanic worked a hand pump to build up initial pressure for starting. Two separate fuel lines ran from the tank to the float bowl so that an alternative was available in case one became fouled or damaged. A faired manifold to a pipe straight to the rear provided a light, simple and effective exhaust solution.

The M93654 type designation of this 4,483cc four was derived from the engine's dimensions of 93 x 165mm (3.66 x 6.50in), followed by the number of cylinders. A power curve taken on engine number 1005, running on a blend of petrol and benzol, showed a peak of 105.5bhp at 3,100rpm. (After World War I for racing in the 1920s the engine's power was increased to 115bhp, a figure which is often quoted for it.) At 2,000rpm its power was 81bhp and its torque 209lb ft. Brake mean effective pressure at that speed was 115psi. The type designation of the vehicle, 18/100, signified taxable horsepower of 18 and maximum power of a nominal 100bhp.

'The sweetest music that I have ever heard is the song of this engine,' reminisced driver Christian Lautenschlager, 'although at 3,500 the vibration was pure hell.' He said that his, the victorious engine at Lyons, was the only one in the team to have such a strong vibration at its peak speed.

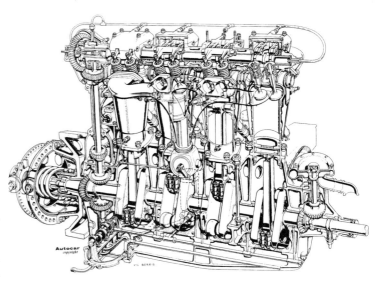

Six Mercedes 18/100s were built in time for the 1914 race, of which one served as a training car. They were granted little or no chance to win against the proven Peugeots, competing on their home ground. Yet they defeated 32 cars of a dozen different marques and finished one–two–three (Lautenschlager, Louis Wagner, Otto Salzer) in the last great race before motor competition was wiped off the European map by a world conflict. Over more than seven hours of racing and 468 miles, the white Mercedes broke the speed and spirit of their opposition by sheer tenacity. It was a lesson the rest of the Grand Prix world would not soon forget.

Opposite above: Although the camshaft itself was enclosed, the coil springs for the four valves per cylinder of the 1914 Mercedes remained in the open. This was considered helpful for valve cooling. Its inlet manifold was made of copper.

Opposite below: As prepared for the 1914 French Grand Prix the 4½-litre Mercedes was extremely purposeful and well tested as a result of previous visits to the circuit at Lyons

Above: A fine drawing by Vic Berris shows the attention given by the Daimler engineers to the strong bottom end of the 18/100 engine, which was designed to be run at speeds that were unprecedentedly high. Great care was taken throughout the engine to provide adequate lubrication.

SPECIFICATIONS

Cylinders	I4
Bore	93.0mm
Stroke	165.0mm
Stroke/bore ratio	1.77:1
Capacity	4,483cc
Main bearing journal diameter	46.0mm
Rod journal diameter	48.0mm
Inlet valve diameter (2 valves)	43.0mm
Exhaust valve diameter (2 valves)	43.0mm
Inlet pressure	1.0Atm
Peak power	106bhp @ 3,100rpm
Piston speed (corrected)	2,520ft/min (12.6m/s)
Peak torque	209lb ft (283Nm) @ 2,000rpm
Peak bmep	116psi
Engine bhp per litre	23.6bhp per litre

1921

DUESENBERG 3-LITRE EIGHT

If reliability is an asset for a racing engine, the 1921 3-litre Duesenberg was so blessed. Jimmy Murphy's Duesenberg crossed the line to win the 1921 French Grand Prix at Le Mans with a hole in its radiator and precious little coolant left in its engine. It nevertheless finished and indeed covered another 10.7-mile safety lap. That's toughness. And other Duesies of the four entered finished fourth and sixth.

That a team of four American racing cars could travel to France to compete in this great race was facilitated by the congruency, since 1920, between the rules of American competition, including the Indianapolis 500 miles, and those of Grand Prix racing. Both of these shared the engine-size limit of 3 litres or 183cu in.

Both in America and Europe racing-car builders were adopting the straight-eight configuration for their 3-litre engines, and Duesenberg was on the brink of introducing a straight-eight production car as well, its Model A. So taking its cars to France would – if successful – win valuable publicity for this new model.

The first 3-litre Duesenberg eights placed third, fourth and sixth at Indy in 1920 and one of the cars placed second in the 1921 '500' two months before the French race. In design their engines were scaled down from a 5-litre predecessor, which in turn had been inspired by work that Fred and August Duesenberg had done during the war on 16-cylinder aviation engines.

To the eyes of Europeans, accustomed as they were to admire elaboration and complexity for their own sake, the Duesenberg engine looked absurdly simple. It made only sparing use of light alloys. Aluminium was employed for the cam cover, the shallow ribbed sump and the finned covers for the water jackets on both sides of the block. Aluminium was employed as well for two covers on the left side of the crankcase through which the pistons and rods could be withdrawn for servicing; these were fitted with tall crankcase breathers. Otherwise the two main castings, the block and the detachable cylinder head, were made of grey iron by a specialist foundry in Chicago.

Its all-iron construction and the use of only three main bearings allowed the Duesenberg's block to be short and stiff. This was helped as well by the relatively small bore diameter of 2.50in (63.5mm) which, when combined with the stroke of 4.625in

(117.5mm) provided a displacement of 2,977cc. The block/crankcase extended down to enclose the crankshaft fully and to allow the one-piece crank to be inserted into a 360-degree plain bearing shell set into the front bulkhead. The centre main was also plain, in a two-piece housing drawn up to the block by cap screws.

The rear main was a number 220 ball bearing with a 7in outer diameter, nested into the rear bulkhead of the block and retained by a cover. This accepted the thrust loadings from the adjacent clutch inside a flywheel which was cap-screwed to the end of the crankshaft. The latter, machined from a single steel billet, was configured like two four-cylinder crankshafts placed end-to-end with one rotated 90° with respect to the other.

The two plain main bearings were 2¼in (57.2mm) in diameter. The rod journals measured 1⅞in (47.6mm) and were of precisely the same width. Riding on them were connecting-rod big ends that were retained by two bolts and surrounded by ribbing for stiffness and cooling. Using a technique that the Duesenbergs had developed through trial and error in racing, the rod big end was tinned and then given a coating of bearing babbit metal that was only ½nd of an inch thick, about three-quarters of a millimetre. They found this method effective in ensuring a rapid transfer of heat away from the bearing and into the metal of the rod.

The rod was machined from a hand forging and given a tubular shank 17.5mm in diameter with walls 3.2mm thick. All its surfaces were ground and polished to eliminate any stress raisers. Measuring 8¾in (222.3mm) from centre to centre, the rod had a split small-end so that it could be clamped around the ¾in (19.1mm) gudgeon pin, which used the aluminium piston as bearing material.

Pressure oil was supplied to the crankshaft by borings in the block to the two plain bearings. The further transfer of oil to the rod big-ends was achieved in an unusual way. The crankshaft webs

Opposite above: Jimmy Murphy's victory at Le Mans in the French Grand Prix of 1921 was a landmark success for American automotive engineering in Europe. The car is shown on one of the smoother parts of the rocky Le Mans circuit.

Opposite below: Striking in its visual simplicity, the Duesenberg engine's block and cylinder head were made of high-quality cast iron. This contributed to its compactness and its strength to cope with high crankshaft speeds.

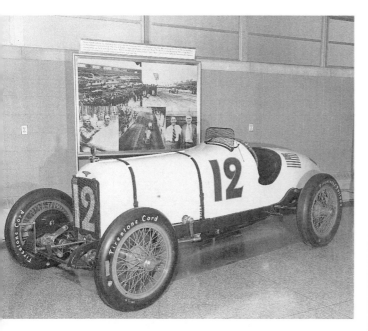

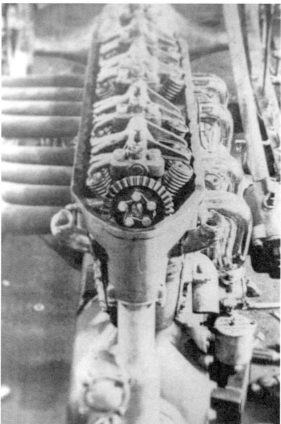

between the offset rod journals were completely circular. Machined into the periphery of each was a groove ³⁄₁₆th of an inch wide and ⁵⁄₁₆th of an inch deep. Covered by a ring – initially of copper and later of steel – shrunken into position and soldered, this groove formed the oil passage between the big-ends. The other crank webs carried counterweights.

At the nose of the crank a small bevel gear drove another bevel at engine speed, and a short shaft running downward to the pumps. Twin gear-type pumps were provided for the dry-sump oiling system. Pressurised oil was supplied to the front bearing of the single overhead camshaft, from which it travelled through the hollow shaft to the cam's other bearings. A passage delivered oil to the shaft on which the valve rocker arms pivoted. A trough below the camshaft collected oil which bathed the cam lobes before draining through the housing that carried the cam drive shaft.

Below the oil pumps was the centrifugal water pump, which delivered coolant to the cylinder block's left front aluminium side plate. From there it flowed back through the block and up to the head through an aperture at the very rear. Intermediate apertures between block and head were avoided for fear that the water column in the long straight-eight engine would confuse coolant flow when the Duesenberg's powerful four-wheel hydraulic brakes were applied.

From the crank's nose bevel gear another shaft ran upward, at engine speed, to a half-speed bevel at the top that drove the single overhead cam. Running in ball bearings, with a steadying plain bearing at its centre, the shaft had its own aluminium housing. A skew gear just below the steady bearing drove a small aviation-type Delco dynamo to top up the 8-volt battery for the engine's coil ignition system. The Delco distributor was driven by a skew gear from the centre of the camshaft and projected from the left side of the head. There it was conveniently placed for the leads to the spark plugs, which projected horizontally into the inlet side of the combustion chamber.

Following the precedent of their aviation-engine designs, the Duesenbergs gave the 3-litre engine one inlet and two exhaust valves. They judged that this gave adequate inlet area while helping to dissipate the heat to which the exhaust valves were subjected. The latter were made of a cobalt-chrome steel alloy and were 27mm in diameter. Tungsten was alloyed with the steel of the single inlet valve, which had a 39mm head. The valves were symmetrically inclined at an included angle of 60° in a chamber that was recessed deeply into the cylinder head. Twin coil springs closed each valve.

The thin-wall aluminium piston was fully-skirted except for cutaways at the sides of its skirt that allowed it to be removed for servicing, past the crankshaft, through the access apertures in the crankcase. Although at the time of the Le Mans race the piston was two-ringed, three rings were later fitted. Protruding well into the chamber, the piston crown was varied in height to adjust the compression ratio, which for Le Mans was a modest 5.2:1.

Running the length of the head, above the camshaft, was a shaft carrying the rocker arms that operated the valves. The cast-steel rocker arms were roller-tipped where they contacted the cam lobe and had high multiplication ratios that gave lift at the valve of 9.5mm for the inlets and 7.9mm for the exhausts. The inlet rocker was T-sectioned. The paired exhaust valves were opened by a forked rocker arm which was drilled, down the centre of each arm, for lightness. Valve clearance was adjusted by filing the tips of the valve stems, although it was not unknown for a mechanic in a hurry to 'adjust' clearance by tweaking the rocker arm.

Induction on the GP-winning car was through two updraught Miller carburettors whose barrel-type throttles were joined by a shaft in torsion. Through a two-branch manifold each fed two ports in the head, within which the inlet ports were siamesed. The ports from the two exhaust valves were siamesed within the head as well, to deliver to an eight-branch exhaust manifold.

Their light reciprocating parts helped these engines reach new highs of crankshaft speed. Before the war no Grand Prix engine developed its peak power at more than 3,000rpm. In sharp contrast the Duesenberg developed its 115bhp output at 4,250rpm and was capable of revving to an astonishing 5,000rpm.

Observers at Le Mans remarked that the engines seemed 'infinitely flexible', which was a benefit with their less-versatile three-speed gearboxes against the four-speeders fitted by others. They were also distinguished by the 'machine-gun-like crackle of their exhaust.' The Americans had come, seen, won – and been heard from.

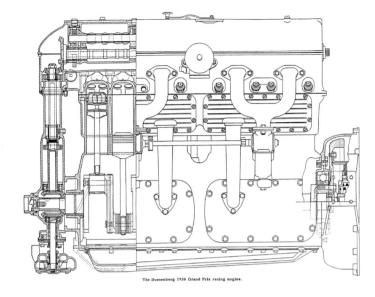

The Duesenberg 1920 Grand Prix racing engine.

Opposite left: Equipped with four-wheel brakes, the 1921 Duesenberg raced without a spare wheel on board. The team's game plan was to limp to the pits for any needed tyre repairs.
Opposite right: Rocker arms from the single overhead camshaft operated the inclined overhead valves of the Duesenberg. The inlet rockers were straightforward, while those for the exhaust valves were forked to operate the paired valves.
Above: Duesenberg used bevel gears and shafts to drive the overhead camshaft, and also the water pump placed low at the front of the engine. Other bevels from the crank nose drove the oil pumps for the dry-sump system.

SPECIFICATIONS	
Cylinders	I8
Bore	63.5mm
Stroke	117.5mm
Stroke/bore ratio	1.85:1
Capacity	2,977cc
Compression ratio	5.2:1
Connecting rod length	222.0mm
Rod/crank radius ratio	3.8:1
Main bearing journal diameter	57.2mm
Rod journal diameter	47.6mm
Inlet valve diameter (1 valve)	39.0mm
Exhaust valve diameter (2 valves)	27.0mm
Inlet pressure	1.0Atm
Peak power	115bhp @ 4,250rpm
Piston speed (corrected)	2,409ft/min (12.0m/s)
Engine bhp per litre	38.6bhp per litre

BUGATTI TYPE 35 2-LITRE EIGHT

It took Ettore Bugatti several years to get the range of his rivals when he began competing in Grand Prix races, but when he did he enjoyed remarkable success. The Type 35 model that he introduced in 1924 established a strong foundation for another decade of Bugatti racing cars. That they enjoyed racing success was important; that they were profitable for Bugatti to build and sell was vital.

Bugatti's base was at Molsheim in Alsace-Lorraine, which was ceded by Germany to France in 1919 by the Treaty of Versailles. This did not prevent such Teutonic engineers as Streicher, Kortz and von Urach from giving Bugatti material assistance in realising his ambitious design ideas. The new 1924 Type 35 was one of the most elegant as well as successful racing cars ever made, but its engine dated from 1922, when it was fitted to a batch of four or five racing cars built to compete under the just-introduced 2-litre Grand Prix limit.

The 2-litre GP Formula continued through 1925, the year in which we will assess the engine of the Type 35. Its major success that season was in Italy's demanding Targa Florio, for at the GP level Bugatti's rivals were by then as committed to supercharging as he was to the atmospheric aspiration he would continue to favour until the end of 1926.

Like the Duesenbergs, who had produced one of his aircraft engines under license in America, Ettore Bugatti had been inspired to pursue the in-line-eight-cylinder engine configuration by his experiences with such units before and during World War I. Again like Duesenberg he employed a shaft-driven single overhead camshaft to open three valves per cylinder, but in the opposite configuration: two inlets and one exhaust.

All the valves were positioned dead vertically. At 35mm the diameter of the exhaust valve was so great that a recess had to be machined in the side of the

Above: Pictured in assembled form, a Type 35 crankshaft shows the wedge-sided tapered bolts that were drawn up to unify the crank from its component parts, so that the connecting rods may have one-piece big ends.

Opposite above: The Type 35 Bugatti's clean lines were in evidence in 1925 at Brooklands where Lieutenant Glen Kidston raced one of the first to be seen in England. While tolerating the imposition of the mandatory Brooklands silencer the Bugatti lapped Brooklands at just over 110 mph.

Opposite below: Built initially as an unsupercharged engine, the 2-litre Bugatti Type 35 was fed by twin carburettors which could be sidedraught or, as here, downdraught units. Although the spark plugs appear to be placed quite low, they were in fact positioned at the tops of the combustion chambers.

combustion chamber to accommodate its opening. Only by virtue of its removable bronze guide could the exhaust valve be withdrawn from the cylinder, which was of monobloc construction with an integral head. Inlet valve diameter was 23.5mm. The lift at the valve was 7.5mm for the inlets and 9.0mm for the exhaust poppet. Valve timing was as follows:

Inlet opens 10°BTDC Exhaust opens 50°BBDC
Inlet closes 35°ABDC Exhaust closes 20°ATDC

Light pivoted fingers were interposed between the cams and valve stems of the Type 35; hardened caps atop the valve stems were varied to set the running clearance. The fingers for the inlet valves on the right side of the engine were pivoted from longitudinal tubes on the left side of the aluminium cambox, and vice versa for the exhaust fingers, each valve having its own cam lobe. The case-hardened fingers had internal oiling channels and multiplied the lobe's lift by a ratio of approximately 1½:1. Each valve was closed by twin concentric coil springs.

Eight bronze bushings in webs in the cambox casting carried the bearing journals of the camshaft, made large enough in diameter to allow the camshaft to be slid in from one end. The cam was in fact made in two pieces and joined at the centre; Bugatti expert Hugh Conway speculated that Bugatti's cam grinder was too short to make a one-piece camshaft. A large bevel gear at its nose gave the reduction to half speed from the vertical drive shaft.

The Type 35's cylinders, with dimensions of 60 x 88mm providing a displacement of 1,991cc, were encased in two four-cylinder head-block units mounted on a common crankcase and topped by a common cambox. Cast from iron, these monoblocs were fully machined. Their tops were

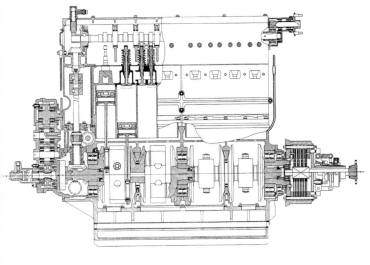

open, closed during assembly by an aluminium plate which was held down by the screwed-in valve guides. Water jackets were cast integral, receiving coolant from a gallery along the right or inlet side running just below the horizontal spark plugs. Water was drawn off the tops of the blocks by a gallery cast into the cambox, also on the inlet side of the engine.

Laurence Pomeroy, Jr memorably wrote of the Type 35 that 'there can be few successful racing engines which have run with so little water in contact with so many hot spots.' Within each block the cylinders were siamesed; no water flowed between them. The importance of adequate water flow around the valve seats was overlooked, with the result that block cracking was not unusual. Mounted at the engine's left front and driven by skew gears from the vertical shaft, the water pump was of elegant large-diameter design.

While each of the eight exhaust valves opened directly on its own port and exhaust pipe, the inlet ports were siamesed into two external apertures for each block. Each of these pairs was fed by its own manifold and carburettor, with a small balance tube connecting the two manifolds. Carburettors were side-draught, either 35mm Solex units or 36mm Zeniths of 'triple diffuser' design with a separate internal venturi to improve fuel vaporisation. To the same end the inlet manifolds were water-jacketed at their centres. Fuels used were proprietary blends of methanol, benzol and acetone such as Elcosine and Dynamin. They were supplied to the carburettors by pressure in the fuel tank generated by a small camshaft-driven pump.

A pattern of ten nuts on short studs attached each block to the top of the barrel-sectioned aluminium crankcase. These nuts were in grooves along the bottom of each block, which were covered by an aluminium strip spring-clipped in place to preserve the elegant rectilinear contours of

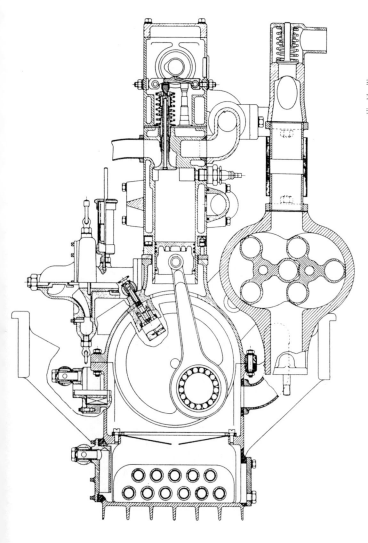

Above: Visible in the sections of the crankshaft are the slinger rings and passages that provided oil to the Bugatti's big-end roller bearings. The cylinders in each block were siamesed, no cooling water passing between them.
***Left:** Unusually for a racing* engine the Bugatti was of wet-sump design, with tubes passing through the oil supply to provide a modicum of cooling. This transverse section of a supercharged engine is taken from the rear, showing the water pump assembly on the left.

BUGATTI TYPE 35 2-LITRE EIGHT

the Type 35 eight. The crankcase was split at the crank centreline. Its bottom portion was an elaborate and deep casting with a finned bottom that constituted the engine's wet sump. From front to rear through the sump ran an array of aluminium tubes providing cooling air to the castor oil which all Bugattis used.

The sump casting itself provided the supporting caps for the front and rear of the Type 35's five main bearings. Individual bearing caps were supplied for the centre three mains. All the main bearings were anti-friction: front, rear and centre were double-row ball bearings with their own inner and outer races, while the other two – those at the centre of each set of four cylinders – were crowded 11mm rollers running directly on a hardened 63.5mm crankshaft journal and in a very deep split outer race which had its own clamping bolts.

Big-end bearings were anti-friction also, each having 17 rollers in bronze cages running on a 45mm crank journal. This and the use of a central ball bearing required the crankshaft to be built up. Bugatti achieved this by the design and precision machining of removable components to make two identical four-cylinder crankshafts which were joined in the centre bearing by a taper. The same taper was used to attach the pot-type flywheel and the clutch that it enclosed. The sections of each four-cylinder crank were firmly and accurately wedged together by pins with tapered flats that were drawn up by nuts.

A gauze filter cleansed the oil reaching the main bearings at the modest pressure of 15psi. This was supplied by a gear-type pump driven at one-fifth engine speed by a skew gear at the nose of the crank. Oil escaping from the main bearings was caught by circular grooves in the crank webs. Bores from these 'slinger rings' supplied the oil to the rod bearings.

Slender and machined all over, the I-section connecting rods were 185mm long. Their stiffening rib ran right around the big end, which was of 61mm diameter. The small end was hardened to bear directly on the surface of the 16mm gudgeon pin. This was carried in a short, fully-skirted Bugatti-made piston. Flat-topped, it typically gave

a compression ratio of 6.0:1. Two compression rings and one oil ring were above the pin and a second oil ring was at the bottom of the skirt.

Ignition was by magneto, usually SEV, this component being mounted in the car's cowl and driven by a shaft with flexible couplings from the back of the camshaft. The shaft was equipped with a Bugatti-designed mechanism that allowed the driver to advance and retard the ignition using a cockpit control.

Rated at 100bhp at 5,000rpm, the unblown 2-litre Type 35 engine could be revved safely to 6,000, giving its driver an ample margin for error. Modest though this output was, it could be counted on to be delivered reliably by a well-maintained engine. It was also put to good use by the Type 35's excellent chassis. Its frame stiffness was enhanced by the bottom half of the engine's crankcase, which was solidly anchored to the side members at four points.

The Type 35 also had room for development. Equipped with a three-lobe Roots-type blower it became the 35C, which enjoyed 14 victories in major events in the seasons from 1928 through 1930 when Grand Prix racing was run without specific displacement limits. In all, nearly 400 of the Type 35 and its derivatives were built by Bugatti – a record for GP car production that will stand for all time.

SPECIFICATIONS	
Cylinders	18
Bore	60.0mm
Stroke	88.0mm
Stroke/bore ratio	1.47:1
Capacity	1,991cc
Compression ratio	6.0:1
Connecting rod length	185.0mm
Rod/crank radius ratio	4.2:1
Main bearing journal diameter	63.5mm
Rod journal diameter	45.0mm
Inlet valve diameter (2 valves)	23.5mm
Exhaust valve diameter (1 valve)	35.0mm
Inlet pressure	1.0Atm
Peak power	100bhp @ 5,000rpm
Piston speed (corrected)	2,384ft/min (11.9m/s)
Engine bhp per litre	50.2bhp per litre

1927

DELAGE 15-S-8 1.5-LITRE EIGHT

Albert Lory's first attempt at a Grand Prix Delage did not work well. Not well at all. The cars were not even ready for the most important race of 1926, the French Grand Prix at Miramas, which went down in history as the poorest-attended GP in history: only three Bugattis started. And when they did race the Delages parboiled their unfortunate drivers. Backed by the wealthy and flamboyant Louis Delage, Lory lost no time in extensively revising the racers for the 1927 season.

With driver Robert Benoist, the 1½-litre Delages swept all before them in 1927. Thereafter Delage retired them with the exception of one car which he entered for Louis Chiron at Indianapolis in 1929, gaining a rewarding seventh place. Young British racing star Richard Seaman acquired another in 1935. Rebuilt and lightened, it was the scourge of the *Voiturette* category in 1936 – a decade after its conception. Here, clearly, was an exceptional racing car.

Built low with an offset seat to suit the new rules of the 1½-litre Grand Prix Formula that took effect in 1926, the Delage chassis was conventional by the standards of the 1920s. What excited admiration was its engine. Albert Lory had assisted Charles Planchon in the development of an ambitious 2-litre V12 GP engine for the preceding Formula. Assisted by Gaultier, Lory was given free rein by Delage to create a new car and its engine under the type number 15-S-8.

Compared to the V12, Lory both shortened the stroke and increased the bore by near enough 4mm each to arrive at the dimensions of 55.8 x 76.0mm (2.20 x 2.99in) for a straight-eight of 1,487cc. The in-line eight was the most popular racing-engine configuration in the 1920s; not for another decade would designers begin considering vee-eights. As originally built in 1926 the Delage eight produced 160bhp at 7,500rpm on a fuel consisting of 40 per cent benzol, 40 per cent petrol, 20 per cent alcohol and a 'zest' of ether to assist starting. Output in 1927 rose to 170bhp from an engine which was capable of revving safely to 8,000.

The 15-S-8 was supercharged by a large single Roots-type blower extending forward from the front of the camshaft gear train, which was at the front of the engine. Running at engine speed, the blower had a capacity of 1.4 litres with its two-lobed rotors 220mm long. The heavy finning of its aluminium housing and its forward placement were both intended to keep the compressor cool, and thus further increase the density of the incoming charge. This was an air/fuel mixture, for the blower drew from a large horizontal Cozette carburettor on its left.

A delivery pipe from the blower ran back along the right side of the engine to the centre of an eight-branch inlet manifold, which was fabricated from steel. At its centre was a blow-off valve to protect the manifolding and blower from backfires. It could also trap the unprepared Delage driver by popping open – and stalling the engine – when he was making a racing start. The maximum boost pressure was moderate at 7psi or about half an atmosphere. Compression ratio was 6.5:1.

After entering the combined block and cylinder head the fresh charge had to slope upward before curving around to enter the combustion chamber through the single inlet valve which – like the exhaust – was steeply sloped at 50° to the vertical. Removable valve guides were essential to allow these valves to be withdrawn from the cylinders. In the hemispherical combustion chamber the valves were large: 31mm inlets and 29mm exhausts. A central 18mm spark plug communicated with the chamber through an 8mm aperture.

Opposite above: The striking lines of the 1927 Grand Prix Delage were reflected on the wet surface of the Miramas track in southern France. Size for size this was the finest racing car yet seen.
Opposite below: Moving the exhaust system to the left on the 1927 Delage helped keep its drivers cooler but no chances were taken with the ample venting of the engine compartment.

Valve timing of the Delage eight was as follows:

Inlet opens 18°BTDC Exhaust opens 58°BBDC
Inlet closes 50°ABDC Exhaust closes 25°ATDC

This gave top-end overlap of 43°. Valve lift was 7mm.

A single iron casting comprised the Delage's complete head-block unit, extending down to the bottom of the cylinders and up almost to the tops of the triple-coil valve springs. Within it the cylinder spacings were equal save for a larger gap at the centre of the row of eight. At their bottoms the water jackets were cast open, allowing better control of the cores, and closed later by steel sheets retained by screws. Flow was provided around the spark plug and the exhaust-valve guides for the

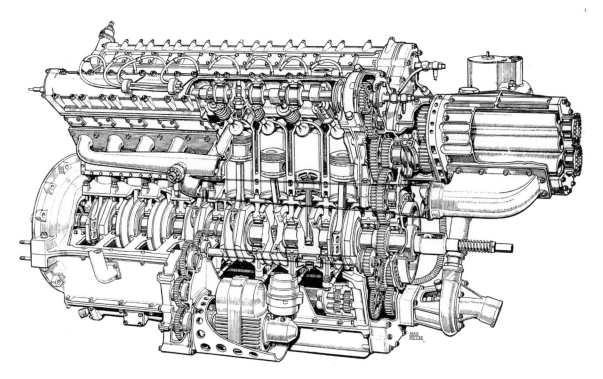

cooling water, which was piped to the exhaust side of the water jacket.

The individual aluminium carriers that held the twin camshafts were attached to the head by long studs that extended to the aluminium cam cover. The two aluminium pieces gripped the outer races of the eight roller bearings that carried each shaft. Apertures in the sides of the cam carriers provided mountings for the pivots of short, light finger followers betwixt cam lobe and valve stem. The carriers had apertures on both sides so the fingers could be positioned as desired; as raced the cam lobes wiped them away from their pivots. Oil entered each hollow nickel-chrome-steel camshaft through a plain bearing and flowed to outlets at each lobe.

The 15-S-8's oiling system had two pressure pumps. One of them lubricated the camshafts, supercharger and the gear trains that drove them and the other accessories. Albert Lory was justifiably proud of the precision of this train of hardened steel gears, pointing out that the pinion that drove the sump-mounted oil pumps was only 3mm wide. The other pressure pump delivered oil to the crankshaft, and a third pump scavenged the dry sump through a screened central pickup.

Within the sump a ladder of pipes along the left-hand side supplied oil at only 1–2 psi to each of the main bearing caps, which were in fact integral with the lower half of the split aluminium crankcase. The nine 49mm main bearings were anti-friction, all rollers except for a double-row ball bearing at the crank nose to take end thrust. The rollers were double-row at the centre and rear mains. Split light-metal cages guided the rollers.

A magnificent piece of machining, the one-piece crankshaft was made of nickel-chrome steel so that its journals could be hardened to serve as the inner races for the roller bearings. This held true as well for the rod journals, which were a modest 32mm in diameter. They were lubricated by oil emerging under centrifugal force from slinger rings in the circular crank cheeks. Lubricant was metered to the slinger rings by small jets adjacent to the main bearing feeds.

With a one-piece crankshaft Lory was obliged to split his connecting-rod big ends and the light-alloy cages that guided the 12 rollers per journal. These ran directly on the surface of the nickel-chrome-steel connecting rod, whose caps were notched to provide secure alignment of the outer race. The I-section rod was 152mm long, exactly twice the stroke, and robust, for Lory was well aware that at

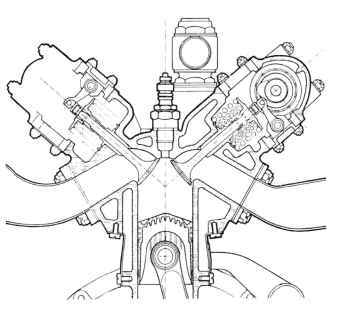

halfway along the engine and powered a gear train that led down to a magneto carried in a cradle alongside the crankcase. For a high-speed engine this was a crucial component; it was made by Bosch.

On the left side of the 15-S-8 a fabricated steel exhaust manifold gathered the exiting gases progressively and fed them to a single exhaust pipe. The eight and its attached five-speed gearbox were offset four inches to the left of the Delage's centreline to balance the driver's weight and allow him to be seated low in the bodywork. The engine and gearbox made up a very long assembly which was attached at its nose and clutch housing to the frame, to which they added little in the way of stiffness. As a result the front of the chassis was prone to weaving during cornering.

Weaver or not, the 15-S-8 Delage was Europe's finest 1½-litre racing car. In all, the Delages were entered in seven races in the 1926–27 period. Twenty race entries resulted in only three retirements attributable to engine trouble. The Delages scored five victories and in two races filled all the podium positions, one of these being the all-important French GP. They were the crowning glories in the career of Louis Delage, who would never again attempt to build racing cars of such sublime extravagance.

the speeds he was intending the tension loads of inertia, not the compression of combustion, would predominate in stressing the rod.

A generous 22mm gudgeon pin joined the rod to a fully-skirted piston which was precision-die-cast of aluminium. Its slightly gable-ridged crown was ribbed underneath, in the longitudinal direction, for both stiffness and cooling. Three rings were above the pin, two for compression and one for oil control. With its rings each piston weighed only 163 grams.

A single centrifugal water pump was placed low at the front of the engine and driven from the accessory gears, all of which were mounted on ball bearings. In total, Laurence Pomeroy Jr calculated, the engine contained no less than 62 ball and roller bearings. From an idler in the front train a gear was driven that turned a shaft running toward the rear of the engine along its right-hand side. It stopped

SPECIFICATIONS	
Cylinders	I8
Bore	55.8mm
Stroke	76.0mm
Stroke/bore ratio	1.36:1
Capacity	1,487cc
Compression ratio	6.5:1
Connecting rod length	152.0mm
Rod/crank radius ratio	4.0:1
Main bearing journal diameter	49.0mm
Rod journal diameter	32.0mm
Inlet valve diameter (1 valve)	31.0mm
Exhaust valve diameter (1 valve)	29.0mm
Inlet pressure	1.5Atm
Peak power	170bhp @ 7,500rpm
Piston speed (corrected)	3,205ft/min (16m/s)
Engine bhp per litre	114.3bhp per litre

1932

ALPHA ROMEO TIPO B 2.7-LITRE EIGHT

Founded in Milan in 1910, the company that became Alfa Romeo after the war was active from its first days in motor sports but it struggled in its efforts to do well in Grand Prix racing. In 1923 Alfa took steps to rectify this by engaging Vittorio Jano, a young engineer who had helped develop Fiat's successful racing cars of the early 1920s. Jano's first GP Alfa, the Tipo P2 of 1924, won its first races and thus marked the arrival on the scene of a brilliant designer of racing cars and engines.

In 1931 Alfa Romeo introduced Jano's latest creation, the 8C 2300. It had an in-line eight-cylinder engine with a significant difference. Jano divided its eight into two cast-iron blocks of four cylinders resting on a common aluminium crankcase. Each block had its own aluminium cylinder head. The crankshaft was made as two separate four-cylinder parts united at the centre by a pair of gears. One of these gears drove the camshafts through a gear train while the other gear drove the supercharger and the oil and water pumps.

Jano's design overcame one of the major disadvantages of the in-line eight: the excessive length of both camshafts and crankshaft that introduced torsional vibrations capable of impairing both valve timing and reliability. A precedent was an 1,100cc eight which was designed for France's Salmson by Emile Petit in 1928. It too had a central gear train to the camshafts, which also drove two superchargers and the magneto. Jano may well have been aware of the elegant little Salmson engine.

The design of the 8C 2300 served as the point of departure for the engine of the Tipo B Alfa Romeo Grand Prix car, the company's first central-seated racer. Between its 1932 debut and mid-1934 the Tipo B took part in 26 races, of which it won 22. It achieved a 92 per cent finishing record from 62 race starts in these years – an impressive achievement. Through much of the 1930s successful Alfas of both sports and GP configurations were powered by engines that were closely related to the Tipo B's 2,655cc (65 x 100mm; 2.56 x 3.94in) straight-eight. Indeed the engine of the great 8C 2900B sports car was virtually identical to that of the 1934 version of the Tipo B.

The Tipo B remained faithful to Jano's successful concept of two four-cylinder engines divided by a camshaft and accessory drive. Instead of detachable cylinder heads, however, it unified each group of four-cylinder heads and blocks into a single monobloc aluminium casting that extended upward to carry the twin overhead camshafts. The cylinder walls were formed by dry steel liners which were inserted from the bottom, shrunk into position and clamped by a small flange, for security, against the top of the crankcase.

Only one casting pattern was needed for the Tipo B monobloc, because the blocks were symmetrical from left to right. The two valves per cylinder were equally inclined at a steep 52° from the vertical and shared the same diameter: 39mm. Valve lift was equal at 9mm and the timing was also strikingly symmetrical as follows:

Inlet opens 20°BTDC Exhaust opens 50°BBDC
Inlet closes 50°ABDC Exhaust closes 20°ATDC

Vittorio Jano was a member of the Fiat school which taught from the early 1920s that two valves in a hemispherical combustion chamber were superior to the four-valve pent-roof chamber that Peugeot, Mercedes, Ballot and others had used so successfully before and after the war. The successful Delages had also relied on two-valve combustion chambers. With the bore sizes then in use and the concurrent concentration on the development of the supercharged engine, the use of two valves could not be gainsaid.

A drawback of the block's symmetry was that the exhaust valves enjoyed no more beneficial water cooling of the valve guides than the inlets, although they needed more. However, good cooling was provided for the 18mm Champion spark plug placed vertically at the centre of the chamber and firing through a masking aperture. All the valves seated directly on the aluminium without the benefit of inserts. While allowing large valves, this made the seats prone to eventual cracking.

Thanks to Jano's use of a cam-follower system

Opposite above: In one of his rare departures from German racing cars Rudy Caracciola competed in an Alfa Romeo Tipo B in 1932. He won the German Grand Prix that year, here tackling the Nürburgring's infamous Karussell.

Opposite below: On this Tipo B engine the inlet manifold was modified to achieve a more balanced mixture distribution among the eight cylinders. Cooling was enhanced by additional finning on the warm-water takeoffs from the top of the cylinder head.

Central gears were bolted to separate camshafts for each block, each being carried by three long plain bearings. Each bearing was retained by an individual cap, held by studs which extended further to hold down the aluminium cam covers. The central cam drive train used spur gears, machined with integral hollow shafts carried by ball bearings.

On the left side of the block a gear train from the crank centre drove a pair of two-lobe Roots-type superchargers, one for each set of four cylinders. Each had rotors 90mm long and a capacity of 1,350cc. Driven at 1.45 times engine speed (the ratio could be changed) they produced a boost pressure of 11psi. Underneath each blower was its own 42mm updraught Weber carburettor, model BS42. Delivery was through a finned aluminium manifold equipped with a pressure-relief or 'blow-off' valve. Thus equipped, the Tipo B engine developed 215bhp at 5,600rpm. Its maximum torque of 210lb ft was produced between 3,500 and 4,000rpm.

With this boost and the fuels of the day a compression ratio of 6.5:1 was appropriate. This was established by the rounded crown of a fully-skirted aluminium piston, which carried its gudgeon pin low to make room for three compression rings and one oil ring above the pin and another oil ring below it. Eighteen millimetres in diameter, the pin fitted in a bronze bushing in the small end of a steel rod 216mm long. Ribs from its I-section shank blended into the two-bolt big end of the rod, which was machined all over. It rode on a 52mm journal.

he had brought to Alfa with the P2, the Tipo B's valves could be short and light. Three springs closed each valve: a large and deep outside spring and two shorter inner springs. Retaining the springs was a mushroom-shaped piece, whose stem surrounded the valve stem and was keyed to the latter so that it couldn't rotate in relation to the valve. Holding this down against the springs was another smaller mushroom-shaped piece which screwed onto the end of the valve stem. Wiped directly by the cam lobe, this was screwed in or out to set valve clearance and was held in place by matching serrations on both its lower surface and the top of the larger 'mushroom' under it.

Jano had enough confidence in plain bearings to use them throughout the Tipo B's bottom end. Ten 61mm babbit main bearings were provided for the crankshaft, an extra one being needed to flank the drive gears at the centre of the engine. Individual main bearing caps were tightened by two studs apiece against the bottom of the magnesium crankcase, which was split at the crank centreline. Enclosing the bottom of the straight-eight was a deep bottom-finned magnesium sump casting which sloped toward an oil pickup located two-thirds of the way along (toward the front).

Gears from the central train drove the

ALPHA ROMEO TIPO B 2.7-LITRE EIGHT

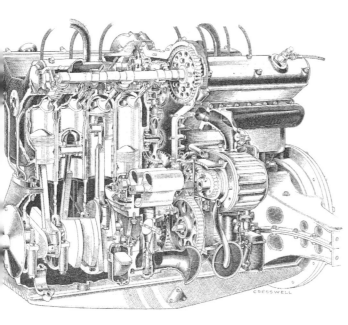

which delivered its output upward to a manifold that supplied coolant to the exhaust side of the water jackets of the two blocks. A take-off at the centre of each of the two cylinder heads transferred warm water back to the radiator. Forward of the gear train was the single Bosch magneto.

In this configuration the Tipo B's engine powered Alfas to signal successes in 1932 and '33, including three victories at Monza, one at an average speed in excess of 110mph. For the 1934 season its bore was increased to 69mm, bringing its capacity to 2,991cc. Thus enhanced, with chassis improvements as well, the Tipo B – also known as the Alfa Romeo P3 in homage to its great predecessor the P2 – won the 1934 Monaco and French Grands Prix.

The same basic engine was enlarged in 1935 to 3,165cc (71 x 100mm) and then to 3,823cc (78 x 100mm) to combat the advances made by the Germans. In the latter form, with a compression ratio of 8.1:1, it produced 330bhp at 5,400rpm. Since 1934 the Alfas were being entered in races by a new team formed by a former employee and racing driver of the Milan company, Enzo Ferrari. His greatest contributions to the sport of motor racing were yet to come.

Opposite above: With beguiling symmetry Vittorio Jano provided separate carburettors and superchargers to feed the front and rear cylinder blocks of the Tipo B's 2.7-litre engine. The rear of the inlet camshaft drove the magneto.
Opposite below: A bottom view of the Alfa Romeo Tipo B crankcase shows the central spur-gear to the camshafts and super-chargers, as well as the plain-bearing journals of the crankshaft.
Above: Simplicity of construction and execution was a hallmark of Jano's design for the Tipo B engine. Dry steel cylinder liners were inserted in the individual four-cylinder blocks.

scavenge and pressure oil pumps mounted on the right side of the engine. Pressurised oil was supplied to the main bearings and, through drillings, to the rod big-ends. Each lubrication system was unique to a four-cylinder module of the engine, for the crankshaft was made in two separate pieces joined together by bolts at the central gear. Machined from forgings, both halves of the crankshaft had full counterweights opposite each rod journal. External oil lines from the crankcase delivered lubricant to passages in the cylinder head.

On the right side of the Tipo B engine the central gear train powered other accessories. To the rear of the gear train was the water pump,

SPECIFICATIONS	
Cylinders	I8
Bore	65.0mm
Stroke	100.0mm
Stroke/bore ratio	1.54:1
Capacity	2,655cc
Compression ratio	6.5:1
Connecting rod length	216.0mm
Rod/crank radius ratio	4.3:1
Main bearing journal diameter	61.0mm
Rod journal diameter	52.0mm
Inlet valve diameter (1 valve)	39.0mm
Exhaust valve diameter (1 valve)	39.0mm
Inlet pressure	1.76Atm
Peak power	215bhp @ 5,600rpm
Piston speed (corrected)	2,963ft/min (14.8m/s)
Peak torque	210lb ft (285Nm) @ 3,750rpm
Peak bmep	196psi
Engine bhp per litre	81.0bhp per litre

1936

AUTO UNION C-TYPE 6-LITRE V16

By any standard the V16 power unit used from 1934 to 1937 by the Auto Union racing cars was an amazing and magnificent achievement. It stands out as the only 16-cylinder ever to achieve consistent success in Grand Prix racing. Its architecture, replete with multiple-purpose surfaces and members and planned with weight-paring ingenuity, is among the most brilliant ever devised for any engine.

Ferdinand Porsche and his engine designer, Josef Kales, were faced with a new formula that fixed a maximum weight for the car: 750kg. They decided to build a large-displacement engine for the Auto Union which could develop high power through high torque at relatively low crank speeds, hence could be stressed at a lower level. Cylinder dimensions were set initially at 68 x 75mm (2.68 x 2.95in) for 4,358cc. Lower structural stresses allowed the block and crankcase to be cast in one piece in thin-wall high-silicon-alloy aluminium. Inserted in it were forged chrome-alloy-steel cylinder liners, exposed to the cooling water.

The V16 had detachable cylinder heads, avoided then by most other GP car builders with the exception of the Maserati brothers. Studs retaining the heads were long, extending well down into the block. The basic engine geometry was architectonic: 45° between cylinder banks, and valves equally disposed at 90° to each other. The valves formed a part-spherical, part-conical combustion chamber which was fired by a single 18mm spark plug.

The V16's integration of valve gear and induction arrangements was masterful. Only one single central overhead camshaft was used, carried in nine bearings. Its 32 lobes opened the inlet valves directly through fingers on parallel shafts. The outboard exhaust valves were opened remotely through finger followers which operated rocker arms at the exhaust valves through horizontal pushrods. This gave the exhaust valve gear the higher reciprocating mass, which was partially compensated for by the smaller size, 32mm, of the exhausts as compared to the 35mm inlet valves.

All the major accessory drives (excluding only the belt-driven water pump) were at the rear of the engine, taken from the crank between the ninth and tenth main bearings. Bevel gears drove a vertical shaft (running at slightly higher than crank speed to reduce the torque loadings) which extended up to the camshaft. From there take-offs drove the fuel pump and the special Bosch oiler, which metered oil from the main pressure system to the supercharger bearings.

Just above the crankshaft, side bevels from the vertical shaft drove the twin eight-cylinder Bosch magnetos. Above them a multiple-disc clutch pack, pre-loaded by a massive coil spring, drove an idler gear which in turn drove the primary lobe of a vertically-placed Roots-type supercharger. Two variants of blowers were used, the original C-type and the later, longer, slimmer S-type with stiffer bearing mounts, both delivering about 2.8 litres per revolution and rotating at slightly more than twice engine speed. On the A-Type Auto Union of 1934 the boost was 9psi on a compression ratio of 7.0:1, producing 295bhp at 4,500rpm.

In its vertical position the blower was offset slightly to the left-hand side of the engine so that its output could be ducted around the vertical shaft to the central inlet passage. With surpassing genius the Porsche designers arranged for the inner surfaces of the heads, covered by the aluminium casting of the camshaft housing, to enclose a volume that served as the inlet manifold. At the front of the engine, at the end of this inlet gallery, a substantial spring-loaded blow-off valve was fitted to relieve the manifold of any overpressure caused by a backfire.

Unusually the bottom of the crankcase was sliced off at an angle as viewed from the side, becoming deeper toward the back of the engine. At its front the crankcase extended down just past the two-bolt main bearing caps, while at the rear it reached all the way down to the bottom of the clutch/flywheel assembly, the split line sloping downward toward the rear at an angle of seven degrees to the crank centreline. This put the most metal where it was needed, at the back of the engine for the all-important attachment to the clutch and transaxle, and

Opposite above: Conceived with a sense of architectural integration rare in racing-car history, the 1936 C-Type Auto Union was the work of the Porsche design office. Here Ernst von Delius is at the wheel.

Opposite below: Although its V16 engine ultimately displaced just over 6 litres, the shrewd construction of the Auto Union kept it within the Formula limit of 750 kilograms without tyres and fluids. Rear suspension was by swing axles.

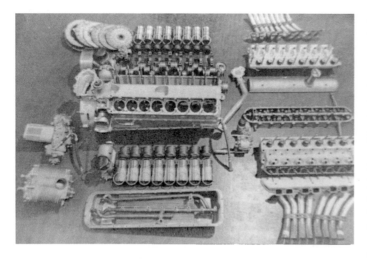

allowed weight to be saved at the front, where all that was needed was a thin-walled sump to catch the oil.

Below the vertical shaft at the rear, worm-and-pinion gears drove the twin gear-type oil pumps at five times engine speed. One of the oil pumps was a scavenger for the dry-sump system, the other a pressure pump drawing from the reservoir. 'Water' is a misnomer for the coolant of these cars, which was usually ethylene glycol pressurised to 5psi.

For a completely new design, so radical that many predicted total disaster for it, the A-Type AU of 1934 was remarkably successful. It equalled its Mercedes-Benz rivals with three victories in important races, including the all-

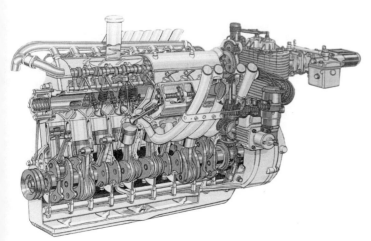

important German Grand Prix. In 1935 the B-Type was a transitional model, and with many experimental features did less well.

Over the following winter the bore was enlarged to 72.5mm, for 4,950cc. Domed pistons were fitted to bring the compression ratio to 8.95:1 and the boost was upped to 11psi. This brought the power to 375bhp at 4,800rpm and the torque from 391 to 478lb ft at a slightly higher speed, 3,000 instead of 2,700rpm – still astonishingly low torque peaks for a racing engine. The almost flat torque curve allowed the Auto Unions to be driven in only two gears on many tracks, and in only *one* gear, with no shifting at all, at Monaco.

As built for 1934 the exhaust manifolds for the V16 collected two cylinders at a time, bringing four pipes on each side into the main exhaust pipes that extended back along the sides of the car. In 1935 AU fitted separate stacks for each cylinder, setting the pattern for all the later Auto Unions and creating the car's distinctive sound, a 'staccato, high-pitched bark'.

The forged chrome-nickel-steel crankshaft of the A-Type AU was carried in tin-bronze main bearing shells, 62mm in diameter, with similar bearings for the 58mm connecting-rod big ends. The 164mm rods had slim I-section shanks and two-bolt caps, conventionally split. Like all the later AU rods the A-Type had an externally-affixed tube along the shank, carrying oil from the big-end to the gudgeon pin, which in later models ran in a needle bearing in the rod. The fully-floating pins were retained by aluminium buttons.

During 1935 the first trials of a new long-stroke crankshaft were made. It required a new crankcase casting to accept larger 70mm main bearings. Its completely new design allowed roller rod bearings to be used, together with a one-piece rod big end stiffened by a single encircling rib. The new rods were also slightly longer, at 168mm centre-to-centre, and the new big-end journals measured 68mm. The crankshaft sections were mated using the Hirth system of face serrations clamped by bolts with differential threads. A Hirth coupling also married the flywheel to the end of the crankshaft.

These new cranks were raced in two engines in mid-1935, retaining the B-Type bore of 72.5mm and extending the stroke to 85mm, giving a

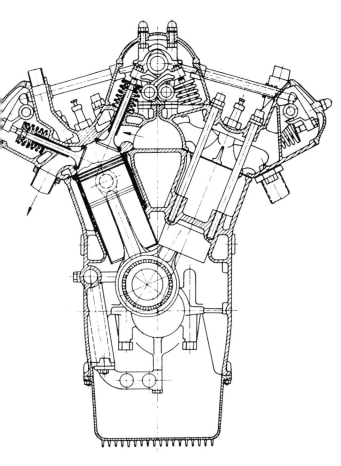

type pump delivered fuel at a pressure of 4psi to the carburettor. All the V16s used the same basic carburettor, a horizontal twin-throat 48mm unit with two float chambers, made by Solex specially for Auto Union by joining two mechanisms of an existing model in a common throttle body. Screen-type air filters were attached and cool air was ducted to them by two tiny scoops protruding from the tail of all the V16 models.

With a 9.2:1 compression ratio and 14psi boost (one atmosphere), the C-Type V16 delivered 520bhp at 5,000rpm. Its torque was a thundering 630lb ft at only 2,500rpm, at which speed it was producing 300 horsepower.

An even more potent version of the engine called the R-Type was developed with a bore 2mm larger for a capacity of 6,330cc and a power output of 545bhp. Nominally this was used only for record breaking, but it may have been used in races as well. In 1937, for example, the engine in Bernd Rosemeyer's Eifelrennen-winning AU was taken out, bench-tested and installed in the envelope-bodied car that set a new Class B flying mile record at 242.1mph on 16 June. So we know – and it does not surprise us – that there was very little difference between the race and record Auto Union engines.

Opposite top: Based on a massive aluminium cylinder-block casting, the Auto Union V16 was brilliantly designed to be light and simple as well as powerful.
Opposite below: At the rear of the Auto Union engine, bevel gears drove a vertical shaft which turned not only the camshaft but also other accessories including the Roots-type supercharger. The nine-bearing crankshaft was built up using the Hirth system.
Above: Although the Auto Union C-Type had dry-sump oiling, its cast-aluminium finned sump was nevertheless quite deep. Individual forged-steel wet cylinder liners were inserted in the aluminium cylinder block.

displacement of 5,610cc. Experiments with this led to the design of the C-Type engine used in 1936 and 1937. This had a further bore enlargement to 75mm for 6,006cc, the largest engine used by any competitor under the 750kg formula.

Driven at one-fifth engine speed from the camshaft, a double-acting DBU diaphragm-

SPECIFICATIONS	
Cylinders	V16
Bore	75.0mm
Stroke	85.0mm
Stroke/bore ratio	1.13:1
Capacity	6,006cc
Compression ratio	9.2:1
Connecting rod length	168.0mm
Rod/crank radius ratio	4.0:1
Main bearing journal diameter	70.0mm
Rod journal diameter	68.0mm
Inlet valve diameter (1 valve)	35.0mm
Exhaust valve diameter (1 valve)	32.0mm
Inlet pressure	1.97Atm
Peak power	520bhp @ 5,000rpm
Piston speed (corrected)	2,620ft/min (13.1m/s)
Peak torque	630lb ft (854Nm) @ 2,500rpm
Peak bmep	260psi
Engine bhp per litre	86.6bhp per litre

1937

AUSTIN SEVEN 744cc FOUR

In 1922 Herbert Austin introduced his Seven, hailed as a big car in miniature. Its creator was that rare British industrialist who also appreciated the value of motor sports as a means of spreading the word about the quality of his products. Originally 696cc, the Seven was soon enlarged to 747cc to bring it nearer the 750cc limit of the international Class H for racing and record-breaking.

In 1923 Austin set up a competition department under Arthur Waite, who later became his son-in-law. Racing versions of the Seven enjoyed great success, so much so in fact that others, notably MG, decided to challenge them for Class H honours. This set the scene for some of racing's most memorable battles.

Blessed with an overhead-cam engine, MG was soon equalling and then surpassing Austin. The bitterest blow fell in 1931 when an MG was the first three-quarter-litre car to be clocked officially at better than 100mph. How was Austin to respond? The answer came serendipitously the following summer when, at Brooklands, one of Waite's men saw a fast white supercharged Ulster-model Seven with a bespectacled engineer at its wheel. This was T. Murray Jamieson, then just 26 years old and employed by supercharger maker Amherst Villiers.

The upshot was that Austin acquired not only the white Ulster and all its supercharger technology from Villiers, but also the services of Jamieson. The latter was instructed to design and build the best possible 750cc racing car. Described by engineering contemporary Harry Mundy as 'a brilliant man, but a bit stubborn,' Jamieson set to work seriously on the project in 1934 with the aid of engineers William Appleby and Tom Brown.

That the new racing Austin single-seaters were built almost regardless of cost was evident from their exquisite engines, by far Britain's finest engineering achievement in this sphere in the 1930s. The only link with previous Austin Sevens was that they had four in-line cylinders. Cylinder dimensions were set at 2⅜ x 2%₆in (60.3 x 65.1mm) for 744cc, remarkably close to 'square' proportions for a 1934 conception. This choice was driven by Jamieson's desire to build an engine capable of 12,000 – some even said 14,000 – revolutions per minute. Five-figure engine speeds were then quite unheard-of.

A mighty valve gear was needed to achieve this goal, and this the little Austin had. Recalled Harry Mundy, 'He'd got triple valve springs, enormous – like front suspension springs – on the tappets to achieve this.' This was an exaggeration, but not by much. The inverted-cup-type tappet was 2.1in (53.3mm) in diameter, drilled around its skirt for lightness, and had a large coil spring beneath its periphery which had no task but to keep the tappet in contact with the cam lobe. The lobes were a full two inches wide to spread the load as widely as possible.

The valve itself was seated by a pair of coil springs. The combined force of the three springs at full lift approached 500lb. They coped with valves that were not lightweights, although the exhaust poppets were hollow-stemmed to allow the use of internal cooling salts. The two valves per cylinder were the same size at 1.50in (38.1mm). They were equally inclined from the cylinder centreline at the wide included angle of 100° and seated on inserts of Monel metal – a nickel alloy of steel – in the RR50 aluminium cylinder head.

Jamieson laid out his baby racing engine with elegance and great attention to detail. Its block/crankcase, also of RR50 aluminium, extended right down to the bottom of the engine, where it spread wider than its narrow waist around the cylinders at the top. A shallow cast finned sump for the dry-sump oiling system closed the bottom. An awareness of the problem of oil churning in the sump was shown by the use of a louvered panel above the sump to collect oil as it was flung from the crankshaft.

All accessories were driven by a train of spur gears at the rear of the engine. Gears set out at each side drove shafts going forward. The left-hand shaft, turning at half engine speed, drove a large water pump whose output – a maximum of 50 gallons per minute – was piped directly to a manifold that was integral with an aluminium jacket around the cylinders. A skew gear set on the pump drive shaft was the access point for the starting crank, inserted at the side of the car.

Opposite above: Looking like a miniature of a big racing car, the twin-cam Austin was driven to victory by Charlie Dodson in the British Empire Trophy race at Donington Park in 1938.

Opposite below: Magneto ignition was provided for the 1937 Austin Seven, which reached its peak output of 116bhp at 7,600rpm. Its inlet manifold was finned for cooling.

On the right side of the gear train the shaft first drove, through a skew gear, a vertical shaft. At its top this drove the 12,000rpm tachometer and at its bottom it turned a stack of oil pumps. The scavenge pump was at the bottom. Above it was a 100psi pressure pump for the bottom end, and above that was a 10psi pump delivering oil to the valve gear. The right-hand shaft continued forward to drive a polar-type inductor magneto, a critical component in a high-speed engine.

The spur-gear train continued to the top of the engine to drive the camshafts, each of which was carried in three wide bearings. Tapped from the rear of the train was a gear drive to a Roots-type supercharger attached to the rear of the block. Driven at 1½ times engine speed, this was sized to provide a boost of 22psi. Its output was supplied through a finned cast light-alloy pipe, equipped with a blow-off or backfire valve, to a finned manifold that mated with the head's internal porting.

The blower drew mixture from a single large SU constant-vacuum carburettor. After inexplicably lean mixtures caused piston-crown failures in early races the SU man suggested the addition of a second float bowl to cope with the lateral g-forces on the engine and this proved to be the solution.

Machined from the solid, the crankshaft was carried by three main bearings. The centre main was a lead-bronze plain bearing carrying a 2.5in (63.5mm) journal, while the other two mains were roller bearings. The rod journals were

1.75in (44.5mm) in diameter and surrounded by white-metal bearings in the rod big-ends. Considering how best to supply oil to these bearings, Murray Jamieson chose the then-novel solution of a feed through the nose of the crank. To seal the delivery he used a pack of finely-ground washers which alternated between static and rotating.

Countersunk screws attached high-density metal to the crank cheeks to increase the counterbalancing mass for the robust fully-machined I-section connecting rods. Five inches (127mm) long, these had two-bolt big ends with triple-ribbed caps and carried slipper-type pistons. The latter were fitted with two compression rings only 1.5mm thick but deep radially; this design overcame an initial blowby problem. One oil ring was fitted. Piston crown heights were varied to try different compression ratios of 6.0, 6.5, 6.8 and 7.5:1; 6.5 was chosen as the most suitable for use with a fuel which was normally 75 per cent methanol, 15 per cent ethanol, 10 per cent water (!) and 3cc of tetraethyl lead per gallon.

Daring to use a detachable head for a highly-boosted engine, Jamieson took care to seal it solidly. Each cylinder comprised a wet nitrided-steel liner. It hung free at its bottom, rubber-sealed to the block, and at its top had a thicker finned section 1¼in deep. This mated with the top of the block, at its bottom, and was a metal-to-metal seal

against the head at its top. Four studs around each cylinder tied the whole together. The wide centre main bearing created a gap at the middle of the engine, so the studs there were duplicated, bringing their total to 12.

Enclosing the 1¼in gap between bottom of head and top of block was an RR50 sandwich piece into which the water pump's output was manifolded. This was rubber-gasketed at its top and bottom. An original plan to use dowels along the sides to locate this piece was found to be unnecessary and in fact an impediment to reliable sealing. From this chamber, water rose into the head, more generously on the inlet side, and then flowed out and up into manifolding on the exhaust side of the head.

The new Austin Class H engine weighed 260lb. Subjected to extensive testing on the dynamometer and 6,000 hard miles at Donington, it gained reliability after the plug was relocated closer to the chamber wall and the SU carburettor was modified. The four developed 116bhp at 7,600rpm and revved easily past 8,000 and indeed higher in sprint events. For longer races it was detuned to 90–100bhp.

No sooner was the new little racer through its teething troubles in 1937 than Austin curtailed its racing programme and Jamieson left to join ERA. Nevertheless the Austins achieved some stunning results. An example was Walter Baumer's 1936 performance in the Freiburg hillclimb, in which he not only won the 1,100cc class but was also a quarter-minute quicker than the best 1½-litre car. New Class H records were set at the end of that season at speeds up to 122mph. In 1938, tragically, the brilliant Jamieson was killed in a freak accident while standing by the pits at Brooklands.

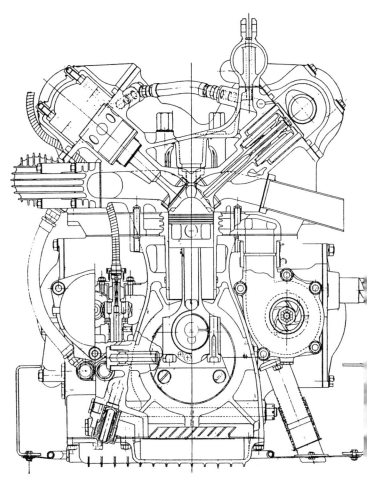

Opposite above: On the left side of the Seven were the aperture for cranking the engine and an inlet duct to the SU carburettor that fed the single Roots-type supercharger.
Opposite below: Designed to rev to well over 10,000rpm, the racing Austin Seven had very large inverted-cup tappets and wide cam lobes.

Its gear drive to the camshafts was at the rear of the cylinder block.
Above: In cross-section the remarkable Austin engine reveals the finning at the top of its inserted steel cylinder liners. Exquisite detail design is evident in all aspects of the structure of the engine and the cooling-water passages from the pump on the left side of the block.

SPECIFICATIONS	
Cylinders	I4
Bore	60.3mm
Stroke	65.1mm
Stroke/bore ratio	1.08:1
Capacity	744cc
Compression ratio	6.5:1
Connecting rod length	127.0mm
Rod/crank radius ratio	3.9:1
Main bearing journal diameter	63.5mm
Rod journal diameter	44.5mm
Inlet valve diameter (1 valve)	38.1mm
Exhaust valve diameter (1 valve)	38.1mm
Inlet pressure	2.5Atm
Engine weight	260lb (118kg)
Peak power	116bhp @ 7,600rpm
Piston speed (corrected)	3,124ft/min (15.6m/s)
Engine bhp per litre	155.9bhp per litre
Engine weight per bhp	2.24lb (1.01kg) per bhp

1937

MERCEDES-BENZ M125 5.7-LITRE EIGHT

Mercedes-Benz was severely challenged by Auto Union in the 1936 GP races. The 1936 M-B racer had been an improved version of its successful 1935 car, but the improvements had evidently been in the wrong direction. Power was a deficiency, which gave Daimler-Benz seriously to think about a substantially new engine for 1937.

Some of its engineers proposed aping Auto Union by building a V16 measuring 75 x 85mm (6,010cc), designated M151. It would have iron liners in a light-alloy cylinder block. But when it became clear that the V16 would not be ready in time, the technical management decided to look for higher power from the existing type of twin-cam 32-valve straight-eight engine.

They created the new F-series engine, officially known as the M125. This in-line eight looked much the same as its predecessors but was longer with its cylinder-centre distance increased from the previous 95mm to 104mm. This allowed a larger bore, its dimensions being 94 x 102mm (3.70 x 4.02in) for 5,560cc. The classic Daimler-Benz cylinder construction of welded sheet-steel water jackets around forged-steel cylinders was retained, built as two four-cylinder blocks with integral heads. These were bolted to a robust aluminium crankcase.

Equally spread at an included angle of 70°, the four valves per cylinder had 39mm head diameters for both inlets and exhausts. They were hollow to permit either sodium or mercury internal cooling. The stem end of the valve was made solid and the filling was added through the centre of the head, permanently sealed after completion. Pivoted fingers were interposed between the cam lobes and the ends of the valve stems. The valve timing (with a cold engine) was as follows:

Inlet opens 15°BTDC Exhaust opens 30°BBDC
Inlet closes 42°ABDC Exhaust closes 3°ATDC

Compression ratio was typically 8.9:1, although toward the end of 1937 it ranged as high as 9.4:1.

A one-piece crankshaft carried I-section connecting rods that had split big ends carrying roller bearings in split cages. The rod big-end bearings had two rows of rollers 8mm in diameter and 10mm wide. The rollers in the mains were 10mm in diameter, varying in width from 18mm downward. Gudgeon-pin diameter was 25mm.

The new engine was built initially with five main bearings, like its predecessors, and also with nine main bearings. Even under the 750kg formula weight was not an issue because the engine with four extra mains gained only 1.1lb (0.5 kg) from this cause, having a crankshaft that was lighter and a crankcase that was heavier than the five-main bearing version. Nine mains were ultimately standardised on the M125. After a failure in early-season testing the rod-bearing size was increased from 63 to 66mm with stronger crank cheeks to match. (In at least one engine the two rod journals closest to the clutch were 66mm in diameter while the others were 63mm. This addressed the need for greater strength closer to the output end of the crank.)

Serious consideration was given to the use of the Hirth built-up crankshaft that was favoured by Auto Union. This allowed lighter one-piece rod big ends. In November 1936 one such shaft was tested in an earlier engine for 12 hours on the dynamometer and 250 miles on the *Autobahn* (one presumes on a section not yet open to traffic) before one of its joining bolts broke. Hirth supplied six complete crank and rod assemblies to suit the nine-main-bearing version of the M125 but these were never seriously committed to competition. One reason was that they were found to be 13 per cent weaker in torsion than the solid crankshaft.

The weight of a single forged-aluminium Mahle piston for this massive engine was precisely 1.1lb (0.5kg). Twin updraught carburettors on the right side of the engine were pressurised by a Roots-type supercharger with rotors 106mm in diameter and 240mm long, mounted vertically at the front of the block. The complete M125 weighed 491lb (223kg). It was destined to produce well in excess of one horsepower per pound.

Expectations for a dramatic power increase had been high since late September 1936, when Mercedes induction-system specialist Georg Scheerer first tried a suction carburation system on a 1935-type engine. Suction systems, in which

Opposite above: Hermann Lang is pictured waiting for a starting signal in his 1937 Mercedes-Benz W125. It was destined to be the dominant car of a season that was hard fought with Auto Union.

Opposite below: The gear train driving the twin overhead camshafts of the 1937 M125 Mercedes-Benz ran up the back of the engine, where it could also turn the Bosch magneto. Mounts for both the pedals and the steering gear were integrated with the castings at the rear of the engine.

gave power increases of 32 per cent at 2,000rpm and 11 per cent at 5,800. Peak output was 488bhp at 5,500. Cautioning that these results did not reflect the changes that would be needed to get smooth throttle response in the car, the engineer estimated that the M125 would deliver 583bhp on the normal racing fuel blend and as high as 597bhp on WW fuel, a blend that was good for power but not fuel economy. It was to happen, but not easily.

A power curve taken on the first M125 in mid-February, with suction carburation, showed 580bhp at 5,800rpm on the standard fuel blend and even better output at medium and low speeds than had been forecast. This was an excellent result. But when installed in a car the eight refused to respond to full throttle smoothly unless carburettor size was drastically reduced. Nor did it want to react quickly to a blip of the throttle for a downshift. After these discouraging trials the 1937 season was started with pressure carburation of the proven type.

The sacrifice in peak power incurred was relatively small, a matter of five to ten horsepower, but the loss was substantially greater at lower engine speeds. Torque was strikingly reduced. A comparison made in June, 1937 on a single engine with the normal test fuel and settings suitable for racing showed the difference:

the supercharger draws a fuel/air mixture from the carburettor and then pumps it to the engine, had been widely adopted by competitors like Auto Union and Alfa Romeo but were not fondly regarded by Mercedes-Benz at Untertürkheim. All its new racing engines since the mid-1920s had superchargers that blew through the carburettors, so the company had a vast fund of knowledge on the operation of pressure-carburation systems.

But Scheerer's findings brooked no argument. Tests on a 1936-type engine with a suction system

	Speed	Boost at valve	Power	Torque
	(rpm)	(psi)	(bhp)	(lbft/Nm)
Pressure carburettors	3,000	6.2	316	553/750
	5,800	13.3	550	498/675
Suction carburettors	3,000	10.2	361	632/857
	5,800	11.3	556	504/683

Above: *Extending to the rear along the right side of the engine from the vertically mounted Roots-type blower at the front, the M125's inlet manifold was shaped to provide equal distribution to all eight cylinders. Each section of the manifold had its own pressure-relief valve to cope with backfires.*
Left: *Carried between the oval-tube frame members*

of the W125, its straight-eight engine had its fuel pump mounted low at the right front. This supplied the carburettor mounted on the left.
Opposite: *Although longer than its predecessors with its displacement of 5,560cc, the W125's M125 straight-eight was remarkably light at 491lb. The connection from carburettor to supercharger is visible at the front of the engine bay.*

MERCEDES-BENZ M125 5.7-LITRE EIGHT

To find a suction-type carburettor that would give the needed throttle response the Daimler-Benz design office reverted to the example of a 1924 2-litre racing Mercedes eight, the M218, which had an updraught instrument incorporating an Automat, a weighted sliding venturi. Much like that unit in principle, the new carburettor had two updraught 62mm throats, each with a 48mm Automat venturi. On the downstream side a two-piece log manifold was provided that was smaller in diameter, 57mm, along the more remote rear block than its 70mm diameter along the front four cylinders.

With this manifold, fed from the front end, one problem consistently troubled the M125 developers: the spark plugs in the two rear cylinders always ran 'oily' or 'wet'. They had to be replaced with a hotter plug, the Bosch 420, while the other cylinders used a colder 450 plug. Realising that fuel was collecting in liquid form at the end of the manifold, Georg Scheerer invented a simple means of releasing it through small orifices – a manifold scavenging system – that piped the fuel back to the supercharger inlet. There it was ingested neat, helping further to seal the compressor's running clearances. This was used, in various forms, on all the suction-carburetted M125 engines.

Dick Seaman, the brilliant young Englishman who placed seventh at Tripoli in his first drive for Mercedes-Benz at the beginning of the 1937 season, was given a suction-carburetted car for the 5 July Vanderbilt Cup event at Roosevelt Raceway near New York. He brought it home in second place, only missing a win because his fuel supply ran short.

A separate Mercedes racing crew had taken a suction-carburettor kit along to the Belgian Grand Prix on 11 July but had not installed it. Seaman's success in America was sufficiently encouraging to lead to the new system's general use in the German Grand Prix on 25 July. There, in the most important event on their calendar, the men from Untertürkheim reaped a well-earned reward for one solid year of the most difficult and exacting experimental work, of literally thousands of test miles in search of a new formula for success that included not only the new M125 engine but also the W125 chassis that carried it. Four out of five starting Mercedes-Benzes finished, two of them in the first two positions.

The M125 set new highs for horsepower output. On the normal fuel blend used for racing the M125 engines leaving the two Scheerer test benches were producing between 550 and 575bhp toward the end of 1937. Auto Union and Alfa Romeo were mere also-rans in 1937 with 520 and 432bhp respectively. And after the M125's career as a GP engine had ended, a special version of the eight, built for record-breaking and hillclimbing, produced a staggering 646 horsepower.

SPECIFICATIONS	
Cylinders	I8
Bore	94.0mm
Stroke	102.0mm
Stroke/bore ratio	1.09:1
Capacity	5,560cc
Compression ratio	8.9:1
Connecting rod length	167.0mm
Rod/crank radius ratio	3.3:1
Main bearing journal diameter	63.0mm
Rod journal diameter	66.0mm
Inlet valve diameter (2 valves)	39.0mm
Exhaust valve diameter (2 valves)	39.0mm
Inlet pressure	1.86Atm
Engine weight	491lb (223kg)
Peak power	575bhp @ 5,500rpm
Piston speed (corrected)	3,534ft/min (17.7m/s)
Peak torque	683ft lb (926Nm) @ 3,000rpm
Peak bmep	304psi
Engine bhp per litre	103.4bhp per litre
Engine weight per bhp	0.85lb (0.39kg) per bhp

1938

AUTO UNION D-TYPE 3-LITRE V12

In 1938 a new Grand Prix formula came into effect that restricted unsupercharged engines to 4½ litres and supercharged units to no more than 3 litres. Prof. Ferdinand Porsche – author of the original Auto Union racer – was very interested in two-stroke engines at this time. He designed a spectacular opposed-piston two-stroke engine for the supercharged 3-litre category, but not for Auto Union. In the 1938–39 period Porsche had switched his allegiance to Daimler-Benz, which was better able to meet his substantial fees.

One might well have expected Auto Union to try building an unsupercharged 4½-litre version of its V16 but its head of development, Robert Eberan von Eberhorst, said that this had not been considered. Instead, he and Werner Strobel carried out a reduction of the V16 concept to create a 3-litre blown V12. This was implemented with remarkable economy which contrasted vividly with the extravagance of design and construction practised by Auto Union's arch-rivals Daimler-Benz.

Racing parts were made in special workshops set up by Auto Union at Zwickau in quantities so small that it was impractical to set up production tooling or special forging dies. Thus many parts had to be machined from solid billets; often only a tenth of the weight of the original metal blank remained after machining. Yet because all the parts had to be fully interchangeable for ease of maintenance in the field, exceptional manufacturing precision was demanded.

Stressed pieces were normally polished. Sliding surfaces, as in the engine, were lapped before assembly to reduce the break-in time required. When possible, new engines were broken in on the dynamometer for four to five hours before power runs were made. And the output figures that were obtained were kept entirely secret, so much so that the mechanics in attendance didn't even tell their friends in the racing department how well the engines were doing.

The 1938 3-litre D-Type V12 resembled the V16 in all its main construction features. A single deep aluminium casting formed the crankcase and cylinder blocks in one unit. As before, forged-steel wet cylinder liners were deeply spigoted into the block and sealed at their tops by the cylinder heads. The bore and stroke of 65 x 75mm (2.56 x 2.95in) were very close to those of the A-Type of 1934. The connecting rod length of 168mm was the same as that of the C-Type as was the main bearing diameter of 70mm.

The new engine started out in 1938 with the same plain main bearings the V16 used. Later a significant horsepower gain was achieved by installing roller main bearings, each with 24 rollers measuring 7 x 10mm. The big ends used 22 rollers each of 7.5 x 11mm, running on the 66mm rod journals of a Hirth built-up crankshaft. All rollers were guided by duralumin cages. While the V16 crankshafts had been only partially counterweighted, in their final editions the V12 cranks were completely counterweighted in acknowledgement of the much higher engine speeds that were being used.

Equal firing-order spacing was achieved by setting the two cylinder banks of the V12 at a 60° angle. This wider spacing rendered impracticable the use of the V16's single-camshaft valve gear. With its pushrods to the exhaust valves that system would have been inadequate, in any case, to cope with the 10,000rpm to which the D-Type's valve gear was successfully tested.

A single central camshaft was retained to open the inlet valves through finger-type followers. It was driven by a vertical shaft and bevel gears at the rear of the engine. The bevel gear at the inlet camshaft was then used to drive bevels to short cross-shafts which extended out to camshafts along the tops of the exhaust valves, again working through finger followers. Double coil springs closed the valves. Made of forged steel, the camshafts turned in plain bearings measuring 30mm in diameter.

Thus the D-Type was a triple-cam engine with inlet/exhaust valves 34/31mm in diameter. They were equally inclined at an included angle of 90° and rested on inserted bronze seats. The valves were made of cobalt-nickel-alloy steel and had solid stems 8mm in diameter. No internal cooling was considered necessary. Nominal valve timing was as follows:

Left: The large filter atop the engine supplied fuel to the carburettors of the Auto Union D-Type in 1938 trim. The drive shafts from the centre to the two outer exhaust camshafts were at the rear of the engine. Below: A downward view of the blower of the 1938 Type D showed an adjustable linkage connecting the two carburettors that allowed their opening to be progressive. Rubber bellows enclosed the shafts that drove the outboard exhaust camshafts.*

Inlet opens 20°BTDC Exhaust opens 20°BBDC
Inlet closes 60°ABDC Exhaust closes 60°ATDC

Other changes from the V16 included an additional oil scavenge pump at the front of the sump, and the use of three compression rings above the gudgeon pin and a single oil ring at the bottom of the full skirt of the Mahle forged piston. Two Bosch six-cylinder magnetos were driven by the bevel gears at the rear of the engine and sparked plugs that were placed centrally at the top of the combustion chambers.

A new scaled-down Roots-type supercharger was designed, with an Elektron (magnesium alloy) case instead of aluminium. Displacing almost 1.4 litres per revolution, it was driven at 2.4 times crank speed – up to 17,000rpm – to produce a boost of 17psi, just over one atmosphere. With this single vertically mounted blower the D-Type engine developed 460bhp at 7,000rpm.

The research-oriented Auto Union engineers well knew how inefficient the Roots-type blower was at such high speeds and pressures. Tests they'd run back in 1936 had shown that the C-Type blower had required 80 horsepower to drive it and the figure was even higher now at higher boost levels. They began work in 1938 on a two-stage layout, one which uses two blowers in series to compress the mixture progressively, giving improved efficiency. They used it for the first time in racing at the French Grand Prix in 1939.

The smaller second-stage blower was a shorter-

lobe version of the one used in 1938, displacing 1.2 litres per revolution. It was driven from the same idler gear as before, but swung around 90° so that the charge passed through it from right to left and was then ducted forward into the engine. To the right of it the larger, first-stage blower was placed, a shorter edition of the S-series supercharger used on the V16 engines, sweeping 2.25 litres per revolution. Both were driven at 1.63 times engine speed, delivering a 24psi supercharge to the engine. Thus equipped the V12 produced 485bhp at 7,000rpm and could attain 500bhp at 7,500, although this wasn't always used in racing. Peak torque was 405lb ft at 4,000rpm, a remarkably low speed for a racing engine.

Under the direction of Eberan von Eberhorst, Auto Union was strong on the conduct of theoretical research into engine operating conditions. On the dynamometer it obtained indicator diagrams of the combustion process, sampling of charge distribution, exhaust gas and spark plug temperatures, fuel consumption rate and supercharger boost pressure, which was read from a mercury manometer. Supercharger development and carburettor mixture formation were subjects of special study.

To feed the D-Type, Solex rearranged the same carburettor parts that had been used for the V16 to make an over-and-under horizontal instrument, better to suit the intake pattern of the vertical Roots supercharger. Then in 1938 for more capacity a third single Solex of the same type was added, at the top, angled to the right while the double instrument was angled off to the left to clear the supplementary unit. The linkage between them gave a progressive throttle opening which produced a smoother application of power and a better mid-range torque output.

To the same end Auto Union developed, with the SUM firm, a special vertical weir-type four-throat carburettor in 1938. It had no float chambers. Each jet block drew from a chamber which was kept full by one fuel pump and was constantly tapped off, at a precise level, by a second pump. All four throats were controlled by a single vertical barrel-type throttle valve, arranged so that it progressively uncovered a second main jet as it opened.

This reliable carburettor was used on the single-stage D-Types in 1939, mounted well to the rear and connected to the blower by a manifold. It was also fitted to the two-stage-blown engines, on which it protruded well out to the right. This required a conspicuous bonnet bulge and a fresh-air supply duct running forward to a point just behind the cockpit.

For von Eberhorst the two-stage blower was only a stopgap measure until he could perfect a vane-type supercharger which, with its internal compression, is a more efficient instrument. Based on the Becke Power-Plus design, one was being developed in 1939 for use on the planned 1½-litre V12 E-Type Auto Union engine. Its construction was well progressed, with single-cylinder tests completed and crankcase castings made, when Germany's motor industry was asked to turn its attention to other matters.

During the 3-litre-formula years Auto Union and Mercedes-Benz used much the same fuel blend, comprised of 86.0 per cent methanol, nitrobenzol 4.4 per cent, acetone 8.8 per cent and sulphuric ether 0.8 per cent. On twisty tracks the 1939 D-Type travelled about 2¾ miles per Imperial gallon of fuel. After winning the final race of 1938 at Donington, driven by Nuvolari, the D-Type scored victories for Auto Union at Monza and Belgrade in 1939. The Yugoslav GP at Belgrade was the last held before the onset of war in Europe.

SPECIFICATIONS	
Cylinders	V12
Bore	65.0mm
Stroke	75.0mm
Stroke/bore ratio	1.15:1
Capacity	5,577cc
Compression ratio	10.0:1
Connecting rod length	168.0mm
Rod/crank radius ratio	4.5:1
Main bearing journal diameter	70.0mm
Rod journal diameter	66.0mm
Inlet valve diameter (1 valve)	34.0mm
Exhaust valve diameter (1 valve)	31.0mm
Inlet pressure	2.66Atm
Peak power	485bhp @ 7,000rpm
Piston speed (corrected)	3,207ft/min (16.0m/s)
Peak torque	405lb ft (549Nm) @ 4,000rpm
Peak bmep	180psi
Engine bhp per litre	87.0bhp per litre

1939

MERCEDES-BENZ M154/M163 3-LITRE V12

After the announcement of the new Grand Prix engine formula for 1938 to 1941 Daimler-Benz concluded early in 1937 that its preference lay in the direction of the 3-litre supercharged alternative, specifically favouring a 60° V12 engine. To cover its flanks it commissioned some studies of 4½-litre unsupercharged units from the Porsche office, but these were never given serious consideration.

As was customary at 'Daimler' the V12's cylinders were individually forged of chrome-alloy steel with integral pent-roof heads. These were welded to common base flanges to form groups of three. Complete with their sheet-steel ports and water jackets, these triple-cylinder blocks were spigoted into a Silumin (high-silicon aluminium) crankcase and retained by short studs. Cylinder dimensions were 67 x 70mm (2.64 x 2.76in) for 2,962cc.

A very deep crankcase fully enveloped the crankshaft, which was supported by seven main bearings. The left-hand cylinder bank was offset 18mm ahead of the right bank to allow for side-by-side connecting-rod big ends on the one-piece forged-steel crankshaft, which carried slinger rings to catch the oil needed for big-end lubrication. The main bearing journals measured 60mm except for the 52mm journal at the front, and ran on 10mm rollers. At the big ends, rollers 8mm in diameter and 12mm long ran on 54mm journals.

Each connecting rod, a forging of nickel-chrome steel, had a two-bolt big end with lateral serrations at the joint face. The centre-to-centre measurement was 155mm. These I-section rods bore much of the responsibility for handling the substantial increase in engine speed that was planned for the M154, as the new unit was known to the engineers. To the workshop it was the 'H-series'. They coped well with it – up to a point. During 1938 the rod was found to be unsafe at any speed above 8,000rpm.

At the back end of the crankshaft a double-roller main bearing was adjacent to the very deep hub of the shallow flywheel. Machined around the outside of this hub were the teeth of the drive pinion for the gear train at the back of the engine, upward to the four camshafts and downward to the oil pressure and scavenge pumps. Development during 1938 led to the addition of two additional external oil scavenge pumps which were driven by shafts, outside the crankcase at the rear, that had originally been intended for fuel-injection pumps. Injection was planned but was not ready in time.

Four bearings supported each camshaft within the full-length aluminium cam housings, also enclosing the finger-type followers and double-coil valve springs. Symmetrically disposed at a 60 degree included angle were four valves per cylinder, each with a 30mm head diameter and 11mm stem.

From the time the new engine first drew breath in January 1938 until the racing season was well under way in May, the V12 was troubled by a limitation on revs caused by valve bounce in the new high-speed regimes that were being reached. This meant early valve contact with the pistons, whose crowns had been pushed exceptionally close to the chamber walls in this large-bore, short-stroke (by previous standards) cylinder to get a compression ratio of 7.8:1 in the first engine. Even so, this was a drop of a full point from the M125. To gain reliability the piston-crown height had to be dropped, reducing the compression ratio of the 1938 H-series engines to the range of 5.9–6.2:1. At some sacrifice in maximum power, this made the engine serviceable for the 1938 season.

Induction was through two Roots-type compressors operating in parallel. Their steel rotors in magnesium casings measured 106mm in diameter and 150mm in length. Protruding forward from the front of the engine, they were driven by a train of spur gears from the nose of the crank at a step-up of 1.5:1. Their pressurised air-fuel mixture was supplied to a single central manifold from which individual branches led downward to the oval inlet ports. Just as had been done on the F-series eight, the Scheerer system of manifold scavenging or 'liquid fuel recirculation' was applied to this manifold to balance out the appetites of all the cylinders.

Opposite above: The sleek lines of the 1939 Mercedes-Benz W154 set a standard for racing-car design that extended well into the 1950s. The Stuttgart engineers ingeniously found places within its body to store the quantities of fuel that its thirsty engine required.

Opposite below: As initially raced in 1938 the 3-litre M154 engine had single-stage supercharging by two Roots-type blowers operating in parallel and feeding a common inlet manifold down the centre of the vee. The engine was angled in the chassis to allow the drive shaft to pass to the left of the low-seated driver.

Left: Painted black, the fabricated steel cylinders of the M154 were made in blocks of three. Drive gears to the four overhead camshafts were placed at the rear of the block.
Below: Mercedes-Benz defied the Fiat-led trend by continuing through the 1930s with four valves per cylinder for its racing engines. This well suited the heavy heat loads that a supercharged engine had to endure. Spur gearing from the nose of the M154 V12 drove the twin two-lobed Roots-type superchargers.
Opposite: A section drawing of the M154 shows the two Bosch fuel-injection pumps at the sides of the crankcase that were originally planned for this engine. Bosses below the exhaust ports show where the injectors were located. The V12 was only raced with carburettors, however.

Within a single aluminium housing the Mercedes design office combined design features of earlier carburettors. At the ends of a long casting were two horizontal throats feeding the two superchargers, each with its own float bowl. The Automat principle of a moving outer venturi was retained, now with the venturi lying on its side and controlled by springs instead of gravity. In the centre of the carburettor a single barrel valve contained a large extra fuel jet. The valve was opened and closed by supercharger boost pressure, acting on a sliding piston mounted on the inlet manifold.

Hermann Lang's engine for Reims showed the highest reading obtained in 1938: 474bhp at 8,000rpm. Lang was fastest qualifier and race leader until his car proved hard to restart after his pit stop – a chronic 1938 problem. The engines sent to Donington Park in October produced between 433 and 444bhp at 8,000rpm.

Racing engineer Rudolf Uhlenhaut set new objectives for the 1939 version of the V12: 'From the driving point of view a speed of 8,500–8,800 would be of great advantage, even if the power remained constant from 8,000–8,500 or fell off slightly.' Standing in the way, he acknowledged, were shortcomings of the valve gear and the connecting rods.

Extensive revisions were made to the base engine for 1939 to improve its ruggedness, serviceability and oil-tightness, leading to a new designation for the unit: to the engineers it was the 'M163' and to the machine shop it was the 'K-series' engine. Both base engines accepted the same supercharger assemblies, the same valves and valve gear and the same accessories. The bore and stroke were unchanged. During 1939 four of these new K-series engines were completed for use by the team.

Break-up of the main-bearing journals, which had been a problem in 1938, was still troubling the V12, as was valve bounce. In order to ensure reliability the racing red line was lowered to 7,200rpm. Thus instead of rising in 1939, as Uhlenhaut had hoped, the speed limit of the V12 engine had to be lowered. Not until this new red line was enforced in the last two races of 1939 was the V12 judged to have attained 'complete operating reliability'.

Another change for 1939 was the adoption of two-stage supercharging. This helped the late-1939 engines produce 7 per cent more power on 10 per cent less manifold pressure than the 1938 engines of the same compression ratio. To explore the potential of a two-stage Roots system for the M154, Daimler-Benz commissioned its consultants, the Porsche organisation, to design one for trials. By

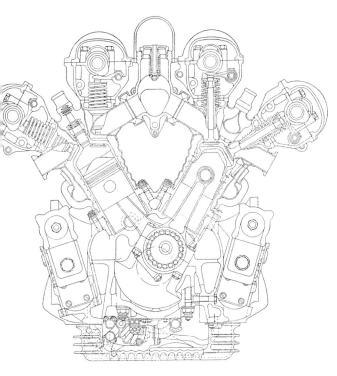

and flanked by the float bowls. A third throttle and its jets were commanded, as before, by the boost pressure in the inlet manifold through a piston and linkage. Controlling this supplementary carburettor on the two-stage-blown engine was made more problematic by its flatter boost curve.

With the two-stage system the blower drive horsepower required was reduced and net engine output was up at every engine speed. The peak power figures of 470 to 480bhp that had been recorded before at 8,000rpm were now achieved at 7,500. Torque was 365lb ft at 5,500rpm. Power was increased by 25 and 30bhp handfuls all the way up the curve while specific fuel consumption remained almost unchanged.

The Mercedes racing engineers were not yet home free. A spate of engine failures in mid-season had them scratching their heads until they diagnosed and solved a fault in the carburettor and its controls. After rectification, the 1939 W154 Mercedes-Benz swept the board in the Swiss Grand Prix on 20 August, placing one–two–three in both a preliminary heat and the final. The Mercedes-Benz V12 was finally fully race-ready – just in time for Grand Prix racing's pre-emption by war.

November 1938 a unit was ready for test. Although not a raceworthy design, it showed that clear benefits would be gained by the use of two-stage boosting.

In the final design for 1939 the rotors of both blower stages were given the same diameter, 125mm, their lengths differing at 220 and 125mm. Both were driven at 1.25 times crankshaft speed. Formerly placed flat, the long axes of the oval blower casings were now angled just off the vertical to accommodate the completely-revised manifolding. The longer primary blower was placed on the right and fed at its inboard port by the carburettor. Around the upper surfaces of the magnesium casings curved the duct between the two compressors, actually cast as part of the finned housing. The smaller left-hand compressor delivered the mixture from its inboard port to the inlet manifold.

A new carburettor was also put in hand. It carried over the same twin horizontal throats of the single-stage model, with their vacuum-responsive Automat venturis, now placed next to each other

SPECIFICATIONS	
Cylinders	V12
Bore	67.0mm
Stroke	70.0mm
Stroke/bore ratio	1.04:1
Capacity	2,962cc
Compression ratio	7.2:1
Connecting rod length	158.0mm
Rod/crank radius ratio	4.5:1
Main bearing journal diameter	54.0mm
Rod journal diameter	60.0mm
Inlet valve diameter (2 valves)	30.0mm
Exhaust valve diameter (2 valves)	30.0mm
Inlet pressure	2.31Atm
Engine weight	603lb (274kg)
Peak power	480bhp @ 7,500rpm
Piston speed (corrected)	3,370ft/min (16.9m/s)
Peak torque	365lb ft (495Nm)
	@ 5,500rpm
Peak bmep	305psi
Engine bhp per litre	162.1bhp per litre
Engine weight per bhp	1.26lb (0.57kg) per bhp

1949

CISITALIA 1.5-LITRE FLAT-12

usio always set his sights on the exceptional. This was the recollection of Giovanni Savonuzzi, who worked for Piero Dusio at his Turin-based Cisitalia company, maker of some of Italy's finest small post-war sports cars and small-capacity racing cars. Setting his sights high, sports-mad Dusio had had a good war as the exclusive supplier of clothing to the Italian army. Now, in 1946, he dreamed of spending some of his considerable wealth on the building of a new Grand Prix car. By the end of 1948 its construction had bankrupted Cisitalia.

Astonishingly, in the confusion that was post-war Europe, contact was made in 1946 between Dusio in Turin and the Porsche engineers, most of whom were still at the sawmill in Gmünd, Austria where they had been relocated during the war. Setting his sights as usual on the exceptional, Dusio asked the Porsche office to design a car for the new Formula 1. The relevant contracts were signed on 3 February 1947. Porsche suggested a rear-engined car and offered the choice of an unblown 4½-litre engine, but Dusio said he preferred the blown 1½-litre alternative.

At first a V12 engine was considered but the final design, Porsche's Type 360, was a flat or 180° V12. This layout allowed the rod big ends of opposite cylinders to share common crankpins, greatly simplifying the bottom end. Mildly oversquare cylinder dimensions of 56 x 50.5mm (2.20 x 1.99in) gave a capacity of 1,493cc. Two valves per cylinder were specified, equally inclined at a 90° included angle just as in the Auto Union D-Type. Although the Porsche office did not design the D-Type it was familiar with it, and on the Cisitalia project it briefly had the guidance and help of one of its creators, Auto Union engineer Eberan von Eberhorst.

Although the 1½-litre's bore was 14 per cent smaller than that of the 3-litre Auto Union V12, the Porsche engineers contrived to fit in valves of much the same size: 34/29mm for inlet/exhaust. One technique they used to achieve this was the omission of valve-seat inserts. The valves seated directly on the high-silicon Y-alloy aluminium cylinder heads. Detachable, the heads were compact castings, nearly symmetrical and differing from top to bottom in having cooling water under the exhaust seats and ports but not the inlets. Long studs attached them to the crankcase.

Split vertically down the crank centreline, the crankcase was formed in two halves, also cast of high-silicon aluminium. Both castings extended downward at the engine's centre to form the complete sump, finned on the bottom. A cylindrical hollow machined at the rear of the sump trapped, between the halves, three barrel-shaped spur-gear pumps, two for sump scavenging and one for delivery, driven by a train of narrow gears at the rear of the crankshaft.

Pressurised oil was fed to the nose of the crankshaft, where it passed through a centrifuge before being fed into the delivery drillings that ran the length of the shaft. An integral supply took oil to the cylinder heads, where it flowed through the cam bearings into the hollow camshafts and was released by small orifices in the flanks of the cam lobes. Tubes at the rear of the lower cam housings returned oil to the sump.

Clamped between each cylinder head and ledges 64mm down in the crankcase were cast-iron wet liners. Although this form of construction mirrored that of the Auto Union engines, it was relatively untested as a means of maintaining a consistent seal at the head joint in a highly supercharged engine. The use of these wet liners allowed the engine to be commendably short, with cylinder centres of 69mm that were compact for a bore of 56mm. They contained high-peaked pistons forged of Duralite aluminium alloy that gave a compression ratio of 7.6:1. Two compression rings and one oil ring encircled the fully skirted pistons above the gudgeon pin.

The Cisitalia's crankshaft was an impressive example of Porsche engineering. Its Hirth built-up construction allowed the use of roller main and rod bearings without splits in their cages and races. Its journals were massive – 55mm for the mains and those for the rods only a smidgeon smaller at 54mm. The cheeks were fully circular, because the opposing rods and pistons effectively counterbalanced each other. The outer steel races of the main bearings were grooved on their

Opposite above: Among the advanced features of the Porsche-designed Cisitalia was four-wheel drive. The drive shafts are visible between the front-suspension trailing arms.

Opposite below: Driven from the noses of the exhaust camshafts, two small-diameter water pumps supplied their respective cylinder banks directly. A flexible crankcase breather pipe rose up and back alongside the carburettor.

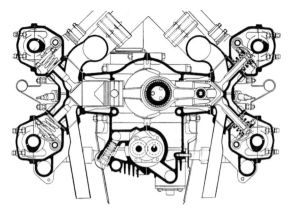

exteriors so they could be firmly seated in their crankcase webs. Seven roller bearings carried the crankshaft. In addition an eighth ball bearing was added at the rear to take the clutch thrust loadings, placed outboard of the gearing that drove the superchargers and camshafts.

With this construction the short connecting rod – 101mm from centre to centre – could have a one-piece big end surrounded by a single stiffening rib. An I-section shank joined it to the small end and its crowded-needle bearing on an 18mm gudgeon pin. This was a rugged bottom end designed to be capable of better than 10,000rpm.

Next to the rearmost roller main bearing a spur gear drove up to another gear which drove an adjacent bevel gear. Other bevels at its sides drove shafts running at engine speed which extended out to the inlet valve housings, where a half-speed bevel pair drove the camshafts. From the inlet cam bevel a matching gear drove another shaft downward to the exhaust camshaft. To stabilise the complete shaft drive train, another shaft extended across the complete engine to join the

two exhaust-cam bevels together, thereby closing the loop.

The cams and valve gear were carried in separate light-alloy housings that were bolted to the head. Dual-coil valve springs seated directly on the head and protruded up through holes in the bottom of the cam housing. Pivoted from hollow shafts running the length of each cam housing were short, light finger cam followers. These were direct-acting, in the sense that the cam lobe was directly above the tip of the valve stem. No positive or negative leverage was provided by the finger. A small cap on the end of the stem was changed to adjust valve clearance. Valve timing was as follows:

Inlet opens   30°BTDC   Exhaust opens 68°BBDC
Inlet closes   61°ABDC   Exhaust closes 22°ATDC

From the top of the compound spur/bevel gear in the crankcase a spur-gear drive was taken to the superchargers atop the engine. Although the original Porsche drawings showed a three-stage Roots blower system overhung above the clutch housing, reconsideration led to the use instead of two vane-type superchargers of Centric design. Vane-type blowers, which had been used by ERA before the war and tested by both Mercedes-Benz and Auto Union, had the asset of internal compression which enhanced efficiency.

Manufactured by Cisitalia, the Centric-type blowers sat side-by-side. An idler in the gear train allowed the blowers to be 'handed' so that they counter-rotated to suit the induction layout. Atop them, feeding both blowers through Y-pipes, were two large-bore Weber downdraught carburettors. The system was planned for a boost above atmospheric of 30psi with drive gears

available in ratios of 49 per cent, 50 per cent and 51 per cent of engine speed.

A separate six-cylinder Bosch magneto for each cylinder bank was driven from the rear of its inlet camshaft, adjacent to the drive bevel. Cables went forward to the 18mm Lodge spark plugs, which were inserted at a steep angle. Each was set back from its combustion chamber and communicated with it through a 6mm orifice. At the fronts of the exhaust camshafts were the two small-diameter water pumps, each serving its own cylinder bank. Water inlet manifolds were cast into the exhaust cam boxes. Water exited from the inlet cam boxes through manifolds.

Because the development of such a small, high-boost engine was unexplored territory for the Porsche people, they specified the design and construction of a single-cylinder test engine for experimentation with various supercharging and timing parameters. At Cisitalia in Turin this little unit, with its lonely horizontal cylinder, was run to

more than 10,000rpm so successfully that Ferry Porsche stated that 'the 400bhp we aimed at could have been reached with only 8,500rpm in spite of the fact that the whole engine was planned for 10,000rpm.'

Using a second-hand dynamometer acquired from Fiat, the complete engine was tested in Turin in the summer of 1949. Although this rig was unsuitable for power development it allowed a number of tests to be made, as a result of which the first engine was well past its best. By this time the Cisitalia company, brought low by the expense approaching $1,000,000 of building the planned five Grand Prix cars, was in the hands of a government receiver. He allowed car and engine to be displayed at the Turin Show in May 1950. In January 1951, however, both were on a boat to Argentina, where Piero Dusio hoped to build a new future with a car-building company called Autoar.

Early in 1953 Autoar approved and commissioned an effort to bring the ex-Cisitalia to life so that it might compete in a race at Buenos Aires that February. Although this was unrealistic – the 'Autoar' was demonstrated there instead – this was the spur to conduct the development that the flat-12 had never had. Remarkably, the Argentine engineers succeeded by April 1953 in measuring a power output of 340bhp at 10,500rpm. Persistent trouble with burned pistons, however, meant that they last ran the car on 18 June 1953. It now rests – still mute – in the Porsche collection in Stuttgart.

Opposite left: To attain optimum weight distribution the Porsche engineers placed the gearbox between the engine and the final-drive gears of the GP Cisitalia. As in the 1938 Auto Union the fuel tanks were side-mounted.
Opposite right: To keep engine width at a minimum the Porsche designers working in Austria specified very short connecting rods for the flat-12, measuring only 4in from *centre to centre. The valves were equally disposed at 90° and opened through finger-type followers.*
Above: When split open, the crankcase of the Cisitalia disclosed the cylindrical package that housed all the oil pumps for the dry-sump system. Also driven from the rear of the crankshaft was a compound gear that carried the bevel which drove the shafts extending out to the camshafts.

SPECIFICATIONS	
Cylinders	F12
Bore	56.0mm
Stroke	50.5mm
Stroke/bore ratio	7.6:1
Capacity	1,493cc
Compression ratio	7.6:1
Connecting rod length	101.6mm
Rod/crank radius ratio	4.0:1
Main bearing journal diameter	55.0mm
Rod journal diameter	54.0mm
Inlet valve diameter (1 valve)	34.0mm
Exhaust valve diameter (1 valve)	29.0mm
Inlet pressure	3.07Atm
Peak power	340bhp @ 10,500rpm
Piston speed (corrected)	3,664ft/min (18.3m/s)
Engine bhp per litre	227.7bhp per litre

1950

MASERATI 4CLT/48 1.5-LITRE FOUR

Adopting the emblem of Neptune's trident, prominent on one of the squares of their home base, Italy's Bologna, the Maserati brothers built and raced cars under their own name from 1927. In all there were six brothers in this generation of Maseratis. Those who survived to be involved in racing cars were – in order of age – Bindo, Alfieri, Ettore and Ernesto. Alfieri's leading role was recognised in the name of the company they founded: Officine Alfieri Maserati.

Beginning in the 1920s with the development of racing cars for Diatto, the Maseratis were soon making Grand Prix cars in their own name. They enjoyed success in the early 1930s before the onslaught of the silver cars in 1934 swept the red ones to one side. Increasingly in that decade Maserati produced successful models to compete in the 1½-litre *Voiturette* category, where both four- and six-cylinder Maseratis offered strong competition to the British ERAs.

A tough new competitor appeared on the *Voiturette* scene in 1938, however, in the form of the Type 158 Alfa Romeo 'Alfetta' with its supercharged straight-eight engine. Lacking the means to compete with the Germans in Grand Prix racing, Milan's Alfa had decided to put more effort into the 1½-litre formula, which many were tipping to be the future Formula 1. In the autumn of 1938 it was rumoured that a new four-cylinder Maserati would soon appear to enhance Italy's *Voiturette* chances. Bindo Maserati announced the Type 4CL in January, 1939, mentioning that it had four valves per cylinder and optional single- or two-stage supercharging.

Launching of the new Type 4CL was made possible by the fresh financial support given to the company by the Modena-based Orsi Group, which took the Maserati company under its wing in 1937. The brothers agreed to remain with the firm for the following decade. In 1940 their operations were moved from Bologna to Modena.

Their new 4CL was single-stage-supercharged at first, developing 220bhp at 6,600rpm. It had a brief baptismal outing in England and then appeared in a team of three cars for the Tripoli GP of May, 1939. There Maserati made history of the wrong kind by retiring all three entries on the first lap. Gigi Villoresi had the satisfaction of setting fastest practice lap in a 4CL capable of 170mph with its spectacular German-designed streamlined body.

These cars survived the conflict to be among the most successful entries in the new post-war Formula 1 for cars of 1½ litres supercharged or 4½ litres naturally-aspirated. In mid-1947 Maserati started supplying parts for a new 4CLT model. This looked like the 4CL but had a tube frame (hence the 'T' designation) instead of box-section and had the promised two-stage supercharging, giving 240bhp.

A year later this engine was inserted in a greatly revised chassis and body, the complete car being called the 4CLT/48. It was nicknamed the 'San Remo' after its first race (and victory). Lower and sleeker, this modern classic of a race car was faster and handled better than its forebears, factors that helped Villoresi split up the winning Alfa trio at Bern in 1948. At Reims that year Tazio Nuvolari put in several fast laps with a 4CLT/48 and called it 'the best Maserati ever'. Revised valve timing and new Roots-type blowers brought its horsepower close to 250.

Several design features contributed to the 4CL engine's competitiveness. One, radical for the year of its introduction, was its use of the 'square' cylinder dimensions of 78 x 78mm (3.07 x 3.07in). At the dawn of motor racing, engines with square stroke/bore ratios were not unusual, but from the 1920s onward it had been the fashion to marry a relatively long stroke with a small bore and two valves in a hemispherical combustion chamber. In adopting square dimensions Maserati was keeping pace with Mercedes-Benz, which gave its 1939 1½-litre M165 oversquare proportions.

Compatible with this decision was the use of four valves per cylinder – another technique which had been widely used in racing's early years but had lapsed in the 1920s and 1930s with the notable exception of Mercedes-Benz. The valves were equally angled at an included 90°. Port faces sloped out at the same degree. Eight individual openings on each side gave an 'eight-cylinder' look to the smooth, simple exhaust manifold. All valves

Opposite above: Among the many successful exponents of the 4CLT/48 Maserati was Thailand's Prince Birabongse, better known as 'B. Bira'. Here he is competing in 1950 at San Remo, the race that gave the Maserati its nickname when Ascari won in this model's first appearance in 1948.

Opposite below: A large triple-throat downdraught Weber carburettor delivered its mixture to the primary blower of the two-stage supercharging system. Gearing from the nose of the crank also drove the camshafts and the magneto along the right side of the block.

Above: Originally created in 1939 by the Maserati brothers, the engine of the 4CLT/48 had four valves for each of its four cylinders. Each valve was given its own individual branch in the exhaust manifold.

Below: This late-type 4CLT/48 Maserati had an enclosed firewall and the oil tank for the dry-sump system was mounted alongside the engine on the right. Cooling water was supplied directly to the tops of the cylinder blocks to help reduce the temperature of the overworked exhaust valves.

Opposite: Like Mercedes-Benz before the war, Maserati introduced a four-valve cylinder head for its 4CL engine. It adopted two-stage supercharging, as shown, in 1947. Illustrated is an earlier version of the 4CLT/48 engine with a smaller Weber carburettor.

were 40mm in diameter. They were closed by coil springs and opened by finger followers – long a Maserati tradition – instead of the cup-type tappets that had been tried on the preceding 4CL and 8CLT.

Heads and blocks were cast integral, avoiding high-boost gasket problems. Although initially the engine's two blocks of two cylinders each were made of cast iron, by 1948 they were being made of aluminium with dry steel liners. Pent-roof combustion chambers gave a compression ratio of 6.0:1. The water jackets were cast open and covered with alloy plates. Neatly encased, the twin overhead cams were turned by a forward-located gear train that also drove the two blowers, one above the other, at engine speed.

The crankshaft was carried in only three bronze-backed main bearings. No separate main-bearing caps were provided. The entire magnesium crankcase (Maserati was a pioneer of the use of the ultra-light metal magnesium in racing car construction) was split horizontally to receive the crank, and was bound together by long bolts. Most of the 4CLT/48 crankshafts were conventional, driven by completely machined I-section connecting rods with split, two-bolt big-ends in which babbit bearing metal was poured directly. As a last-ditch effort to maintain competitiveness in the middle of 1951, the Orsi shop produced a massive built-up crankshaft which allowed one-piece rods and roller-type big-end bearings.

Lubrication was dry-sump, a feature which kept many of these well-worn 'Masers' in the race in later years when they held oil like a colander. 4CL and 4CLT models had an oil reservoir stowed under the driver's seat, in obeisance to Maserati tradition, but the 4CLT/48 had a side-saddle tank slung to the right of the engine.

A huge Weber twin-throat carburettor fed the big bottom primary blower with a brew of 85 per cent methanol, eight per cent benzol, five per cent acetone and two per cent castor oil. The acetone and castor oil were primarily for cooling the valves and piston heads and lubricating the lobes of the blower. Boost reached 25psi, piped through a simple log manifold with two blow-off or 'backfire' valves. In early editions the water pump and magneto were located just under the manifold on the right; late cars mounted the pump on the nose of the secondary blower, under the radiator header tank. This had the benefit of speeding up the pump to overcome cooling difficulties.

These engines varied in detail, but most were rated at 260bhp at 7,500rpm. Later Orsi cars may have been nearer 290 with 30psi boost at the same revs, but it was too little and too late – although still commendable for that engine. By the 1950s the 4CLT/48s were getting tired and oily and very much in need of new factory parts, which were not readily available. As a result, some of these machines were privately reworked to keep their original condition or even to improve upon it.

Typical of one approach was Reg Parnell's car, which eventually had an engine that was more English than Italian. It had bronze cylinder blocks, a special crankshaft and a longer-than-standard primary blower, among many other amendments. Nor had the Maserati brothers entirely abandoned their brainchild. Having left Maserati in 1947 to found OSCA in Bologna, they developed and built a 295bhp 4½-litre V12 which fitted perfectly into the San Remo chassis. Prince Bira had such an installation made, which put him back in the running for some minor 1951 events.

The successes of cars powered by the 4CL engine depended almost entirely on the efforts of private teams, as Maserati's official team entries were very occasional. Nevertheless Maserati cars filled the bulk of the starting grids through 1950, a typical figure being 11 out of 24 starters for the 1949 Italian GP. The 4CL prefix connoted light weight, ruggedness, simplicity for easy maintenance, and power that was usually adequate and occasionally exceptional.

One team that went the extra mile with the San Remo was the Scuderia Milan of the Ruggieri brothers. Motivated by a $9,000 bonus promised by the organisers of the Italian Grand Prix to any team that brought two new cars to Monza in 1949, they set about the substantial improvement of their 4CLT/48s. They fitted wider brakes to two cars, and installed high-boost engines of a type developed by Prof. Mario Speluzzi from the basic Maserati 4CL four for speedboat racing. Called 'Milans', the cars driven by Nino Farina and Piero Taruffi went remarkably well at Monza although the temperamental Farina abruptly parked his for no obvious mechanical reason.

By 1952, when most race promoters had

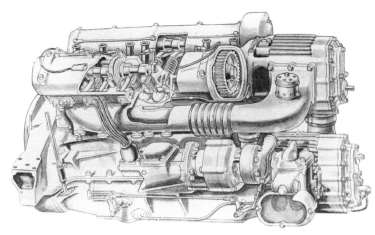

turned to the unblown 2-litre Formula 2, Maserati owners faced a new challenge. The resourceful Enrico Platé stripped the blowers from his brace of 4CLT/48s, fitted new blocks and crankshafts to bring the engines to the larger size and chopped eight inches out of their wheelbases. With two twin-throat Weber 35DCO carbs they produced some 150 horsepower. In spite of a weight disadvantage they gave Harry Schell and Emanuel de Graffenried some very good races. These cars, plus an experimental Orsi-Maserati based on them, were rebodied as 'Buranos' for the film *The Racers*.

SPECIFICATIONS	
Cylinders	I4
Bore	78.0mm
Stroke	78.0mm
Stroke/bore ratio	1.0:1
Capacity	1,491cc
Compression ratio	6.0:1
Connecting rod length	161.0mm
Rod/crank radius ratio	4.1:1
Main bearing journal diameter	62.0mm
Rod journal diameter	52.0mm
Inlet valve diameter (2 valves)	40.0mm
Exhaust valve diameter (2 valves)	40.0mm
Inlet pressure	2.72Atm
Engine weight	364lb (165kg)
Peak power	260bhp @ 7,500rpm
Piston speed (corrected)	3,839ft/min (19.2m/s)
Engine bhp per litre	174.4bhp per litre
Engine weight per bhp	1.40lb (0.64kg) per bhp

1951

ALFA ROMEO 159 1.5-LITRE EIGHT

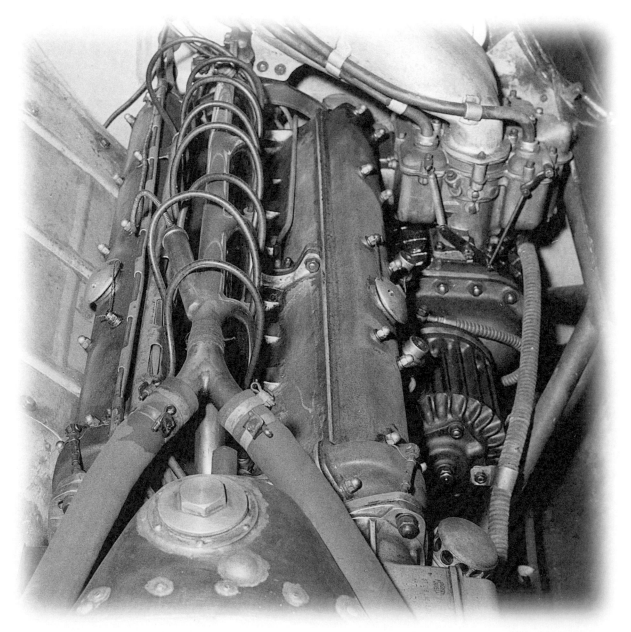

When in 1937 it was rumoured that Alfa Romeo was about to produce a new car for the current *Voiturette* category or 'Formula 2' of the day, good things were naturally expected. What could not have been expected was that essentially the same car would be dominating major Grand Prix events in 1951, eight full years of racing later. Laurence Pomeroy, Jr gave due attention to the fabulous record of the Type 158 Alfa Romeo in Volume II of *The Grand Prix Car*. Wrote Pomeroy,

'In this period (1947 through 1951 only) the company made 99 separate entries in 35 races. Of these they won all but four, so they had 31 victories together with 19 second places and 15 thirds. They made fastest lap in 23 of the races and suffered only 28 retirements. Taking into account retirements, the cars raced a total of 18,153 miles under Formula 1 (plus 854 miles in 1946), an average of 6,800 racing miles per car for an overall reliability factor of 81 per cent. This is a record of reliability and success without parallel in motor racing history.'

This achievement was the product of a fallow period in Alfa Romeo's participation in Grand Prix racing. Under the 2-litre formula of the 1920s Milan's Alfa had enjoyed sudden and remarkable success, thanks to the designs of Vittorio Jano. In the races of the early 1930s the Tipo B Alfa had kept the firm's banner aloft through its nationalisation in 1933. By 1937, however, it was evident that Jano's further efforts were not likely to bring Grand Prix victories to Alfa Romeo. Jano was dismissed and his assistant since 1924, Gioachino Colombo, was made responsible for racing car engineering.

After revising the existing cars for racing in 1938, Colombo and his team set about designing a new engine family. This comprised a straight-eight of 1½ litres for *Voiturette* racing and a V16 of 3 litres for Grand Prix competition, using two of the eights on a common crankcase, with twin crankshafts geared together. Initially these engines were dubbed '308' and '316' respectively. By the winter of 1937 Colombo had completed the drawings for the '308', and manufacture of its components was put in hand.

The first four examples of this new *Voiturette* were assembled and tested at the Modena works of Enzo Ferrari, whose team or Scuderia was contracted to serve as Alfa Romeo's racing arm.

First to check out the new little Alfa or 'Alfetta', as the public nicknamed it, was the Scuderia's head tester, Attilio Marinoni. He pronounced it – in June of 1938 – an eminently satisfactory motor car. A month later, two out of three cars entered went through to take first and second places in the Coppa Ciano at Leghorn, a debut which was not deceptive. They were soon given the designation with which they became world-famous: Type 158.

On the test bench in 1938 the supercharged eight gave 180bhp at 7,000rpm on 7psi boost. As raced in 1938 its output was 205bhp at 7,000 and in 1939 it reached 225bhp at 7,500. Thus those pre-war years were chiefly devoted to raising the reliable rev limit of the engine and thereby increasing its output. A two-stage Roots-type blower group had already been planned for the 158 before the war. In peacetime this was manufactured and tested under Colombo's supervision and fitted to some of the team cars in races in 1947. It brought power output to 254bhp at 7,500rpm in that year.

The Alfettas were carefully hidden away during the war. Their first post-war race was on 9 June 1946, when both Nino Farina and Jean Pierre Wimille broke their cars at St Cloud. This sorry day is worthy of mention only because Alfa Romeo did not lose another Grand Prix race until 14 July 1951 – and it entered all the big ones, except for a rest year in 1949.

Development of the 158 was steady, power being up to 265 in 1947. The following year Wimille drove a new version with bigger primary blower in Reims practice and in the Italian GP. This type, the 158/47, delivered 310bhp at 7,500rpm. Some engines were rated as high as 335bhp at 8,000rpm. The Alfa eight was already displaying the appetite for power that would take its drivers to the first two Formula 1 world championships.

The Type 158 engine was classic in layout and dimensions. Even in the 1950s the straight-eight configuration remained statistically the most successful in Grand Prix racing. With cylinder

Opposite above: Although essentially a pre-war Voiturette *design, designed by Gioachino Colombo and built in the workshops of Enzo Ferrari, the Alfa Romeo 158 evolved into the Type 159 of 1951. It was the mount of the world champion in both 1950 and '51.*

Opposite below: Heavy shielding surrounded the exhaust pipes of the 159 Alfa Romeo of 1951, fed with air to keep them cool. A trunk from a cowl inlet admitted air under dynamic pressure to the Weber carburettor, which had separate pipes to the float bowls to ensure that they were under similar pressure.

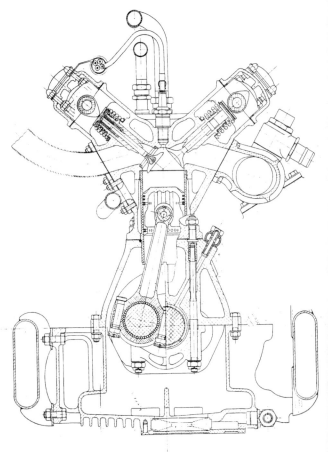

dimensions of 58 x 70mm (2.28 x 2.76in) the Alfa had a relatively long stroke, which kept the engine short. Though it was much criticised for this characteristic in an era when 'square' or 'oversquare' proportions were the norm, the 158's compact combustion chambers (7.5:1 compression ratio) and high-velocity ports were very well-suited to high supercharge and combustion pressures.

Gasketing problems were avoided by combining the block and head in a single monobloc casting. It was made of aluminium alloy and had thin-wall screwed-in wet steel cylinders and shrunk-in valve-seat inserts. The two 36mm valves per cylinder were equally splayed at the wide included angle of 100°. The Elektron (magnesium alloy) crankcase was split on the crankshaft centreline, and housed seven 52mm plain main bearings plus one outrigger bearing next to the flywheel and multi-disc clutch. I-section connecting rods were used and crowded needles served as the big-end bearings in developed versions of the engine.

Unlike Jano's designs of the early 1930s, which had the gear train at the centre of the engine, the 158's gear drive to the twin overhead cams ran up the front of the engine. Step-up gearing of 1.35:1 and a short, flexibly-jointed shaft on the left turned the small secondary blower, which in turn was geared to the big primary Roots-type unit. On top of the latter was a triple-barrel downdraught Weber 50 DR3C carburettor, its throttle valves arranged to give a progressive opening action. At first this was fitted with a long 'elephant's trunk' air intake drawing from below and behind the slanting radiator with its integral header tank. Small pipes from this duct vented the float bowls to balance the fuel surface pressure with that in the inlet duct.

Initially a single magneto for all eight centrally-placed Lodge spark plugs was stowed under the exhaust manifold, next to the water intake piping. This was replaced by two four-plug magnetos at the camshaft noses, where the environment was cooler. Oil from the blower drive drained into the rear of the deeply finned sump, which was scavenged by two pumps. An oil reservoir was in the car's cowl, while a cooler sat under the radiator. To its right was a duct leading to a shroud around the exhaust manifold, carrying heat rapidly away from it.

Because the opposition hadn't moved greatly forward in Alfa's rest year of 1949, the Type 158/47 was able to reappear in 1950 practically unchanged. Later in that season Ferrari's unblown 4½-litre cars started to menace, so boost was raised to 20psi, bringing the output to 350bhp at 8,500rpm – near enough one horsepower per pound for the 363lb (165kg) eight. The basic engine remained little changed; in fact only nine engines of this type were ever produced, and all of those before 1942.

In 1951, several victories by Ferrari provoked an occasional hint of desperation in the once-invincible Alfa team; but their engineers worked miracles to wring more power reliably from the straight-eight. Sustaining high output depended heavily on the use of Shell's 98.5 per cent-methanol Dynamin fuel as an internal coolant for pistons and valves. Valve overlap was deliberately made extreme to force a high-pressure draught through the head at top dead centre in what was characterised as a 'fifth stroke'. The cars were burning more than 150 litres per 100 kilometres. To accommodate this thirst, big side fuel tanks were fitted in 1951 to give a total capacity of 225 litres.

Major engine revisions and boost up to 30psi allowed the 159 to scream up to 10,500 revs on the test bed and to develop 420bhp at 9,300rpm by the time of the final 1951 race – well over double its original rating. The power required to drive the superchargers was 135bhp. Cool water was now pumped directly to alternate exhaust-valve guides to dissipate heat from these vital components. After long use of a single exhaust pipe, twin manifolds and pipes were again fitted to reduce heat loadings. Traction became a serious problem, and the Alfas were exceeding 190mph on the faster courses such as Spa and Reims.

Alfa just eked out a world championship for Juan Fangio in 1951 with the type 159A, which was used in only two races. These cars drew carburettor air from the cockpit or alternatively from a cowl scoop, depending on the weather. Fangio recalled that he felt a real surge of power when he opened the scoop to the outside air; engineers estimated a benefit of as much as 25 horsepower. The reshaped Alfettas, now bulkier and more purposeful, had a new, shrill blower whine that recalled the 1939 Mercedes-Benz. Their speed in 1951, their final season, was such that Mercedes thought better of trying to challenge them during that Grand Prix Formula.

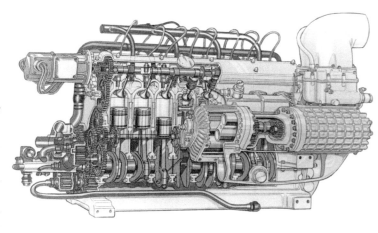

Opposite left: As first raced as a Voiturette *in 1940 the Type 158 Alfa had but a single Roots-type supercharger flanked by crankcase breathers. In this form it produced 225bhp at 7,500rpm.*

Opposite right: A transverse section of the Type 159 shows the small-diameter needle bearings used for the connecting-rod big ends, and the way in which the studs retaining

the main-bearing caps travelled up through the magnesium crankcase to retain the cylinder block. Valve gear is not unlike that of the 1932 Alfa Tipo B. **Above:** *The drive shaft from the gear train at the front of the Type 159 engine powered both blowers in the two-stage system, the drive reaching the big primary blower through the internal gears of the smaller secondary unit.*

SPECIFICATIONS	
Cylinders	I8
Bore	58.0mm
Stroke	70.0mm
Stroke/bore ratio	1.21:1
Capacity	1,480cc
Compression ratio	7.5:1
Connecting rod length	147.0mm
Rod/crank radius ratio	4.2:1
Main bearing journal diameter	52.0mm
Rod journal diameter	46.0mm
Inlet valve diameter (1 valve)	36.0mm
Exhaust valve diameter (1 valve)	36.0mm
Inlet pressure	3.10Atm
Engine weight	363lb (165kg)
Peak power	420bhp @ 9,300rpm
Piston speed (corrected)	3,888ft/min (19.4m/s)
Engine bhp per litre	283.9bhp per litre
Engine weight per bhp	0.86lb (0.39kg) per bhp

1951

BRM TYPE 15 1.5-LITRE V16

It began with a dream such as you and I might have if we were to plan over a few pints of bitter the racing car we could build if we had lots of money and time. Raymond Mays had never been one to think on a small scale if a large scale were handy. While still a young man at school in England, Mays had discovered that charm, persuasion and unswerving faith in one's own abilities could bring any dream to reality. Raymond Mays dreamed of motor racing. His passion for it led to the creation of the astonishing supercharged 1½-litre V16 BRM Grand Prix car.

Before World War II no British car had dared to challenge the crack German and Italian teams. After the war, Britons found that they had access to some – but not all – of the Axis secrets of racing success. Leading the search for financing to build a car that would exploit this knowledge was Mays, who in the 1930s had played a key role in the formation of the privately backed ERA company and had driven ERA racing cars to many wins in events of sub-Grand-Prix status. With support in cash and kind from British industry, Mays and self-taught engineer Peter Berthon designed and built the Type 15 BRM.

The exotic essence of the BRM was its engine, which packed no more than 1,500cc into no less than 16 cylinders. The bore and stroke dimensions were 1.95 x 1.90in (49.5 x 48.3mm), defining the smallest individual cylinders ever used in Grand Prix racing. They were arranged in a vee at a 135° angle which gave even firing intervals, excellent balance and daunting complexity. Mays and Berthon aimed to build a car that would fully flower in the last years of the Formula in 1951 and 1952, having enough potential to defeat anything else that might come along. The target peak speed was 12,000rpm, a brave goal for 1947.

High supercharging boost pressure was the responsibility of the engineers of Rolls-Royce, which would build the blowers. They recommended a compact two-stage centrifugal supercharger. Although this was a heretical concept in road racing, in which positive-displacement blowers of the Roots and vane type had been favoured for their strong output throughout the engine speed range, the Rolls-Royce men argued that they could build a two-stage centrifugal charger for the BRM that would start delivering useful boost pressure at 6,000 engine rpm, half the engine's peak speed.

Detail design of the BRM V16 engine proceeded along these lines in the hands of Eric Richter, assisted by Harry Mundy and Frank May. Their work began in 1946 and was largely completed by the spring of 1947. The first orders for parts were placed well before the end of that year.

This dream engine of Berthon and Mays abounded with ingenious and complex features. The gear drive to its overhead camshafts was taken up through the centre of the engine, dividing it into two 750cc 135° V8 engines placed end to end. This diminished the chances of torsional vibration problems by keeping each individual section of crankshaft (two) and camshaft (eight) at a short, stiff and manageable four-cylinder length. Flanking the centre main bearing were two drive gears, one for each cylinder bank to take into account the offset of the banks. From each drive gear a self-contained two-stage gear pack carried the drive up from the crankshaft to the train of gears in its cylinder head.

All 16 cylinder bores were carried in a single RR50 aluminium-alloy casting. Wet cylinder liners of high-tensile cast iron were held down against Neoprene sealing rings by the pressure of the detachable cylinder head against a flange at the top of the liner. The crank's two fully counterweighted halves joined together at the central drive gear. The crankshaft was carried in ten plain Vandervell thin-wall bearings, their caps tied into the supporting webs by cross-bolts as well as studs. I-section connecting rods measured 4.125in (104.8mm) from centre to centre.

The two central drive gears were also used as the means of extracting power from the engine. Below the pair of 27-tooth crankshaft gears was a mating pair of spur gears of 52 teeth that drove a hollow sub-shaft extending rearward to the clutch. Thus when the crankshaft was spinning at 10,000rpm the clutch was doing only 5,200, a normal rate for the drive-line technology of the time. In order to maintain clockwise drive-line rotation the engineers elected to rotate the engine counter-clockwise.

The sub-shaft was carried in a deep magnesium

Opposite above: Although one of the handsomest racing cars of all time in its original 1951 form, seen competing in the British Grand Prix at Silverstone, the Type 15 BRM failed to achieve its potential during the racing formula for which it was designed.

Opposite below: Under its rounded bonnet the BRM packed a mass of machinery. The low-placed radiator required the use of a header tank positioned high at the rear of the engine compartment.

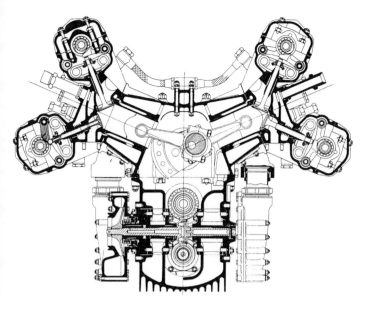

Firing each cylinder through a small aperture was a 14mm Lodge spark plug. The sparks were generated by a battery-powered coil ignition system. A four-cylinder distributor was driven from the front of each camshaft and supplied with its own spark coil. Each Lucas distributor had three sets of points. One made contact, one broke it, and one (manually selected) gave a retarded timing for starting the engine.

Not until June 1949 was the first 525lb (238kg) Type 15 engine running. Its output was disappointing – only 295bhp at 10,000rpm with a boost pressure of 24psi. The V16 produced only 110bhp at 6,000rpm and 200bhp at 8,000. Going back to their drawing boards, the Rolls-Royce men uprated their compressor. At the cost of doubling the power required to drive it at 10,000rpm (from 75 to 150bhp), the drive ratio of the supercharger was stepped up from 3.25 to 4.00:1. The first-stage impeller was enlarged from 6 to 6½in in diameter.

With this compressor the power rose to 360bhp at 9,000rpm, 395bhp at 10,000 and 430bhp at 11,000. These figures weren't reliably deliverable, however, until several years after the engine first ran. The highest actual dynamometer test figure achieved by the engine was given by Harry Mundy as 482bhp at 12,000rpm in its 1952 form. Outputs as much as 100 horsepower higher than this have been quoted, but these have been educated guesses from boost pressures registered on the dashboard gauge.

In 1950 the BRMs competed in only one world-class race, a non-championship GP at Barcelona. There outside observers could see clearly for the first time that the cars had nothing like the fabulous power output that had been forecast and indeed feared. (The actual figures, given above, remained secret for more than a decade.) Both cars retired in the race, one with gearbox oil leaks and the other with a sheared blower drive shaft, prompted by a faulty bearing.

In 1951, the last full season of world championship racing with 1½-litre supercharged cars, the BRMs competed in only one qualifying event, the British Grand Prix at Silverstone. There, as usual, they arrived on the morning of the race without having practised and started from the back of the grid, surviving to place fifth and seventh in the GP, thanks to restraining the peak engine speed to 9,500rpm.

Persistent and frustrating engine failures from

casting that formed the main vertical bulk of the engine. It incorporated the chassis mounts and most of the accessory drives, and also served as the oil collector for the dry-sump lubrication system. Spiral gears on the sub-shaft drove two transverse shafts that powered the four pressure and scavenge oil pumps mounted in the casing walls and also drove the two externally placed water pumps.

Below the large gear on the sub-shaft yet another shaft was driven, this one at 1.285 times crankshaft speed. It went forward, in roller bearings, to the pair of step-up gears that drove the Rolls-Royce supercharger at the front of the engine. This shaft was designed to flex in torsion and was given a bronze-faced clutch at its forward end. Initially the supercharger had two nickel-steel impellers, 6in in diameter in the first stage and 5½in in the second.

The four separate cylinder heads were cast of RR53 aluminium alloy. Combustion chambers were traditional hemispheres, bounded by valves symmetrically inclined at a 90° included angle. The inlet valve head measured 1.25in (31.8mm) over a 1.1in port, while the exhaust valve diameter was 1.09in (27.8mm). Sodium-cooled, the exhaust valves had inserted wet guides that were finned where they contacted the cooling water. Light and compact hairpin-type valve springs and finger-type cam followers were used. Valve opening duration and lift on the inlet side were 300° and 0.2in (5.1mm) respectively.

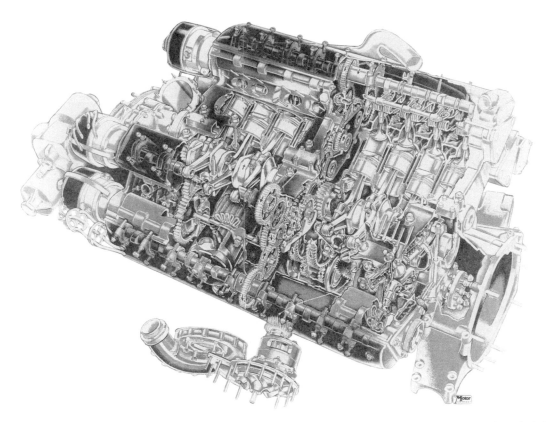

1949 to 1951 were finally traced to the flawed design of the V16's cylinders. The choice of a wet cylinder liner that sealed against a shoulder close to its bottom end proved unwise. When the engine was run at high boost and power the liners pressed down against their Neoprene bottom seals, which flexed just enough to allow a gap between the top of the liner and the cylinder head that admitted small amounts of cooling water the instant the throttle was slightly closed. This injection of water into the hot chamber had a literally explosive effect on the engine.

With this fault diagnosed, the shrieking sixteens from Bourne were to run in 38 more races from

1952 to 1955, at last with reasonable reliability. None of them, however, was an event of importance. A daring dream had to give way to harsh reality.

Above: As a 1½-litre engine the V16 BRM was unsurpassed in its complexity. Critical shortcomings of the design were inadequate valve lift and unreliable sealing of the all-important joint between the cylinder head and the liner.

Opposite above: Carried in roller bearings, the camshafts opened the valves through finger-type followers placed on alternate sides of the cam chambers. Hairpin-type springs closed the valves. Finned exhaust-valve guides were directly exposed to the engine coolant.

SPECIFICATIONS	
Cylinders	V16
Bore	49.5mm
Stroke	48.3mm
Stroke/bore ratio	0.98:1
Capacity	1,487cc
Compression ratio	7.5:1
Connecting rod length	104.8mm
Rod/crank radius ratio	4.3:1
Main bearing journal diameter	58.4mm
Rod journal diameter	38.1mm
Inlet valve diameter (1 valve)	31.8mm
Exhaust valve diameter (1 valve)	37.8mm
Inlet pressure	4.85Atm
Engine weight	525lb (238kg)
Peak power	430bhp @ 11,000rpm
Piston speed (corrected)	3,529ft/min (17.6m/s)
Engine bhp per litre	289.1bhp per litre
Engine weight per bhp	1.22lb (0.55kg) per bhp

1952

KÜCHEN 2-LITRE V8

Many remarkable tales of ingenuity and improvisation can be told of post-war German motor racing, but this tops them all. This four-cam 2-litre V8 engine was by a good margin the most powerful GP powerplant of its formula and time. Yet it was not the product of one of the established German factories. A mere three of these two-litre V8s were built for the post-war Formula 2 by a private individual in his own workshops, primarily as a hobby. This dalliance delivered 200 horsepower in 1951, a figure that Ferrari and Maserati were only able to reach in 1953.

Küchen was a great name in German design circles, especially those involved with motorcycle engines. Born in 1897, Richard Küchen built his first car at the age of 13, using a de Dion powerplant. Further landmarks in the Küchen career included a four-valve motorcycle engine which featured ram-tuned intakes and exhausts in 1929. When in 1934 he had the task of dieting the Auto Union GP car to regulation weight; Küchen trimmed off 17lb (7.7kg) by minimising the size of every nut on the car.

After V-E day motor racing struggled to life in Germany against the most depressing practical odds. By 1949 Egon Brütsch (known as a builder of tiny egg-shaped vehicles in Stuttgart) was far enough along in his racing plans to order a two-litre racing engine from Küchen for his new EBS monoposto. He wasn't able to collect it, though, and pre-war ace Hans Stuck stepped in to acquire one engine. Another was sold in Switzerland while the third remained in Küchen's Ingolstadt shops. Stuck's engine was installed in his AFM chassis, built by Alex von Falkenhausen of Munich. The combination made its first racing appearance in the German Grand Prix on 20 August 1950.

At 216lb (98kg) the Küchen V8 came breathtakingly close to one horsepower per pound. Its crankcase was made in two Silumin (silicon-aluminium) alloy pieces split horizontally at the crankshaft centreline. The upper half extended only to the bottoms of the cylinders. Less structural was the liberally finned lower half, which offered some lateral bracing to the main bearing caps. The bottom of the crankcase was sealed by a finned casting which sloped toward a central oil pickup for the dry-sump system.

An early-type Hirth built-up crankshaft was chosen, a construction which eliminated split bearing races and cages with their associated problems. All main bearings were single-row roller type except for the double-row rear main, which shared space with a ball bearing to take thrust loadings. The mains were surrounded by steel outer races which were clamped between the upper crankcase and deep two-stud main bearing caps of light alloy.

Oil reached the mains through a tubular gallery running along the bottoms of the caps. As it escaped from the main journals it was flung outward, directed by lips on the outer races, into slinger rings recessed in the crank cheeks. Oil collected in these rings reached the rod journals and their bearing rollers through angled and then radial drillings. The capability of Ing. Küchen's workshop facilities was indicated by the fact that he made his own rollers for all the roller bearings.

Logical design and beautiful finish were features of the rods, which extended the I-section of the shank all the way around the big end to give maximum support to the rollers. Circlips retained the internally-tapered gudgeon pins in the pistons, forged by Mahle. Three narrow compression rings and one oil ring were carried above the full skirt. Bore and stroke were square at 68mm (2.68in) each for 1,976cc.

Assembly of the heads and cylinders of the Küchen V8 was accomplished in a manner utterly foreign to automotive engines. The wet cylinder barrels were straight tubes of chrome-nickel steel, chrome-plated to a thickness of 0.0016in and finely dimpled to retard wear that had previously rendered them unusable after about five races. Externally threaded at the top, these barrels were screwed directly into the cylinder head at the combustion chambers – in itself not unusual. Around the liners a water jacket was then bolted to the cylinder head to obtain a water seal.

Protruding through holes in the bottom of the water jacket, the bottom ends of the barrels were threaded to allow steel rings to be turned up

concluded that the valves were too small at 30° and not enough larger at 45° to warrant the accompanying increase in area of the combustion chamber walls. The middle figure was chosen, giving an included angle of 74°.

Deeply tuliped, the head of the inlet valve was 38mm in diameter, while the solid-stemmed exhaust poppet measured 35mm. They seated directly on the cylinder head, without inserts. After four or five long races, as a result, the seats would erode to a sponge-like condition, beginning with the casting pores. Had he another opportunity, Küchen would have inserted cast-iron 'chills' in the mould adjacent to the seats-to-be. These would have caused the Silumin to cool more quickly and hence form a denser, less porous structure at the seats.

All four detachable camboxes were machined from a single basic casting, thanks to the symmetry of the design. These bolted down over triple-coil valve springs, which together exerted 220lb (100kg) per valve. The hollow camshafts were carried in four roller bearings each, spaced to give maximum support to the lobes. Thin steel outer bearing races were held in place by pairs of cap screws from the cambox exterior.

A shaft ran the length of each cambox to act as the pivot for the neat and light (1½ ounces) roller-tipped finger followers. In its open centre each finger carried a narrow 20mm diameter roller on needle bearings, the side arms of the finger being drilled for lightness in some cases. This valve gear was wholly satisfactory up to 10,000rpm, well beyond the engine's limit of about 8,200. Valve lift was 9.8mm and timing was as follows:

Inlet opens   50°BTDC   Exhaust opens 78°BBDC
Inlet closes   78°ABDC   Exhaust closes 50°ATDC

Separable castings at the front of the engine enclosed the twin gear trains to the cylinder banks. Drilled to reduce inertia, the narrow spur gears were carried on double-row ball bearings and oiled at their meshing points through exterior piping – one of the few installations on the engine that had a homebuilt look. A gear also drove downward to the double scavenge and single pressure oil pumps mounted within a separate housing at the front of the crankcase. Spun by the same shaft as the scavenge pumps was a double-outlet water pump

against the jacket to form – with the aid of O-rings – a water seal at the bottom. The complete head-cylinder assembly was finally bolted to the upper crankcase through flanges on the bottom of the water jacket. Thus the barrels themselves anchored the head to the crankcase, under tension from the head to the rings abutting against the water jacket – which in turn was fastened to the crankcase.

A common casting was used for both cylinder heads. Ing. Küchen experimented with valve stem angles (from the vertical) of 30°, 37° and 45° and

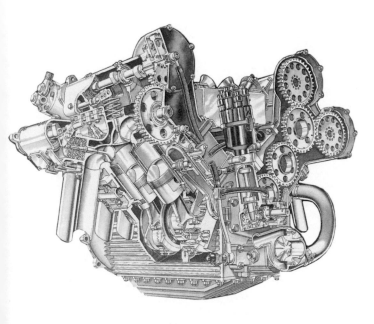

that delivered coolant to the outside of each bank through a bolted-on manifold.

A dog-driven extension shaft from the crank nose engaged a skew-gear drive to two angled vertical shafts which were capped by Bosch distributors. Marelli magnetos were tried, but Küchen felt that distributors plus a small battery were lighter and no less effective. Two spark plugs per cylinder were placed wide apart and at a slight included angle. A compression ratio of 14:1 was used, requiring a fuel of 90 per cent methanol laced with 10 per cent benzol.

On the original engines Ing. Küchen fitted an array of eight Amal carburettors each 28mm in diameter, served by a mass of piping and controlled by two sets of lever arms. Although Küchen devised improved control mechanisms for the Amals, Hans Stuck tired of their vicissitudes and had a pair of two-throat 32mm downdraught Webers installed in 1951.

The V8's power and torque (116lb ft) were sufficient for Stuck's AFM to leave the works Ferraris standing on the grid on several occasions in 1951, Monza on 13 May being a prime example. However, several elements in the engine suffered periodic deterioration resulting in retirement. Gremlins in both car and engine relaxed enough to allow Stuck to win the Grenzlandring Formula 2 race at better than 127mph on 9 September 1951 and to set a new record for the Aosta–San Bernardo hillclimb in the same year.

In anticipation of further development Ing. Küchen had laid out a complete port fuel-injection system with the assistance of Bosch technicians.

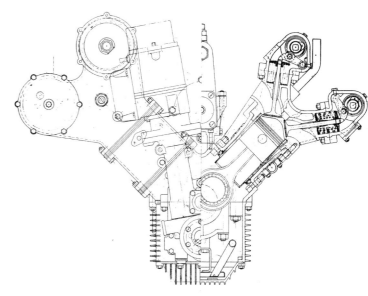

The ignition drive would have been spaced forward and a gear train inserted to drive two four-piston injection pumps placed in line down the central vee, convenient to injection nozzles in the inlet ports. These plans were shelved when, in late 1952, the new formula for 1954 was announced and Küchen decided to develop the engine no further.

Opposite above: *As originally built, the Küchen V8 (seen from the rear) had eight individual motorcycle-type Amal carburettors opened by a sector-geared linkage. Precise synchronisation of these was difficult.*
Opposite: *A cutaway drawing by Tom Fornander shows the roller-bearing big ends and Hirth crankshaft of the Küchen V8. Also exposed are its roller-tipped cam followers, which were drilled for lightness.*

Above: *Richard Küchen was successful in keeping to a minimum the aluminium cylinder-head masses of his V8 engine. Shown is the way in which the steel cylinders, threaded into the heads, acted to retain them within the crankcase as well. Here Küchen also shows a position in the central vee for a Bosch fuel-injection pump, which however was never installed in this engine.*

SPECIFICATIONS	
Cylinders	V8
Bore	68.0mm
Stroke	68.0mm
Stroke/bore ratio	1.0:1
Capacity	1,976cc
Compression ratio	14.0:1
Connecting rod length	138.0mm
Rod/crank radius ratio	4.1:1
Main bearing journal diameter	52.0mm
Rod journal diameter	52.0mm
Inlet valve diameter (1 valve)	38.0mm
Exhaust valve diameter (1 valve)	35.0mm
Inlet pressure	1.0Atm
Engine weight	216lb (98kg)
Peak power	200bhp @ 8,000rpm
Piston speed (corrected)	3,570ft/min (17.9m/s)
Peak torque	116lb ft (157Nm) @ 7,000rpm
Peak bmep	145psi
Engine bhp per litre	101.2bhp per litre
Engine weight per bhp	1.08lb (0.49kg) per bhp

1953
FERRARI 500 2-LITRE FOUR

Technical director Aurelio Lampredi was in his office at Maranello one Sunday morning, as usual, in early June 1951 when the matter was resolved. He and Enzo Ferrari had been debating the sort of engine to build for the coming 1954 Formula 1, ideally an engine that could also be used in 2-litre form in the meantime in Formula 2. Ferrari was already competing in Formula 2 successfully with his single-overhead-cam 166 F2 V12.

Ferrari and Lampredi had considered uprating to 2 litres the failed supercharged 1½-litre four-cam V12, the work of Lampredi's predecessor Gioachino Colombo. Indeed they had even built and tested such an engine. But this was a heavier solution when lightness and agility were needed. In 1950 John Heath's Alta-engined HWMs had pressed the works team of two-litre Ferrari V12s and had done so with only four cylinders.

Enzo Ferrari could appreciate that a four-cylinder engine had torque and weight characteristics that were well-suited to the twisty circuits that predominated in European racing. Mulling it over, he plumped for the four, as he told Lampredi that June morning. The engineer forgot his plans for the Sabbath afternoon. He reached for T-square and triangle and in a few hours had sketched the essentials of the Tipo 500, destined to be one of Ferrari's most successful engines.

Some have described the 500 as a 'simple' engine. It was anything but. Lampredi lavished all his skill and ingenuity on this, the first Ferrari engine he designed from scratch. He had been responsible for the unsupercharged 4½-litre GP engine of 1950–51 but this was a continuation of the Colombo V12 concept and, to boot, was also used as a production-car engine. In contrast, he said, 'the 500 was born as a racing car. I did everything possible to improve the engine's design.' It was simple solely in that it had only four cylinders.

Just as he had done with his big V12, Lampredi took no chances with the 500's cylinder-head construction. Like many racing engines of the 1920s and 1930s, its head was unified with the block in an aluminium-alloy casting that extended down three-quarters of the length of the cylinder. Screwed into this head/block unit, reaching right up to its combustion chambers, were four cast-iron wet cylinders. Each had a castellated flange at its lower extremity that was gripped by a special wrench to screw it in or out. Two grooves below the flange carried the rubber O-rings that sealed the bottom of the cylinder into the top of the crankcase, which was a separate casting.

Lampredi specified a bore and stroke of 90 x 78mm (3.54 x 3.07in) to give 1,985cc. He disposed the stems of the two valves per cylinder equally at an included angle of 58°; thanks to the removable cylinders the valves could easily be extracted from the head/block unit. Very thin guides were inserted for the valves, which were thick-stemmed and hollow for lightness. Diameters were 48mm and 44mm for the inlets and exhausts respectively.

Lampredi took no chances with his valve gear. He brought to Ferrari elements of a W18 aircraft engine he had worked on at Officine Reggiane in 1942–44, which had narrow cam lobes working against roller followers. Also credited with contributing to the selection of a roller cam follower was Ferrari's long-serving and hugely experienced technician, Luigi Bazzi.

Carried over from other Ferrari engines were hairpin-type valve springs, which permitted short and light valves. Above each valve was a steel-tipped light-alloy follower with a circular top, into which was set a large-diameter roller. Pressing up against this circular top were two relatively-light concentric coil springs whose only task was to keep the roller in steady contact with its cam lobe. The function of controlling the follower was separated from that of closing the valve. This unique valve gear virtually eliminated cam and valve problems from the Ferrari lexicon. It also allowed the cam lobe to be narrow: 8mm wide.

The followers slid in thin-wall iron guides which stabilised both their circular top and their stem, into which a hollow steel tip was inserted at the point of contact with the valve stem. Different tips

Opposite above: Fewer cylinders meant more speed for the cars of Enzo Ferrari, which moved from twelve to four cylinders to compete in the 2-litre Formula 2 in 1952. This proved to be the right direction for the Ferrari Type 500, driven here by Piero Taruffi.

Opposite below: By the time of the German Grand Prix in August 1953 the Ferrari Type 500 was fed by two twin-throat Weber carburettors. These were specially designed to suit the inlet port spacing of the Ferrari engine.

so another gear pair was needed to step the magnetos up to half-speed again. They fired Champion 14mm plugs which were placed in slightly-splayed positions with their electrodes recessed from the surface of the hemispherical combustion chamber.

The magnetos were an Achilles' heel of the engine, Lampredi said: 'I always used to tell the drivers they could do what they liked with the gears, because no matter what happened the engine would not break. They couldn't rev the engine above 7,500–7,800rpm even when going flat out because of the poor ignition.' Assisting in this unburstability was the dry-sump lubrication system, with its gear-type pumps also driven from the crank nose. A triple-gear scavenge pump had inlets for two pickups at the front and rear of the shallow magnesium sump.

Remarkably, the cylinder block was innocent of major oil galleries. Instead, Shell oil under pressure was delivered to all five main bearings through pipes in the sump and banjo-type unions at the base of each aluminium main cap. The latter were inserted snugly into their webs in the deep crankcase and retained by two studs. From the grooved mains the oil flowed into the crankshaft drillings and thence to the rod journals. The main bearings were 60mm in diameter and 28mm wide except for the critical centre main, which was 35mm wide.

Above: On the test bench at Modena in February 1952 the new four-cylinder engine designed by Aurelio Lampredi showed the original rear mounting of the two magnetos needed for its dual ignition.
Below: By mid-1952 the heads and front gearcase had been revised to provide access plates at the fronts of the camshafts. Induction was provided by four individual horizontal Weber carburettors.
Opposite: With its steel liners screwed into the cylinder block, the Ferrari Type 500 had no head-gasket problems. The artist has exaggerated the width of the camshaft drive gears, which in fact were commendably light and narrow.

were inserted to adjust the valve clearance. The iron guides in turn were set into a magnesium tappet and cam carrier that was bolted to the head. Five thin babbited bearings carried each hollow-core camshaft. Attached to the front of the block and crankcase was an aluminium-alloy cover which supported the outer ball bearings of the gear drive to the camshafts. The gears were strikingly thin and light to minimise space, weight and rotating mass.

Initially the twin Marelli magnetos for the 500's dual ignition were driven from the backs of the camshafts and protruded through the firewall into the cockpit. During 1952 they were relocated to the front of the engine and given their own drive from the gear turned by the crank nose. This first gear above the crankshaft rotated at less than half engine speed,

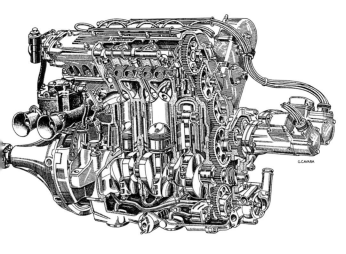

Machined from the solid, the steel crankshaft had four counterbalancing masses – two flanking the centre main and two adjacent to the front and rear main bearings. To minimise the mass to be balanced the rod journals were heavily drilled internally and sealed by plugs. These drillings were part of the crankshaft's oil passages, which were continuous from one end to the other to ensure ample availability of oil. The two drillings to feed oil to each rod bearing emerged at 90° to the radius of the throw to avoid the pressure-reducing effects of centrifugal force at high revs. Rod journals were 50mm with a 20mm width. Thin-wall Vandervell bearings were used.

Two bolts retained the big-end caps of connecting rods with I-section shanks which were virtually the same in width from top to bottom. The length of the rod, forged from GNM-alloy steel, was 142mm. Precision-cast by Borgo, the fully skirted aluminium pistons were ribbed under the crown for stiffness. They carried two very thin compression rings and two oil rings, one above and one below the gudgeon pin, which was retained by aluminium buttons. The domed crown provided a compression ratio of 13:1 for the methanol-based Shell Super F fuel, in spite of having to be doubly flatted to provide clearance for the valves at overlap.

Cast integral with the 500's crankcase were the four legs that rubber-mounted it to the chassis. Lampredi gave the aluminium crankcase a rounded barrel shape. It was double-walled, with the interior wall closely patterning the path of the big

end of the connecting rod as it rotated. Coolant from the front-mounted pump was delivered to the right side of the crankcase, where it entered cast-in passages that both cooled the tops of the front and rear main bearing pairs and led upward to the cylinders and head. Above the centre main bearing a passage was drilled vertically in both the crankcase and block to carry oil up to the camshaft bearings and cams.

Short stubs bolted to the cylinder head carried twin-throat Weber 50 DCOA carburettors. With these, at the end of 1953 the Tipo 500 – named for the capacity of one of its cylinders – produced 185bhp at 7,500rpm. Peak torque was an excellent 152lb ft at 5,700rpm.

With this engine powering the 'Starlet' – as an admiring public nicknamed this 'little' Ferrari – Alberto Ascari won five of 1952's seven championship GP races to become world champion. A sixth was won by Ferrari-mounted Piero Taruffi. Ascari performed identically and was champion again in 1953, when it was Mike Hawthorn's turn to win a sixth of the seven races for the prancing-horse stable. Including non-championship races, these Ferraris won 32 of their 35 starts in 1952–53 – a phenomenal record of success.

SPECIFICATIONS	
Cylinders	I4
Bore	90.0mm
Stroke	78.0mm
Stroke/bore ratio	0.87:1
Capacity	1,985cc
Compression ratio	13.0:1
Connecting rod length	142.0mm
Rod/crank radius ratio	3.6:1
Main bearing journal diameter	60.0mm
Rod journal diameter	50.0mm
Inlet valve diameter (1valve)	48.0mm
Exhaust valve diameter (1valve)	44.0mm
Inlet pressure	1.0Atm
Engine weight	348lb (158 kg)
Peak power	185bhp @ 7,500rpm
Piston speed (corrected)	4,123ft/min (20.6m/s)
Peak torque	152lb ft (206Nm) @ 5,700rpm
Peak bmep	190psi
Engine bhp per litre	93.2bhp per litre

1954

JAGUAR XK 3.4-LITRE SIX

Among those production engines that have benefited from racing inspiration the Jaguar XK six must be included. With its twin overhead camshafts and hemispherical combustion chamber it joined Alfa Romeo and Lagonda among series-production engines that were inspired by racing advances. It hadn't started out that way; various other valve arrangements were experimented with by William Heynes, Wally Hassan and Harry Mundy before they settled on the chain-driven twin-cam head. But as conceived the 3,442cc six became one of the great engines of all time – and a sound base for development for racing.

Jaguar was not an obvious choice for racing greatness. Its pre-war models had been built more for show than go, with the SS100 an honourable exception. However, with his commitment to an all-new engine to power his cars, Jaguar chief William Lyons needed a venue to demonstrate its excellence. Essaying a tentative foray to France in 1950 with XK120s, Lyons found that venue in the Le Mans 24-Hour Race. Jaguar first set its seal on the race with its victory in 1951 with the C-Type and subsequently developed the D-Type with Le Mans expressly in mind.

After a defeat by 2½ miles in 1954 by Ferrari the D-Type Jaguar went on to win Le Mans in 1955, 1956 and 1957 – always with the faithful XK twin-cam engine. As used in the C-Type and the production version of the D-Type the cast-iron block, forged-steel connecting rods and forged EN16 steel crankshaft differed only in minor machining from standard Mark VII parts. In the early and production D-Types the cylinder head was a modified aluminium-alloy C-type casting.

Vandervell indium-lead-bronze plain bearings were fitted to the seven main and six rod journals, which were 2.750 and 2.086in (69.9 and 53.0mm) in diameter respectively. The crank was not fully counterweighted, the designers' view being that torsional vibration would be more of a problem than bearing loads; a large steel-mass vibration damper was fitted at the front.

The two-bolt I-section connecting rod was drilled to lubricate the fully-floating gudgeon pin, which was held in the full-skirted Aerolite piston by circlips. A special Dykes design for the centrifugally cast top piston rings greatly reduced blow-by at high piston speeds, an important consideration in such a long-stroke (88 x 106mm,

3.46 x 4.17in) engine. A single Maxilite oil control ring was used.

A two-stage Renold duplex roller chain, controlled by a Weller spring tensioner, drove the twin overhead camshafts, which in turn operated the valves through inverted cups sliding in inserted cast-iron guides. In the production D the cam contours retained the ⅜in (9.5mm) lift of the M and C cams but increased inlet duration by 30° to a total of 270°.

The valves were symmetrically deployed with an included angle of 70° and were returned to their seats by double springs. Head diameters were 1⅞in (47.6mm) for the inlets and 1⅝in (41.3mm) for the exhausts. Aided by a half-point compression ratio increase to 9.0:1 over that of the C-Type, these passed enough air and fuel to bring the power of the production D to 246bhp at 5,800rpm and 250bhp at 6,000rpm, a bonus of 30bhp over the C. Torque was 242lb ft at 4,000rpm. The works recommended that speeds above 5,750rpm be held for short periods only, and that upshifts should be made at 5,500.

The porting of the racing engine was unchanged from the original layout as planned with the assistance of Harry Weslake, the inlet passage being slightly curved to provide turbulence. The Champion spark plug was at the side of the hemispherical chamber, positioned to initiate a flame front moving away from the inlet valve. Ignition was conventional by means of a Lucas single-breaker automatic-advance distributor fed sparks by a chassis-mounted Lucas HV12 coil.

So much room was needed for the three twin-choke type 45 DCO3 Weber carburettors and their associated plumbing that the D-Type's engine had to be canted by 8½° to the left on its three-point mounting to provide sufficient space at the top. Giving a 45mm bore and 38mm venturi for each cylinder, the Webers supplied accurate mixtures at high lateral G-forces, thanks to their centrally-disposed emulsion tubes and jets. Short ram tubes drew air from a grille-supplied balance box, and

Opposite above: No sports-racing car engaged in international competition has made better use of a series-based engine than the D-Type Jaguar. In this it was helped by an advanced monocoque frame and excellent aerodynamics.

Opposite below: From 1955 the works D-Types were fitted with a new cylinder head that gave the inlet valves a greater inclination to allow them to be increased in diameter. As shown here the head had provisions for dual ignition but this was not in fact used in racing.

fuel arrived via a single flexible line from two SU pumps on the rear bulkhead. Two fabricated three-branch exhaust manifolds fed, first, short flex pipes and then the outside twin pipes, which ended just before the rear wheel.

Partly to facilitate oil cooling but chiefly to reduce engine height by 2¾in, a dry-sump oil system was used for the D-Type. A transverse shaft at the front of the engine, skew-gear-driven from the crankshaft, turned the scavenge pump on the left and the pressure pump on the right. The steel drive gear of the scavenge pump engaged with two cast-iron idlers so that it could draw separately from two oil pickups at the front and rear of the shallow sump. This pump delivered oil to the 11-litre reservoir which rested behind the left front wheel and was vented to the crankcase. The single-idler pressure pump drew SAE 30 oil from the reservoir and pumped it at 45–50psi through an oil cooler and back to a transfer block which then supplied the main gallery along the right side of the crankcase.

Front-end space in the D-Type was shared by a vertical oil radiator and a Marston light-alloy water matrix, which was connected to a separate header tank by two hoses. The tank in turn received hot water from a gallery in the casting that carried the carburettors. A valve on the header tank kept the system under a pressure of around 4psi. Recommended operating temperature was 70°C.

The specification of the production D-Type engine as described resembled that of the works

Le Mans cars of 1954. Expecting stiff competition in 1955 from the new 300SLR Mercedes-Benz, Jaguar decided that some engine uprating would be in order for its team cars. A special crankshaft forged of EN40.3/4 steel was supplied, with an increased diameter at its nose. Most important was an entirely new head configuration which breathed so well that more power was realised at lower revs and the peak torque speed was raised by 1,000rpm. The 1955 output figure was 270bhp for Le Mans.

In the new head, also developed with the help of Harry Weslake, the inlet valve remained inclined at 35° to the vertical but the exhaust stem was 5° more steeply sloped at 40°. Identifiable by a square instead of circular front inspection plate, the new design made provision for dual ignition, although this was not used initially. It provided a 9.0:1 compression ratio and accommodated valve diameters of 50.8mm for inlets and 42.9mm for exhausts. Weslake clearly subscribed to the idea that it was easier to push gases out of a cylinder than to persuade them to enter.

Later in 1955, after several years of experiments, Jaguar began seriously testing the fuel-injected version of this engine which first raced at Sebring in March 1956. That season its output, with Lucas port-type injection and slide-type throttles, was typically 270bhp at 6,000rpm. Nevertheless the Weber-carburetted engine was still capable of excellent performance. Webers were fitted to the most powerful 3½-litre engine

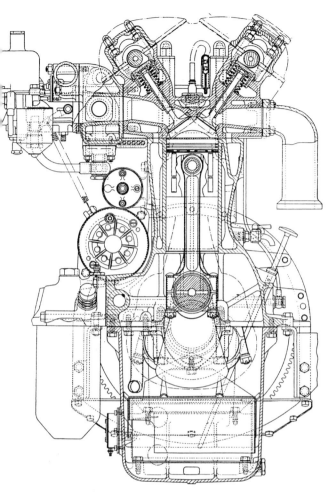

active in racing when the works withdrew after 1956. Momo bored out some blocks to 87.3mm (from the standard 83mm) to raise displacement to 3,807cc and fitted new California-made JE pistons. Jaguar tested one in January 1957 and, finding it good, approved an increase to 87mm (3.43in) for 3,781cc, thus creating the '3.8' engine. Its best output in 1957 was 307bhp at 5,500rpm with fuel injection and 297bhp at the same speed on Webers.

This was not quite the limit for Jaguar's own exploitation of its six in racing trim. At the end of 1958 it began testing cylinder heads with inlet valves of 53.2mm diameter, a 4.7 per cent enlargement. In May 1962 an injected six of this type produced 324bhp for use in a lightweight E-Type being entered by John Coombs. Two years later the impressive figure of 344bhp at 6,500rpm was registered on the engine installed in Peter Lindner's Le Mans E-Type.

The Jaguar six didn't like to be smaller. Efforts to race it at displacements of 2½ and 3 litres, to meet various handicap and capacity limits, were failures. Neither was the use of an aluminium cylinder block for the lightweight E-Types a great success. But as a big iron-block engine it was a winner – the best of its kind.

SPECIFICATIONS	
Cylinders	I6
Bore	83.0mm
Stroke	106.0mm
Stroke/bore ratio	1.28:1
Capacity	3,441cc
Compression ratio	9.0:1
Connecting rod length	196.9mm
Rod/crank radius ratio	3.7:1
Main bearing journal diameter	69.9mm
Rod journal diameter	53.0mm
Inlet valve diameter (1valve)	47.6mm
Exhaust valve diameter (1valve)	41.3mm
Inlet pressure	1.0Atm
Engine weight	530lb (241kg)
Peak power	250bhp @ 6,000rpm
Piston speed (corrected)	3,693ft/min (18.5m/s)
Peak torque	242lb ft (328Nm) @ 4,000rpm
Peak bmep	174psi
Engine bhp per litre	72.7bhp per litre
Engine weight per bhp	2.12lb (0.96kg) per bhp

ever built by Jaguar, which delivered 279bhp at 5,750rpm in November 1956 as prepared by the works for the Ecurie Ecosse team.

The next step in the development of the Jaguar six for racing was engineered in Woodside, New York by Alfred Momo, the experienced Italian in charge of racing preparation for Briggs Cunningham's team. Cunningham, then Eastern US distributor for Jaguar, kept the leaping cat

Opposite left: With its cast-aluminium sump the dry-sumped Jaguar six was significantly shallower than standard. It is shown as raced in 1954 and as subsequently fitted to the production D-Types.
Opposite right: In 1956 in the D-Type, the Jaguar six

was first raced with Lucas port-type fuel injection, which used a slide throttle.
Above: *A lateral section of the standard XK120 engine displays its long-stroke architecture, excellent porting and inverted-cup tappets. The outer profile of the cast-iron block is subtly shaped.*

FERRARI 553 2.5-LITRE FOUR

Enzo Ferrari and his chief engineer Aurelio Lampredi were well satisfied with their decision to build four-cylinder engines to compete in the 2-litre Formula 2 that was adopted for the world championship in 1952 and '53. Two championships for Alberto Ascari could hardly be seen as a poor dividend for that investment. Accordingly the main thrust of their challenge for the new 2½-litre Formula 1 starting in 1954 was also with four-cylinder engines. Starting from a proven base, they had every reason to hope for an early harvest of championship points.

From the earlier Type 500 the Type 625 was evolved, its designation again referring to the capacity of one cylinder. This measured 94 x 90mm (3.70 x 3.54in). With a 13:1 compression ratio the Type 625 was stated to produce 250bhp at 7,200rpm in 1954. It was installed in a chassis that was, as well, an evolution of the Type 500.

Lampredi also prepared a new chassis, the Type 553, with a revised transaxle and side-mounted fuel tanks that gave it a rounded look and the nickname *Squalo* or 'Shark'. For this he prepared a substantially new engine. He hoped that his new four would be able to run reliably at high revs – the immediate goal was 7,500 – and that its top end could breathe well enough to be useful at this speed. Both requirements led to the strongly oversquare dimensions of 100.0 x 79.5mm (3.94 x 3.13in) for a displacement of 2,496cc.

To get a perspective on this rpm objective, we may consider Lampredi's 90 x 78mm Formula 2 four of 1953, which was reliable at 7,500. An examination of comparable piston speed showed that with similar standards of structural design the 553 engine could be expected to be trouble-free at 7,050rpm only, so some kind of breakthrough in Lampredi's thinking was going to be required if the desired revolutions were to be reached reliably.

As in Lampredi's V12 Ferrari engines, the cylinder head and water jacketing of the 553 were cast of Silumin alloy in one piece which included the entire housing at the front for the camshaft drive gear train. Cast-iron cylinder liners, which were screwed up into the combustion chambers, hung down below the bottom edge of the water jacketing. When the head/jacket unit was bolted down to the deep crankcase these liners were made water-tight with the latter by a close fit plus rubber O-rings. This head-cum-cylinder assembly was attached to the flat top of the crankcase by four studs at its corners and by eight long studs which emerged between the cam boxes in the centre of the engine.

About half the height of the entire engine, the light-alloy crankcase was notable for its smooth, unribbed sides and considerable width. New Lampredi thinking was evidenced by its octagonal cross-section, which he adopted to try to reduce internal windage losses and eliminate sludge-generating atmospheric breathers. The crankshaft was carried in five main bearings, Vandervell thin-wall shells being used exclusively. Finished all over, the deep-throated rods were conventional in layout, while the pistons had full skirts carrying one of the four rings below the gudgeon pin. At the bottom the crankcase sides curved inward to a very shallow finned oil pan.

Like the later Dino V6, the Type 553 four housed many of its accessories in a cover plate bolted to the front of the crankcase. The scavenge and pressure pumps for the dry-sump oiling system were at the lower right and left of the cover. Between them and a bit higher – just below the crank centreline – was the usual Fimac mechanical fuel pump. At the upper left and right of the cover, at both sides of the crank nose, were the two Marelli magnetos which rested horizontally pointing forward.

Driven from a bevel gear above and between the magnetos was the horizontally placed water pump with double outlets. These delivered cool water to the engine through the centre of the side of the crankcase, thus near the heavily loaded centre main bearing. From there water flowed upward to emerge from risers cast above the centre of each combustion chamber and returned to the radiator through a manifold.

A train of narrow gears rose from the crank nose to drive the twin camshafts. Because the head/water jacket casting was so short, the highest central gear protruded up above the central valley of the head. It was found necessary in 1954 to add small external oil pumps to feed oil to the bearings

Opposite above: Although the 'Squalo' chassis was initially unsatisfactory, the Type 553 engine gave better results and was installed in the more conventional Ferraris raced in the 1954 and '55 seasons. Mike Hawthorn drove this one at Aintree in the latter year.

Opposite below: Although square and wide-spaced cam boxes gave the impression of extreme valve angles, the included angle was not excessive for the era at 85°. Weber carburettors with twin throats of 58mm were the largest available at that time.

shouldered steel plug was inserted. This came from the machine shop unfinished at the tip which contacted the valve-stem end. Clearance was set and maintained by grinding this tip the necessary amount. The short, sturdy valve itself was closed by a massive pair of hairpin springs, which together exerted about 400lb (182kg) compressed. The rotational speed of the *Squalo* engine was not limited by its valve gear, which could cope with 10,000rpm.

Inlet valves of 50mm diameter were inclined at 40° from the vertical – 5° less than the smaller exhausts – and received their mixture from tapering ports. Double-bodied Weber carbs, eventually of 58mm bore size, were mounted on small steel frameworks which in turn were bolted to the chassis frame to reduce float-bowl frothing caused by vibration of the engine, which was connected to the carbs by lengths of flanged rubber piping. The high-rev objective was indicated by the large diameter of the high-mounted exhaust system, which first collected the gases from cylinder pairs 1-4 and 2-3 before merging into a single tailpipe. The latter was also longer than that used on the earlier two-litre four.

The difficulty attendant upon the design of a very large combustion chamber manifested itself in the 553's compression ratio, which at 12:1 was a full point below that of the Type 625 four of the same displacement. Weighing 352lb (160kg), the 1954 553 engine was rated by Ferrari at between 265 and 270bhp at 7,600rpm. At the same time this was the peak speed that the

of these cam drive gears; a fracture, probably from vibration, of the feed to this piping led to González's retirement in the French GP in 1954. Carried in five bearings in detachable tappet boxes, the large-diameter camshafts were hollow.

The 553's valve gear was a further development of the gear used with satisfaction in the Type 500 Formula 2 engines. The narrow cam lobe attacked a roller, which was shaft-mounted in the upper face of a wide aluminium mushroom tappet. In earlier designs two thin-wire coil springs were used to hold the tappet assembly against the cam, but in the *Squalo* a single heavy spring exerting about 125lb (57kg) compressed was fitted.

In the hollow stem of the tappet mushroom a

FERRARI 553 2.5-LITRE FOUR

magneto ignition permitted; this acted as an informal rev limiter.

The *Squalo* proved a tricky car to drive, but improvements to its mass distribution allowed Nino Farina to give hot chase in one to Fangio's winning Maserati at Spa in 1954 until a piston broke. The same failure befell González, symptomatic of the liberties that Lampredi was trying to take with piston speed. The engine's power was also to the fore at the fast Reims track, where the *Squalos* were the only cars to stay within sight of the flying Mercedes-Benz W196 on its debut. Neither was the Type 553 a sluggard at Monza for the Italian GP, where Froilán González set the fastest lap of the race on his second lap.

That Ferrari considered the 553 engine to be useful was indicated by his installation of it in several of his Type 625 chassis for GP races after mid-1954. For 1955 the 553 engine became the Type 555 through a number of detail changes which altered its appearance only slightly. The new 555 became the standard Ferrari racing engine for the '55 season, installed both in the 625 chassis and in the Type 555 *Supersqualo* car. Although radical in appearance, this was essentially the late-1954 Type 625 with a special transaxle, side tanks, a reinforced frame and a sexy new Scaglietti body.

To incorporate internal oil lines and to simplify assembly, the 555's cam-drive gearcase was split vertically in two. The hold-down studs for the tappet boxes were moved outside instead of inside the boxes to provide more room for a wider type of hairpin valve spring. Acknowledging the reality that ignition and structural constraints would not allow the four to exceed 7,500rpm consistently, its tuning was realigned

to give 265–270 horsepower at 7,000 to 7,200rpm.

In 1955, with Mercedes-Benz, Maserati and Lancia all well into their strides, Ferrari had a patchy record. The 555 four won at Monaco in the 625 chassis after all the Mercedes retired. In the *Supersqualo* it achieved third place in the Belgian GP at Spa behind the two cars from Stuttgart, a tremendous performance by Guiseppe 'Nino' Farina in what turned out to be his final Grand Prix. When in mid-season Ferrari was given the D50 Lancias with their V8 engines, the fate of Lampredi's four – and indeed of Lampredi as Ferrari's chief engineer – was sealed.

Opposite left: The Type 553 4-cylinder engine was conceived as the power unit for the radical new 'Squalo' Ferrari built for the 1954 racing season. The size of its exhaust pipes indicated optimism concerning its potential output.
Opposite right: A squat, rectangular crankcase was a new departure for engines designed by Aurelio Lampredi.

From the horizontal water pump at the front, pipes were fed on each side to a point in the crankcase close to the critical centre main bearing.
Above: Strongly oversquare at 100 x 79.5mm for 2,496cc, the Type 553 four produced 270bhp at 7,600rpm. This pushed its corrected piston speed to a level not consistently attained in racing until the late 1960s.

SPECIFICATIONS	
Cylinders	I4
Bore	100.0mm
Stroke	79.5mm
Stroke/bore ratio	0.80:1
Capacity	2,496cc
Compression ratio	12.0:1
Connecting rod length	138.0mm
Rod/crank radius ratio	3.5:1
Main bearing journal diameter	60.0mm
Rod journal diameter	50.0mm
Inlet valve diameter (1valve)	50.0mm
Exhaust valve diameter (1 valve)	46.0mm
Inlet pressure	1.0Atm
Engine weight	352lb (160kg)
Peak power	270bhp @ 7,600rpm
Piston speed (corrected)	4,446ft/min (22.2m/s)
Engine bhp per litre	108.2bhp per litre
Engine weight per bhp	1.30lb (0.59kg) per bhp

1955

LANCIA D50 2.5-LITRE V8

Remarkably, in view of the great success that the Cosworth-built Ford V8 was later to enjoy, few V8 engines had been built for Grand Prix racing before Vittorio Jano and his design team produced theirs for the Lancia D50 that first raced at the end of 1954. The 1939 Mercedes-Benz W165 was V8-powered, but it was a *Voiturette*, not a GP car. For a French national racing effort of 1947–48 Albert Lory, author of the superb 1927 Delage, built a four-cam V8, but the CTA-Arsenal was not a success.

For Jano the D50's 2,490cc V8 engine was a logical progression from the four-cam V6 engines he and Francesco De Virgilio had designed for the sports-racing Lancias of 1952–53. Like those it used chains to drive its overhead cams, a solution that was then unique among Grand Prix cars. The double-roller chain for each head ran straight across between the two cam sprockets and then over an adjustable idler placed just below the left-hand cam sprocket of each bank.

A one-piece high-silicon aluminium-alloy block and crankcase was the heart of the V8. Ferrous wet liners were inserted to form the cylinders. The top of the liner had a flange which met the cylinder head (through a gasket), and three-quarters of an inch below the top was a shaped and notched flange which butted against a counterbore in the block casting. Between these two flanges at the top of the liner all the stress of the cylinder-head seal was absorbed. From this point downward the liner had only to guide the piston and was subject to no compression stresses. Sealing at the bottom of the cylinder was assured by a close fit plus two synthetic O-rings grooved into the liner.

The water jackets of adjacent cylinders were completely separate except for a transverse passage at the top just below the head face. Coolant entered the block through manifolds low at each side and exited through ducts alongside the inlet valve seats. Distribution of water in the heads was very good, with flow around all the valve seats and a wet, finned section of the exhaust valve guide. The water pump was driven from a small gear train at the nose of the crank and had an integrally cast duct to the cylinder manifolds.

Each cylinder head and its joint seal was treated as a unit in itself, the water jackets acting only as structural supports. The crankcase was a third design unit. The bottom of the block was machined off on the centreline of the crank and the five main bearings were supported by deep, thick webs. Attached to them by two big studs close in and two smaller ones farther out were massive webbed aluminium main bearing caps. Carried in them was a fully machined alloy-steel crankshaft whose mass was kept as low as possible to aid responsiveness and acceleration.

Drawing oil from the close-fitting light-alloy sump was a large scavenge pump mounted low at the front, sucking oil through a series of collectors hung from the main caps. An oil reservoir was in the tail of the car and a core-type oil cooler was mounted in the front of the left-hand pontoon with a scoop on the outboard side. The pressure oil pump body was offset to the right of the crank nose and was integral with the top of an oil filter housing. Virtually all the oil feeds and ducts were incorporated in the block casting.

Unusually for a racing engine, the big ends of the I-section connecting rods were split diagonally so they could be pulled up through the cylinders for rebuilding.

At first the pistons were high-domed with full skirts which carried five rings each – one below the big gudgeon pin. Heavy ribs under the crown curved down to carry loads to the pin bosses. Very shallow cutaways for valve-head clearance displayed unusual confidence in the valve gear.

Early D50 prototypes had long slim fingers separating the cam lobe from the valve-stem end. Hairpin springs were fitted to keep the stems short and valve weight down. This arrangement, while good of its type, was still too heavy for the exacting Jano. During development in 1954 the fingers were dispensed with after the rest of the engine was proven and Jano inserted the compact

Opposite above: Among the many radical features of the 1955 Lancia D50 was its V8 engine. This was a configuration that hitherto had been used extremely rarely in Formula 1.
Opposite below: Like the Mercedes-Benz of 1939 and the BRM of 1951 the Lancia D50 angled its vee-type engine in the chassis to allow the driver to sit alongside an engine-speed propeller shaft to a rear transaxle. Each cylinder was fired by two spark plugs.

type of tappet that he first developed for Alfa Romeo. The simple mushroom tappet was screwed directly to the valve stem, in some versions with a surrounding collar for extra security. Valve clearance was easily set by rotating the tappet in relation to the valve and locked by a series of notches under the pressure of the coil valve springs.

Thanks to the detachable head there were no mechanical restrictions on the valve dimensions, which were large by any standards: 46.0mm for the inlet and 44.5mm for the exhaust. They were symmetrically inclined at an 80° included angle. Stems were substantial and the heads were deeply tuliped. The inlet valve stem was nearly an inch longer than the exhaust stem to allow plenty of room for a big smoothly-curving port from the carbs.

Early engine drawings showed special Weber carburettors with throttle bodies angled to mate with the Lancia inlet ports. These were built but not used at the D50's debut, when the V8 was fed by four twin-throat Type 40 PII Solexes supplied by a small-diameter fuel-line network down the centre of the group. Twin Marelli magnetos were driven off the back ends of the inlet cams and protruded through the firewall into the cockpit.

At the rear of the V8 was naught but a small cover for oil sealing and a direct connection to the drive shaft which, like the engine, was angled from right front to left rear of the chassis to allow a low profile. The engine sat in a deeply-trussed tubular frame to which it made a major structural contribution. Attaching the cowl and firewall to the structure carrying the front suspension was the V8 itself. Lugs cast into the front and back of each cylinder head were bolted into the frame. In addition, two lugs at the 'bottom' of each head mated with mounts welded to the bottom frame members, adding substantially to frame and beam stiffness. The cylinders and crankcase hung suspended between the cylinder heads in this unique and pioneering installation.

Early power figures quoted for the V8 ranged between 230 and 260bhp, a typical figure being 250bhp at 7,700rpm. Lancia's experiments with direct fuel injection were marred by a tendency for fuel to find its way down the cylinder walls

into the oil supply, so the Solexes were used instead. They also tried two bore/stroke combinations: 76 x 68.5mm and 73.6 x 73.1mm, finally settling on the latter (2.90 x 2.88in). First set at 8,100, the rev limit crept up to 8,400. Mike Hawthorn took one engine to 8,900 at the end of '55.

Assisted by Jano, Ferrari commenced a range of experiments with the V8 after he was given the cars in 1955. Prior to the 1956 season the original Weber carbs were given another try. They produced ten more horsepower at the top than

the Solexes, but were weak in the middle rev ranges. Reinstatement of the Solexes, allied with the use of a separate tuned pipe for each exhaust port, brought the power in at 5,000rpm instead of 6,500 and raised peak output from the 1955 level. By 1956 quoted power rose to 265bhp at 8,000rpm. The cars were geared for 8,200–8,600 on the fastest straight of a given course and drivers were asked to stay under 8,100 in the gears.

Before mid-1956 the structure of the engine was heavily reworked. Ferrari elected to use the oversquare dimensions that had previously been rejected. To raise compression new pistons were made and gaskets between the heads and block were eliminated. A heavier oil pan was also cast to contribute more stiffness to the bottom end. Chiefly for ease of installation, Ferrari gave up the use of the engine as an element of the car's chassis frame.

These amendments resulted in an engine that would stay together at 9,000rpm but would blow sky-high at 9,100. Fangio proved the point in Belgium, where he left a broken car with 9,200 showing on the tell-tale. Reliability improved after Fangio obtained the dedicated services of a particular mechanic; this helped him win his fourth world championship behind the D50 V8.

For the 1957 season a major rework of the V8 brought new 80 x 62mm (3.15 x 2.44in) cylinder dimensions and a reduction in compression ratio from 11.9 to 11.5:1. New Solex carburettors were fitted, angled to give a straighter air path to the valves. Output of the new Ferrari designated the '801' was now rated at 285bhp at 8,800rpm with an improved torque curve that added 18bhp from 4,500 to 7,000rpm. In this last season for unlimited fuel Ferrari experimented with exotic brews, using 6 per cent nitromethane in some early-season races with inconsistent results. In that final year for the V8, it seemed, Fangio and Maserati had the edge in the exploitation of oxygen-bearing fuel additives.

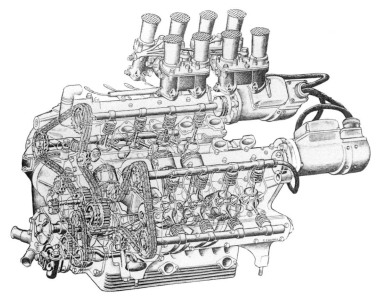

Opposite above: For Lancia the evolution of a 90-degree V8 from its earlier 60-degree V6 racing engines was an easy enough transition. Bosses at the front and below the cylinder head show the way in which the V8 was made an integral part of the car's chassis.

Opposite below: Fine design judgement is evident in every detail of the aluminium cylinder block of the D50 V8

with its inserted ferrous wet liners. The engine's design was the work of Ettore Zaccone Mina.

Above: A sharp departure from racing convention was Lancia's choice of a chain drive to turn the camshafts of a high-speed Grand Prix engine. Project director Vittorio Jano judged that this had proved satisfactory in the sports-racing Lancia engines.

SPECIFICATIONS	
Cylinders	V8
Bore	73.6mm
Stroke	73.1mm
Stroke/bore ratio	0.99:1
Capacity	2,490cc
Compression ratio	11.9:1
Connecting rod length	135.0mm
Rod/crank radius ratio	3.7:1
Main bearing journal diameter	60.0mm
Rod journal diameter	50.0mm
Inlet valve diameter (1 valve)	46.0mm
Exhaust valve diameter (1 valve)	44.5mm
Inlet pressure	1.0Atm
Peak power	250bhp @ 7,700rpm
Piston speed (corrected)	3,706ft/min (18.5m/s)
Engine bhp per litre	100.4bhp per litre

1955

MERCEDES-BENZ M196 2.5-LITRE EIGHT

In the first months of 1952 Daimler-Benz set up a special group in its racing-car design department to create the engine that the company would use in its Grand Prix car for the 1954 2½-litre Formula 1. Under 50-year-old Hans Gassmann, an ingenious and inquisitive engineer, they began planning an engine that would be known as the M196.

A V12 was considered, but rejected in view of its relatively high centre of gravity, weight and complexity. Analysis of other alternatives favoured a straight-eight because it could be inclined in the chassis to place its weight very low. Taking the drive from the end of its crankshaft, however, would induce torsional stresses which were calculated to be 'so high that a crankshaft damper could only cope with them with difficulty.' More favourable conditions were given by a drive take-off geared to the centre of the crankshaft. This design was chosen, with the central gear train used also to drive the camshafts and engine accessories such as injection pump, dual magneto and water and oil pumps.

Initially a traditional four-valve cylinder head was tested for this eight in a 310cc single-cylinder engine. At high revs, however, valve bounce was occurring, demanding deep cut-outs in the piston crowns that degraded the high compression ratio that was essential if the engine were to perform well unsupercharged. Seeking some way out of this dilemma, Hans Gassmann had little else on his mind on the evening of 20 May 1952 when he boarded the trolley-bus at Untertürkheim to ride to his home in suburban Stuttgart. Seated in the trolley-bus on his way to work the next morning, Gassmann pulled an envelope from his pocket and made some sketches on it. In the office he showed the envelope to his colleagues and said, matter-of-factly, 'This is how we will do it.'

The historic sketches of Hans Gassmann showed two cam lobes controlling each valve. One lobe opened it in the normal manner. The other, a D-shaped lobe working through an L-shaped rocker, pulled it closed again. Independently Gassmann had reinvented the desmodromic valve gear with which both Delage and Th. Schneider had raced in the 1914 French GP – and been defeated by Mercedes.

Having conceived the desmodromic gear, Hans Gassmann realised that it could be used to open and close much larger, heavier valves than the ones in their test engine. This led his group to change its design to a two-valve combustion chamber machined as a perfect hemisphere. This was a smoother and less-broken-up chamber that promised lower heat losses and a higher usable compression ratio.

Valve lifts of 10mm were tried at first, then increased to 12mm for the exhausts and 13mm for the inlets. The final valve timing remained unchanged through 1954 and 1955 and was as follows:

Inlet opens 20°BTDC Exhaust opens 50°BBDC
Inlet closes 56°ABDC Exhaust closes 14°ATDC

Traditional Daimler-Benz forged-steel integral cylinders and heads were used, welded to their 1.0–1.5mm sheet steel water jackets to form four-cylinder blocks. The absence of any valve-seat inserts – not needed by the forged-steel cylinder – allowed very large valves to be fitted. Inclined at an angle of 43° from the vertical, the inlet valve was 50mm in head diameter with a 10mm stem. The exhaust was inclined at 45°, with a 43mm head and a stem of 12mm to permit internal drilling and two-thirds filling, from the head end, with sodium salts for cooling. These diameters were very large in relation to the cylinder dimensions, set well oversquare at 76.0 x 68.8mm (2.99 x 2.71in) for 2,496cc.

Opposite above: With its wind-cheating lines, inboard brakes and advanced space frame the 1954 Mercedes-Benz W196 was no ordinary racing car. Neither was its M196 straight-eight engine particularly commonplace.
Opposite below: With the 2½-litre engine canted steeply to the right in the chassis, a view from the front of the car showed the cylinder heads topped by the plenum chamber feeding the eight individual inlet ports. Twin ignition made changing the sixteen spark plugs no sinecure.

A distinctive feature of the design was its downdraught inlet porting, coming in through the top of the cylinder head. This was well-suited to the engine's placement in the car, angled to the right at 37° to the horizontal, and to the layout of its auxiliaries. This port was favoured because it directed the incoming air flow away from the exhaust valve, which reduced the tendency for the hot exhaust valve to heat up the fresh charge and thus lessen its density. Each cylinder was fired by two 14mm Bosch spark plugs.

After good results were obtained in 1952 with direct-injection tests in the 300SL engine it was certain that the Grand Prix engine would be designed from scratch to be injected. Nozzle positions in the inlet port as well as in the cylinder were tried. Selected was a point on the cylinder wall just below the inlet valve, with the centreline of the nozzle angled upward at 12.5°. Fuel flow began 30° after top dead centre on the inlet stroke and continued for 160°.

From a 'shopping list' of 25 different fuel blends supplied by Esso, seven were tested. The best results, as a combination of power with fuel economy, were given by blend RD1, which contained 45 per cent benzol, 25 per cent methyl alcohol, 25 per cent 110/130 octane gasoline, 3 per cent acetone and 2 per cent nitro-benzene. Resistance to knocking at the 12.5:1 compression ratio used was increased by the addition of 0.03 per cent by volume of tetra-ethyl lead. Nitromethane additives were tried but not used because they were too knock-sensitive.

The fully skirted piston was an aluminium-alloy forging by Mahle with a high and heavy dome, weighing 1.05lb (0.48kg) with its rings, gudgeon pin and retaining clips. The spacing of the top two compression rings was kept wide by the need to ensure that hot gas could at no time push its way down past both rings through the small hole in the cylinder wall for the injector nozzle. Two additional plain rings above and below the pin were profiled on their lower faces to act as oil scrapers.

At the bottom end of the engine a complete commitment was made to roller bearings and built-up Hirth crankshaft components. The individual sections of the crankshaft were joined together by radial serrations, tightened by a massive differentially-threaded screw inside each bearing journal. Unusually, the main bearing journals were smaller at 51mm than those of the rod big ends at 55mm. Lubrication of the big-end rollers was by oil escaping from the mains into slinger rings in the crank cheeks. One-piece I-section connecting rods were steel forgings braced by twin ribs around both large and small eyes.

A deep Silumin crankcase fully enclosed the rotating equipment. Main bearings at both ends were held by the bolted-on covers that completed the open-ended construction of the crankcase. This design gave added importance to the use of lateral cap screws to tie the lower ends of the dural caps

for the other eight main bearings into the crankcase walls. The bearing caps were retained by long studs coming through the crankcase from the hold-down points for the cylinder blocks.

The rear cover of the crankcase also incorporated a flange for the clutch housing and a steady bearing for the output drive shaft. Driven from the engine's central gear train, the 20mm shaft inside the sump turned at 0.89 engine speed to power the clutch and drive line in the conventional clockwise manner. Hence the crankshaft turned counterclockwise, as viewed from the front of the car. (In this respect Daimler-Benz reached the same conclusion as the designers of the V16 BRM.) The offset mounting of the output shaft and the clutch allowed the heaviest elements of the engine to be placed some 2.5in closer to the ground than would have been possible if the clutch had been attached directly to the end of the crankshaft. The engine weighed a hefty 451lb (205kg).

Castrol R lubricant was brought by a supply pump from the dry-sump reservoir to an oil filter built into the crankcase. From the filter the oil went to a large pressure pump for the main bearings and two small pumps for the inlet and exhaust cam bearings respectively. A five-section

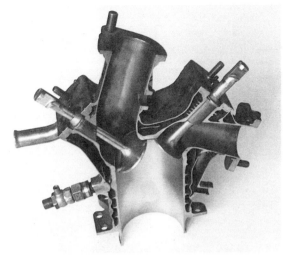

scavenge pump was mounted outside the sump. At 8,000rpm the system completely recirculated all the oil in the M196 every minute.

The exhaust ports were fitted with 47mm downpipes which were grouped into two main 65mm exhaust pipes. The four centre cylinders were gathered into one pipe and the other four into the other. On the inlet side curved ram pipes 9½in long were fed by a plenum chamber similar to that on the 300SL. For 1955 the ram pipes were made straight to improve correlation between the dynamometer tests and the track results.

In its first 1954 race appearances the rated power of the M196 was 257bhp at 8,250rpm. It combined this power with remarkable output lower down its range: 220bhp at 6,300rpm, for example, that also being the speed of its maximum torque, 183lb ft. Refinements to the injection nozzles, piston crowns and port contours brought the output to 290bhp at 8,500rpm by the end of 1955 and filled out a sagging section of the torque curve at 5,000rpm.

The redline was 8,700rpm, which could be held for 20 seconds at a time, and 9,000 was allowed for momentary excesses of 3 seconds. These limits were observed with but a few exceptions by Juan Fangio as he drove the W196 to world championships in 1954 and 1955.

Opposite above: Viewed from the front, the M196 engine shown here is canted at approximately the angle at which it was fitted in the car. The breather on the right would be vertical. In the foreground are the two Bosch magnetos and the vibration damper fitted to the front of the crankshaft.

Opposite below: Built up by means of the Hirth system, the M196 crankshaft was a work of art in its own right. Because the drive to the clutch was taken from its centre it was possible to fit a vibration damper at both ends.

Above top: A sectioned M196 cylinder (they were made in blocks of four)

reveals the elegance of the traditional Daimler-Benz method of fabricating these components from forged and sheet steel. This method allows both the exterior of the cylinder wall and the exhaust-valve guide to be finned for improved cooling. Close control is possible over all sections of the unit.

Above bottom: The crowning glory of the M196 Grand Prix engine was its successful employment of desmodromic valve gear, which uses cams to close as well as open the valves. Closing was the function of the large D-shaped cam, pressing a lever and fork that raised the valve when required.

SPECIFICATIONS	
Cylinders	I8
Bore	76.0mm
Stroke	68.8mm
Stroke/bore ratio	0.91:1
Capacity	2,496cc
Compression ratio	12.5:1
Connecting rod length	137.5mm
Rod/crank radius ratio	4.0:1
Main bearing journal diameter	51.0mm
Rod journal diameter	55.0mm
Inlet valve diameter (1 valve)	50.0mm
Exhaust valve diameter (1 valve)	43.0mm
Inlet pressure	1.0Atm
Engine weight	451lb (205kg)
Peak power	290bhp @ 8,500rpm
Piston speed (corrected)	4,033ft/min (20.2m/s)
Peak torque	183lb ft (248Nm) @ 6,300rpm
Peak bmep	182psi
Engine bhp per litre	116.2bhp per litre
Engine weight per bhp	1.56lb (0.71kg) per bhp

1955

PORSCHE 547 1.5-LITRE FLAT-4

Porsche built the cars first, and then the engines. Racing appearances were made in 1953 by the first Type 550 Porsches, mid-engined two-seaters that were the first cars that Porsche built expressly for competition. They competed with pushrod units until the engine intended to power them was ready, as it was in the summer of 1953. It was a radical new four-cam flat-four that was destined to serve Porsche in various forms until 1966, ending its career in the Type 904 Carrera GTS.

The new engine's displacement was to be 1.5 litres to suit the international racing and record-breaking Class F – one in which Porsche was already very active. Its designer, the young Ernst Fuhrmann, gave his flat-opposed four a stroke/bore ratio of 0.78:1, which was exceptionally low for that time. Its cylinder dimensions were 85 x 66mm (3.35 x 2.60in) for 1,498cc. The short stroke of the Type 547 – as it was known – increased the overlap between its main and rod bearing journals, which made the crankshaft stronger at that critical point, and also helped keep the width of the engine within reasonable bounds.

Fuhrmann chose a classic hemispherical combustion chamber. Placed in a vertical plane, its two valves were equally inclined at an angle of 39° from the cylinder centreline. Head diameters were 48mm for the inlet valves and 41mm for the exhausts.

Few difficulties in the design of this engine were more taxing than providing a light, simple and positive means of opening and closing four widely-spaced pairs of valves. The drive was taken to one cam on each bank – as in the Type 360 Cisitalia engine, though in a different sequence – and was then carried to the adjoining camshaft. The drive to the cams was taken from a gear at the flywheel or output end of the crankshaft. There a pair of helical gears drove a half-speed shaft in the sump, directly below the crankshaft. At the other end of the crank, below the engine's centre main bearing, the half-speed shaft (called the 'countershaft' by Porsche) carried back-to-back spiral bevel gears. These in turn rotated smaller gears on hollow shafts which extended straight out to the left and right. At its respective side of the engine, each shaft turned a gear at the centre of the lower exhaust camshaft. From that point another shaft rose vertically to turn spiral bevel gears at the centre of the inlet camshaft.

Oil reached each cylinder head through the hollow centre of the drive shaft to that head. Once in the head, the oil was carried to the bushings and the cam lobes by drillings and by the hollow core of each camshaft. The cam lobes were made separately and keyed to the shaft that carried them. This method, which resembled that of motorcycle engine design, made it easier to choose the right cam contour as well as the best material for the lobe surface.

To transmit the cam action to the valve, Ernst Fuhrmann improved upon another technique that had been used in the Type 360 Cisitalia: a pivoted finger follower. A single shaft could not be used as a hinge for the pairs of side-by-side fingers because one of the cam drive shafts passed between the fingers. Instead, Fuhrmann used a bronze spherical pivot, with the end of the finger being held against the pivot by a small coil spring. The cam was offset 10mm from the valve stem toward the finger pivot, so that the valve clearance could be adjusted by raising or lowering the pivot by turning the threaded stud on which it was mounted.

Flats for valve clearance were machined in the top of the domed piston, which was cast by Mahle out of 124 aluminium alloy. Deep-skirted, the piston had one oil ring below the gudgeon pin and three compression rings above it. The pins were free to float in both the piston and the small end of the connecting rod. Because the crankshaft was a built-up Hirth component with roller main and rod bearings, the connecting rod could have a one-piece big end.

Each throw of the crankshaft was as heavily counterweighted as the limited space between the opposed cylinders would permit. Since this was not quite adequate, cylindrical slugs of heavier metal were inserted into the cheeks of the four counterweights. Lubricant – SAE 30 – was pumped to the three main bearings through brass metering jets. As the oil escaped it was centrifuged outward and caught by slinger rings, from which it was carried by passages to the rod journals.

Opposite above: When Porsche decided to build a car expressly for sports-racing competition it made a very good fist of it with the Type 550, here breaking records at Monthléry in 1955. In 1953 the car was married with the Type 547 engine designed to power it.

Opposite below: As a flat-four engine the Type 547 was in the Porsche tradition; it was designed to be able to fit into the standard Porsche chassis. Radically, in the sports-racing Type 550 Spyder it was positioned forward of the rear wheels.

Oil was delivered to the various galleries by the pressure section of a two-sided oil pump which was driven by a gear at the tip of the half-speed countershaft. It was housed, together with a scavenging pump of more than twice the capacity, in a cylindrical casting which fitted into a matching cavity formed by the two halves of the crankcase. This ingenious design detail was transferred directly by Fuhrmann from the engine of the GP Cisitalia.

To keep the engine's profile low and to provide enough oil and oil-cooling capacity, the 547 had dry-sump lubrication. The narrow, bottom-finned sump was cast as part of the aluminium-alloy crankcase, which was a two-part assembly split vertically down its middle. Four long studs around each cylinder clamped the cylinder head (one to each pair of cylinders) down against the finned cylinder, which was spigoted deeply into both the crankcase and the head. The individual cylinders, made of aluminium with chrome-plated bores, were produced by Mahle and the intricate deeply-finned cylinder heads were permanent-mould cast in aluminium.

Arranging enough air cooling for the heads of this high-performance engine posed a major challenge. Air flowing downward would pick up heat from the upper, inlet side of the head before continuing downward to cool the hotter exhaust-valve area. This was acceptable to the Porsche designers because the inlet side of the engine had to be kept cool in order to maintain high

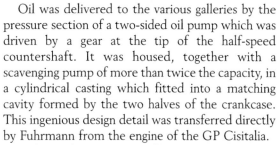

Above left: The business end of the Type 547 showed the twin camshaft-driven distributors for its dual ignition and the very sophisticated design of its cooling blower.
Above top: In his design of the Type 547 four, engineer Ernst Fuhrmann relied on Porsche's traditional shafts to drive its overhead cams. Generous cylinder-head finning provided the additional cooling that a competition engine required.
Above bottom: Removing

the cover of an inlet camshaft revealed the spiral-bevel drive that crossed the head from the exhaust side to rotate the camshaft. The twin-throat down-draught carburettors were by Solex.*
Opposite: *Section drawings portray the built-up crankshaft of the Type 547, its roller-bearing bottom end and the shaft drive to its camshafts. Spherical pivots carried the very light fingers that were interposed between the cam lobes and valve stems.*

volumetric efficiency. As well, in building this special racing engine they could afford to use expensive fine and deep finning to conduct the heat away from the exhaust side and toward the cooling air. The total cooling-fin area was increased from 2,600 square inches on the normal Porsche engines to 3,600 on the Type 547.

A special cooling blower was also needed; Porsche expertise was equal to the task. A radial-outflow fan was chosen with backward-curved blades, the most efficient albeit also the most space-consuming design. The fan was double-sided, drawing air from both the front and back of the engine. The generator, in the middle, acted as the fan's drive shaft and support. The front and back sections of the fan fed completely separate cooling ducts to the front and rear opposing cylinder pairs of the engine. The fan ran at a one-to-one ratio and was so efficient – requiring only 8.8 drive horsepower at 7,300rpm – that it could still be driven by a simple vee-belt.

Fuhrmann gave each combustion chamber two spark plugs and fired them with two Bosch distributors, which were driven from the ends of the upper, inlet camshafts. The latter had fittings at both ends so the distributors could be on either the front or the back of the engine, to suit the installation, and also so that the same basic cylinder head casting could be used on both sides of the engine – an important economy.

Developed in parallel with the engine were new carburettors from Solex: the 40 PII (also known as 40 PJJ) units that were used on the modified 1500 Super engines in the first 550s. For the Type 547 engine the 40mm bores were fitted with venturis 34mm in diameter.

By the autumn of 1952 Fuhrmann's design was complete and its fabrication began. On 2 April it ran under its own power for the first time in a test cell at Zuffenhausen. When the engine was first shown in public at the Paris Salon in late 1953 its output was quoted as 110bhp at 7,000rpm; the same net figure, albeit at 6,200rpm, was quoted for the series-built 550 Spyder of 1955. By Le Mans 1954 the four was producing 114bhp at 6,800 and could be revved safely to 7,500.

Steady increases in the engine's output were made to power successive generations of Porsche Spyders. By 1959, when Porsche built a single-seater for use in Formula 2, it was producing 155bhp and was safe to more than 8,000rpm. In

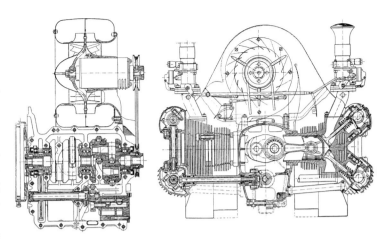

1961 and early 1962 it powered the Formula 1 Porsches, also with Kugelfischer fuel injection that helped improve the torque curve.

Final efforts to upgrade the Fuhrmann four included experiments with desmodromic valve gear, a flat-mounted cooling fan and Bosch fuel injection. Michael May used the latter two techniques in the engines he prepared at Porsche early in 1962, which produced 185bhp. Versions of the four measuring 1.6 and 2.0 litres were also made both for racing purposes and production Carrera models. One powered the 1966 904 coupé at the rate of 190bhp.

SPECIFICATIONS	
Cylinders	F4
Bore	85.0mm
Stroke	66.0mm
Stroke/bore ratio	0.78:1
Capacity	1,498cc
Compression ratio	9.5:1
Connecting rod length	132.0mm
Rod/crank radius ratio	4.0:1
Main bearing journal diameter	52.0mm
Rod journal diameter	52.0mm
Inlet valve diameter (1 valve)	48.0mm
Exhaust valve diameter (1 valve)	41.0mm
Inlet pressure	1.0Atm
Engine weight	225lb (102kg)
Peak power	125bhp @ 6,500rpm
Piston speed (corrected)	3,195ft/min (15.98m/s)
Peak torque	95lb ft (129Nm) @ 5,500rpm
Peak bmep	157psi
Engine bhp per litre	83.4bhp per litre
Engine weight per bhp	1.80lb (0.82kg) per bhp

1955

FERRARI 750 MONZA 3-LITRE FOUR

Making good use of his material, as was his wont, the canny Ferrari was quick to begin deploying his new four-cylinder engines in sports cars as well as Grand Prix cars. One of his first such efforts was the Mondial of 1953, which used a detuned (160bhp) version of the Type 500 Formula 2 engine in an attractive sports car. As bigger versions of the fours were developed they appeared in sports cars too.

Experimental 3-litre four-cylinder sports Ferraris initially had 102 x 90mm cylinder dimensions for 2,942cc and produced some 225bhp at 6,800rpm. A spyder version of this Type 735S made a promising but troublesome appearance at Senigallia in 1953. In January of 1954 that car was taken to an endurance race in Buenos Aires, where it had the measure of one of the regular Ferrari twelves until the torque of the four shattered the final drive after a pit stop. A newly built 735S was driven to a conservative fifth place.

Their experience with these cars and also with the new Type 553 Formula 1 engine allowed Aurelio Lampredi and his team to lay out a new sports car, the Type 750S. Its first appearance was at Monza on 27 June 1954, when Hawthorn/Maglioli took first and González/Trintignant second in the 1000 Kilometre Super corte-maggiore sports car GP. The name 'Monza' came naturally enough to this new model, a series of which was produced over the winter of 1954–55.

The main line of development toward the Monza was via its engine, which was designated Type 105 by the Ferrari drawing office. In classic Lampredi style its head and cylinders were integrated in an aluminium casting which included the ports, combustion chambers and water jackets, but not the cylinders themselves, which were separately cast of iron and screwed up into the chambers. Dimensions were 103 x 90mm (4.06 x 3.54in), which came daringly close to the Class D limit at 2,999.6cc.

Inlet valves were inclined at 45° from the vertical and exhausts at 40°, the latter having sodium-filled stems. Both valves seated on shrunk-in inserts. The combustion chamber was a modified hemisphere, with special contouring around the spark-plug holes. Placed at the fore and aft ends of the chamber, the twin plugs were closest to the exhaust valve, a position which, with a bore of over four inches, was vital to the proper ignition of a thinly-spread mixture.

Lampredi's proven techniques were incorporated in the Monza's elaborate valve gear. Twin hairpin springs, placed in a fore-and-aft plane, closed the valves through a collar retained by split keepers. Above this the tappets and camshaft were carried in separate cast light-alloy boxes. T-shaped in cross section, light-alloy tappets were guided by their stems and carried narrow rollers which protruded only slightly from their wide tops. The lower parts of the rollers rode in vertical slots and thus prevented the tappet from rotating. To ensure that this assembly was held in contact with the cam, a pair of light concentric coil springs acted against each tappet only, leaving the hairpin springs to cope solely with the valves.

Above: Made of light alloy, the Monza's tappets carried a large roller which contacted the narrow cam lobe. Inserted in the bottom of the tappet was a steel tip whose thickness was ground to establish the correct valve clearance.

Opposite above: That the Ferrari 750 Monza could drift corners in the hands of a driver like Mike Hawthorn at Goodwood in 1955 was indisputable. Its torque-rich 3-litre four-cylinder engine helped maintain precise control.

Opposite below: With a damascened finish on its firewall, owner George Tilp went the extra mile in the appearance of his Ferrari Monza. At the front of its engine a vertical dynamo is prominent.

The separate tappet box, which accounted for the unusually high and wide Monza cam boxes, allowed thorough lubrication of cams and followers without forcing leakage down the valve stems. This tappet and spring system was effective in keeping the valves in contact with cams that provided 310° of inlet duration and 98° of overlap. Lobes little more than a centimetre wide were carried on large-diameter tubular camshafts, which in turn rested in five plain white-metal bearings each.

Exhaust porting was generous, the outer opening being flared considerably from its size at the valve. Tuned manifolding was used, with the pipes paired 1-4 and 2-3 and these two later joined at a single expansion chamber. Induction was by means of two 58 DCOA3 Weber twin-choke carburettors, fitted with 44mm venturis. Abbreviated angled alloy

pipes connected the carburettors to the ports and stubby ram pipes were fitted. A heavy throttle linkage cross-shaft was carried in two ball bearings.

The short head-cum-cylinder unit bolted directly to the very deep Silumin crankcase, with rubber O-rings forming water seals at the bottoms of the individual cylinders. Solid webbing supported each of the five main bearings, which were 60mm in diameter and available in four undersizes. The webbing continued down an inch-and-a-half beyond the crank centreline to give the deep, I-sectioned bearing caps some lateral support. Two studs retained each cap.

So that it could carry the oil supply to the crank and the big ends, the centre main was made 14mm wider than its 28mm brethren. Devoid of elaborate balance weighting, the forged steel crankshaft carried 50mm big-end journals. Aluminium-bronze Vandervell thin-wall bearings were fitted here, as at the mains, and four undersizes were again available.

Connecting rods were short and simple, the sides of the I-section shank being perfect tangents to the outer diameter of the gudgeon-pin end. Two bolts retained the big-end cap, while the fully floating pin received its lubrication from splash alone. Fully

skirted pistons carried two compression and two oil rings, one of the latter being below the pin.

In the transition from the 735S to the 750 the peak-power speed was cut back from 6,800 to 6,000rpm – 250bhp for the Monza. Nevertheless the four big pistons continued to impose a high level of stress on the rest of the engine and drive train. As a result the standard Monza's full-bore racing capability deteriorated after the first seven hours. Beyond that its tune lapsed and clearances became excessive, calling for a complete rebuild and renewal of bearings, pistons, etc. Lengthy endurance races were thus seldom the Monza's cup of tea.

An alloy cover at the front of the engine concealed the accessory and camshaft drive-train of 10mm-wide spur gears. The upper gears drove the cams while the water and oil pumps were placed low at the front. Dry-sump lubrication was used. Two screened pickups scavenged the front and rear of the intricately finned cast light-alloy sump. The scavenge oil pump had two idlers, to ensure that it kept up with demand, and it supplied a riveted tank on the right-hand side of the engine bay.

A single-idler pressure pump drew from the

side. Some of the 1955 Grand Prix cars with the Type 555 engine used this bottom end and accessory box with a cover plate over the generator drive. Earlier 3-litre sports cars used magnetos, but coil ignition was deemed superior for the Monza for all-round 'sports car' use.

A Fimac mechanical pump driven from the rear of the exhaust camshaft supplied fuel to the back end of the carburettor pipework, while the front end was fed by a rear-mounted Autolex electric pump.

The starter motor protruded rearward from the top of the shallow clutch housing, which enclosed a 10in dry double-plate clutch with flexible disc centres. A short extension supported the Hooke-type universal joint at the forward end of the drive shaft to the rear transaxle. Four heavy crankcase brackets mounted the engine package to the chassis on rubber inserts.

The many Monzas sold brought great success to private owners in all parts of the globe, especially in America. They were neither the most powerful nor the fastest sports cars of their day, but like the Type 35 Bugattis they won many contests by sheer weight of numbers. As a works racing car the Monza was displaced by the better-developed 860 Monza, whose longer stroke (102 x 105mm for 3,432cc) made it the largest four-cylinder engine ever produced by Ferrari. It was the Sebring 12-Hour winner in 1956.

reservoir and replenished the mains through a sump-mounted full-flow filter. Reluctant to complicate his crankcases with too many cast or drilled-in oil passages, Lampredi relied heavily on external and internal piping to carry the oil around.

Simplicity marked the cooling system, which was kept in circulation by a twin-outlet pump adjacent to the scavenged oil supply. Drawing from the bottom of the gilled-tube radiator, the pump sent the coolest water to both sides of the crankcase, where it could absorb some of the heat generated by the main bearings. From there it rose past the cylinders to outlets directly above each combustion chamber. Thus the water was at its warmest when it reached the exhaust valves, which were not favoured with a high-velocity cooling stream. The use of sodium-filled valve stems was fully justified. Though it was thus placed lower than the cylinder head, the header tank was integral with the radiator.

An extension from the cam gear train bevel-drove a cross-shaft within a magnesium-alloy box at the engine's front. Further bevels rotated the central 12-volt generator and the Marelli distributors at each

Opposite: A box of gearing at the front of the Type 750 four drove not only its dynamo but also the two distributors for the engine's dual ignition. Below that was the water pump with its twin outlets supplying

coolant to the centre of the crankcase on both sides.
Above: Twin-throat Weber carburettors 58mm in diameter met the induction requirements of the Monza, which reached its peak power (250bhp) at 6,000rpm.

SPECIFICATIONS

Cylinders	I4
Bore	103.0mm
Stroke	90.0mm
Stroke/bore ratio	0.87:1
Capacity	3,000cc
Compression ratio	9.2:1
Connecting rod length	142.0mm
Rod/crank radius ratio	3.2:1
Main bearing journal diameter	60.0mm
Rod journal diameter	50.0mm
Inlet valve diameter (1 valve)	50.0mm
Exhaust valve diameter (1 valve)	46.0mm
Inlet pressure	1.0Atm
Engine weight	353lb (160kg)
Peak power	250bhp @ 6,000rpm
Piston speed (corrected)	3,791ft/min (19.0m/s)
Engine bhp per litre	8,383bhp per litre
Engine weight per bhp	1.41lb (0.64kg) per bhp

1956

NOVI 3-LITRE V8

In 1940 Lewis Welch, a businessman in Novi, Michigan, decided to sponsor the construction of a new supercharged V8 engine for entry in the Indianapolis 500-mile race, which at that time was run under Grand Prix rules specifying a 3-litre limit for blown engines. Welch approached Fred Offenhauser, maker of the 'Offy' four, providing the necessary funds if Fred would handle all the design and construction responsibilities. Offenhauser in turn obtained the services of the man who was America's only full-time racing-engine designer, Leo Goossen.

The cylinder dimensions chosen by Welch and his engineering advisor, William 'Bud' Winfield, for their V8 were 3.185 x 2.84in (80.9 x 72.1mm). These oversquare proportions – unusual at the Novi's conception – produced a compact powerplant and provided a firm foundation for its long and successful design life. The same may be said for the traditional Miller type of block design used, with the cylinder head integral with the cylinders and jackets. This was an ideal choice on Goossen's part for a highly supercharged racing engine.

The large oval inlet and exhaust ports curved out and down from the valve seats in a 'dated' manner which was, however, well-suited to the gas-flow requirements of the manifolding. Spark plugs in the first Novi blocks were placed at the centre of the hemispherical chambers in recesses which were cast open, then closed by a conical, spun-steel insert in a classical Miller manner.

A complex casting by Alcoa, the aluminium crankcase gained rigidity through its full-barrel construction. Integral with the crankcase was the narrow finned dry sump, with horizontal baffling just below the crankshaft. Also integral was the bellhousing, the cases for primary drives to camshafts, blower and accessories, and the main oil and water passages.

Ford history, and the 1940 state of the engine bearing art, influenced the Welch-Winfield choice of three main bearings for the Novi. Each was 60.3mm in diameter and an exceptional 66.0mm wide, carried in a steel-backed nickel-babbitt bearing shell. The bearings in turn were held by split bronze circular carriers, each of which was attached to a crankcase web by eight studs. The bronze carriers were larger toward the rear of the engine so they could be assembled on the crankshaft, which was then lowered into the up-ended crankcase from the clutch end during the build process.

Machined from a billet of SAE 4130 steel, the crankshaft was of the 180° or single-plane layout, which offered a simple, strong crankshaft with minimal low-inertia counterweighting. A half-speed gear pair below the crank nose turned the big scavenge pump for the dry-sump lubrication system and the pressure pump, which supplied the integral rifle-drilled galleries at 100psi.

A forward extension from the half-speed gear drove the six-blade impeller of the water pump, which had twin outlets. These were piped directly to the front of the block, within which the coolant flowed through drilled passages to four 0.44in holes leading to the exhaust side of each block. Two 0.25in holes on top of each block returned the coolant to the radiator through a simple manifold. As on all Miller-pattern engines, this inlet–outlet differential in number and size of coolant holes tended to restrict the outflow of warm coolant, producing an internal block pressure of the order of 30psi.

At the output end of the V8 a heavy flange joined the crankshaft to a beautifully machined part that served a number of purposes. Nominally a flywheel, it was also the outer housing of the multiple-disc clutch. Just inboard of the rear oil seal, which ran against its surface, this flywheel was hobbed to form the 55-tooth primary drive gear for the camshafts and the supercharger.

The twin camshafts of each block were served by a short, symmetrical gear tower carrying three gears on two centres in a two-piece aluminium housing. Six bearings supported each of the camshafts, the extra one bridging the wide centre of each block. The camshafts were housed in two-piece aluminium cases attached to the block by a dozen long studs each.

Miller-pattern valve gear was employed, with a flat-topped 1.53in (38.9mm) inverted-cup tappet

Opposite above: Paul Russo was a frequent pilot of the powerful Novi racing cars, which competed chiefly at Indianapolis. They often qualified at the front and led the race but never succeeded in winning the 500-mile classic.
Opposite below: Until 1955 the Novi V8 powered a front-wheel-drive racing car, designed like the engine by Leo Goossen. In 1956, as shown, it was mounted in a rear-wheel-drive chassis.

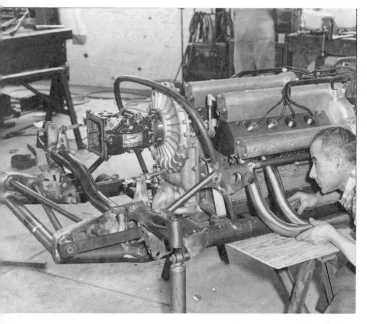

completely enclosing twin coil valve springs. Removable valve guides, needed in any case to allow the valves to be extracted from the integral heads, were retained by the inner valve springs. Two valves per cylinder were equally inclined at an included angle of 84°. Their heads measured 1.5in (38.1mm) for the inlets and 1.44in (36.6mm) for the exhausts.

The Duesenberg-Miller tradition of centrifugal supercharging was maintained for the Novi. Gearing at the rear of the crankshaft drove a shaft – serving to cushion the drive – at 1.25 times engine speed running to the opposite end of the engine. The drive speed was stepped up further at the front by a pair of spur gears that gave alternative overall ratios of 5.35 or 5.00:1.

The supercharger impeller's 16 straight blades were machined from a billet of Duralumin akin to heat-treated SAE AA2014. The original 10in impeller (later reduced in size) reached 42,000rpm at an engine speed of 8,000rpm, which was equivalent to a tip speed of 1,835 feet per second or Mach 1.67 – extremely high. The BRM V16 blower, for example, never exceeded 1,360 feet per second or Mach 1.24.

The induction system included an intercooler nestling in the vee that presented a T-shaped path to the entering fuel/air mixture. Four ports at each side of the intercooler led to cast manifolds which retraced the T-shaped flow back to the

inlet ports, passing a large blow-off valve on each side. Bud Winfield selected three downdraught carburettors of his brother Ed's design to feed the thirsty V8. Fuel mixtures varied over the engine's long development life, but it was primarily designed for alcohol. A typical blend was 80 per cent methyl alcohol with 20 per cent gasoline.

At the rear of the engine a gear above the drive to the blower turned a short shaft to a bevel gear which supplied an engine-speed drive to a single Bosch magneto mounted on the left side of the bellhousing.

A single example of this complex engine was designed, built and made race-ready for Indianapolis 1941 in the space of only nine months. It was rated at 450bhp at 8,000rpm on a boost of 30psi and weighed 660lb (300kg). By detail refinements after the war within the original design framework, output was increased to 500, then to 530 horsepower, still at the same rpm and boost and modest compression ratio of 6.2:1. At these higher ratings, and under prolonged full-throttle conditions, the combustion chamber roof tended to crack between the central spark plug hole and the exhaust valve seat.

For 1951 a major rework was carried out to solve this and other problems by Frenchman Jean Marcenac, who had been with the team since 1946. Before his death in 1950 Bud Winfield had specified new cylinder blocks which carried the spark plugs offset from the chamber centre and inclined toward the centre of the block. The plug wells were made integral with the block casting. This allowed the chamber roof to be strengthened while enlarging the inlet valve by ⅛in (3.2mm) to 41.3mm. Originally cast aluminium, the pistons were now machined from forged alloy billets.

New connecting rods also came into use by 1951, replacing the tubular-shank rods first fitted. The new rods were forged with an I-section shank carrying a drilled oil passage to the small-end bushing. Centre-to-centre length remained 5½in (139.7mm). The plain big-end bearings measured 2 ⁵⁄₁₆in (58.7mm) in diameter. Higher piston crowns gave the 1951 Novi engine a compression ratio of almost 9:1, helping increase the output to 550bhp at 7,800rpm. Another 1951 change was the use of a single Holley aircraft carburettor with a large rectangular throat, mounted downdraught like the Winfields it replaced.

After both Novis broke their blower drive shafts in the 1952 500-mile race the blower shafts were strengthened for 1953 and the crankshaft cheeks which were not supported by main bearings were made fully round instead of straight. Removal of the intercooler reduced engine weight by 75lb (34kg) to 585lb (266kg) and raised the net boost to 35psi above atmospheric. This allowed the output to remain at 550bhp while the safe engine speed was reduced to 7,500rpm to improve reliability.

The career of the V8 as the power of front-wheel-drive chassis ended in 1956, when new Kurtis rear-wheel-drive chassis and bodies were built. Experience with the non-intercooled

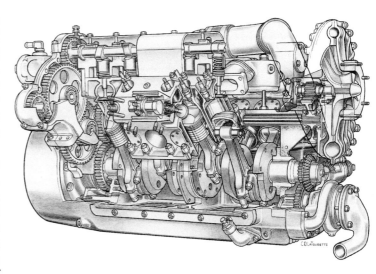

Novi engine allowed Jean Marcenac to increase its output to 650bhp for 1956, using one horizontal Holley aircraft carburettor after trying two Bendix units in 1954. This was the final year for the Novi in its original 3-litre form, for the Indy rules changed the following year. This potent V8 continued to be developed in 2,750cc form until, by 1963, it was producing 742bhp at 8,200rpm and was able to rev to 9,000 safely. Through most of its lifetime the Novi was the most powerful engine used in any circuit-racing single-seater car.

Opposite left: At the Kurtis workshop in California the Novi was installed in its new rear-wheel-drive chassis. Its centrifugal supercharger was fed by a single horizontal Holley aircraft carburettor.
Opposite right: In classic Miller engineering fashion the Novi carried two cast-iron cylinder blocks set atop an aluminium crankcase. The
gear drive to the overhead camshafts was at the rear adjacent to the flywheel.
Above: Clarence LaTourette's drawing reveals the shaft running the length of the engine that drove the supercharger at its front. Machined from the solid, the crankshaft had three very wide main bearings. The dual-ignition version of the engine is shown.

SPECIFICATIONS	
Cylinders	V8
Bore	81.0mm
Stroke	72.1mm
Stroke/bore ratio	0.89:1
Capacity	2,972cc
Compression ratio	9.0:1
Connecting rod length	139.7mm
Rod/crank radius ratio	3.9:1
Main bearing journal diameter	60.3mm
Rod journal diameter	58.7mm
Inlet valve diameter (1 valve)	41.3mm
Exhaust valve diameter (1 valve)	36.6mm
Inlet pressure	3.4Atm
Engine weight	585lb (266kg)
Peak power	550bhp @ 7,500rpm
Piston speed (corrected)	3,761ft/min (18.8m/s)
Engine bhp per litre	185.0bhp per litre
Engine weight per bhp	1.06lb (0.48kg) per bhp

1957

MASERATI 250F 2.5-LITRE SIX

Few engines have been granted a more classic status in the racing pantheon than that of the Maserati 250F Grand Prix car. The 250F was ultra-competitive on its debut at the beginning of the 2½-litre Formula 1 in 1954 and – after serving as Fangio's world championship mount in 1957 – was still capable of providing the odd competitive ride in 1958. Indeed, a 250F competed in the final race of the 2½-litre era at Riverside in 1960. In long-stroke form its straight-six engine also powered the successful 300S Maserati sports-racing car.

Gestation of the 250F's engine was not untroubled. Gioachino Colombo had joined the strength at Maserati in time to make significant improvements in its 1953 2-litre GP car and to put forward his ideas for the engine for the new car, which included a large bore in relation to the stroke. After disagreements over policy at board level Colombo left during 1953. Work on the engine was completed by engineers Bellentani and Nicola. Their six powered the 250F to victory in its first two races – an exceptional achievement – in the hands of Juan Fangio, who gained therewith valuable points in his successful bid for the 1954 world championship.

Cylinder dimensions of the 250F six were well oversquare, as Colombo had recommended, at 84 x 75mm (3.31 x 2.95in) for 2,493cc. Its sister, the 300S sports-car engine, had the same bore size and a stroke of 90mm (3.54in) for 2,991cc. While the 300S reached its peak power (260bhp) at 6,500rpm and was not generally revved higher than 6,700, the 250F was red-lined at 8,200 in 1956–57. Assisted by Maserati's mastery of the value of a small amount of nitromethane in the methanol fuel, peak output reached 285–290bhp at 7,500rpm by 1957. The works engines often survived speeds well in excess of 8,000rpm. Maximum torque was 209lb ft at 6,000rpm from an engine that weighed 434lb (197kg).

Above: The Maserati connecting rods were machined all over and polished to eliminate stress raisers. Inserted aluminium plugs held the gudgeon pin in place.
Opposite above: First conceived in 1953 for the 1954 Formula 1 season, the Maserati 250F was transformed by 1957 when Fangio drove it to his fifth world championship. The engine remained essentially the same, however.
Opposite below: In 1956 Maserati experimented with direct fuel injection to the cylinders along Mercedes-Benz lines, using an adapted diesel injection pump with a regulating cam driven by the throttle linkage. Although a power advantage was gained, it was judged unsuitable for use with the tyres then available.

The cylinder block of the 250F extended from the centreline of its crankshaft to the top of the cylinders, which were capped by a conventional detachable head. The upper one-third of the block served as an aluminium-alloy coolant tank surrounding six nitrided-iron wet cylinder liners. Over their bottom two-thirds these liners were a shrink fit in the block, which before their insertion was immersed in an oil bath at 160°C.

With the bottom of the block being machined off at the crankshaft centreline, no direct lateral bracing was provided for the seven main bearing caps. Each had four retaining studs, however. Heavy ribbed webbing within the block supported the main bearings. The fully-counterweighted nitrided-steel crankshaft was machined from a billet.

A deep casting at the front was bolted to the assembled block-sump unit and carried the scavenge and pressure oil pumps, the water and mechanical fuel (Fimac or Mona) pumps – plus the helical and spur gear drives to these units – and all fluid inlets and outlets. The crank nose carried two helical gears, one to drive this unit and the other to rotate the gear train in the block. This latter consisted of two big drilled gears vertically disposed to drive the two pairs of cam-drive gears in the head, plus two short longitudinal shafts with bevels which turned the twin Marelli magnetos.

A bulkhead divided the very deep Elektron (magnesium alloy) sump into two separately-scavenged sections with a longitudinal baffle, placed at an angle, which scooped excess oil splash off the crankshaft and directed it downward. The scavenge pumps drew from two screened pickups and pumped the oil through a cooler and back the whole length of the car to a tail-mounted 20-litre reservoir. Crankcase breather pipes ducted directly from the oil pickups to the left-hand side of the engine removed air from the system at this critical point. This helped suppress

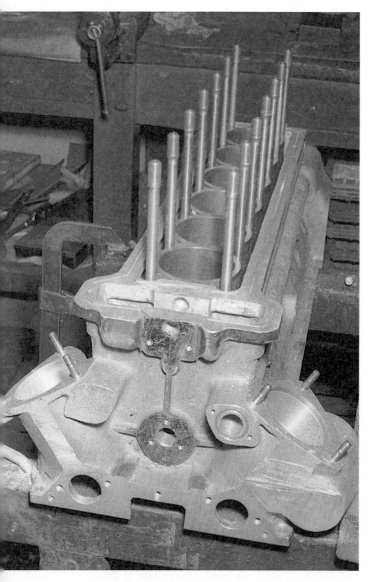

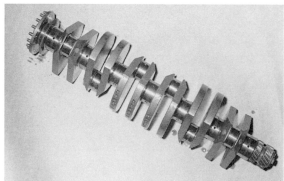

oil made up for its lower viscosity by its addition of an anti-scuffing compound to cope with the high loadings between the cam lobes and the finger followers.)

All the bottom-end bearing shells were Vandervell lead-indium type and all mains were 60mm in diameter. Front and rear bearings were 32mm wide while the five inner shells measured 19mm. Big-end journals were 51mm in diameter and 19mm wide. Short connecting rods were forged steel with heavy I-section shanks and two bolts per cap. These were fully polished and given bronze gudgeon pin bushings 25mm in diameter. Both circlips and aluminium plugs held the pins in place in the pistons of the 300S version of the six, which was rather like Maserati team manager Nello Ugolini's habit of wearing a belt and braces at the same time. With steep peaks providing compression ratios of up to 12.5:1 the pistons were made by Borgo and carried two compression rings and one oil ring by Kiklos above the gudgeon pin. Below it was another oil ring on the full skirt.

Colombo brought from Alfa Romeo his successful system for providing a supply of cool water directly to the exhaust valve guides and seats. The output of the centrifugal pump was split, sending a small amount of water directly to the block via a gallery on the left-hand side, but directing most of the coolant to the exhaust-valve guides and seats by means of a dedicated manifold down the centre of the head. A similar manifold above the inlet valves returned hot water to the radiator.

Helical timing gears were used all the way up to the last idler, which shared a shaft with the spur gear that drove the spur gear on the end of each camshaft. Each cam rotated in seven wide babbit

an oil-foaming problem that troubled the 250F in its first race.

The pressure pump drew from the reservoir and fed the full-flow filter which was normally on the left side of the block (at the front on the rare fuel-injected engines) at 100–110psi. Oil entered the centre main bearing from the left and passed through to an external gallery on the right-hand side. This fed the rest of the mains. During 1956 this gallery was roughly quadrupled in diameter to improve flow and offer a reserve of cool oil near the bearings. (Although Italian-entered 250Fs used oil of SAE 60 viscosity, BP produced a special SAE 40 oil specifically for this engine. This BP Corsa 40

bearings with thrust surfaces at the centre journal, which also received the oil for the camshaft and its bearings. Cam side thrust was absorbed by pivoted fingers between the lobes and the valve stem. The finger pivot shaft was hollow to carry oil to each finger and, through a hole drilled in the base of the finger, to deliver oil to the critical sliding surfaces. Each triple-coil valve spring could support between 265 and 300lb (between 120 and 136kg) when compressed, depending on the individual engine.

Valve inclinations from vertical were 36° for the inlets and 41° for the exhausts, giving an included angle of 77°. In the developed 250F the inlet valve was 46mm in diameter while the exhaust measured 40mm; initial diameters had been 42 and 38mm respectively. Lift was 8mm. The combustion chamber was a clean hemisphere, with the vertically-placed twin 14mm Lodge spark plugs flanking the inserted valve seats.

Inlet port diameter was 45mm, which matched the 45mm bodies of the three twin-choke Weber 45 DCO3 carburettors. Air was drawn through ram tubes from a recessed air box. Oval exhaust ports 44mm across at their widest point lined up with two three-branch collectors. On early 250Fs these faired into two pipes, but from late 1956 the works cars blended them together into one large pipe. The normal fuel blend for the 250F consisted of 50 per cent methanol, 35 per cent benzene, 10 per cent acetone and 5 per cent benzol. For racing in hot weather the proportions of the major ingredients were shifted to 60 per cent/25 per cent.

In 1956, when it had the services of Stirling Moss and Jean Behra, Maserati tried several tricks to extract more power from the 250F six. In that year and 1957, the last for unlimited fuels, it tried two fuel blends that combined oxygen-bearing nitromethane with methanol, butyl alcohol and benzene. This was burned with new cylinder heads with 10mm spark plugs, creating a more compact combustion chamber. More power was

there, but so was higher fuel consumption. Desmodromic valve gear was built and tested, but never committed to a race.

More progress was made with fuel injection, continuing work that had begun with the 2-litre six of 1953. Maserati chief engineer Giulio Alfieri fitted a modified OM diesel injection pump along the left side of the block and drove it with a triple chain from the gear train at the front. Injection was direct, feeding nozzles that were placed just at the top of the cylinder wall – no easy task with a wet-liner engine – and spraying against the inlet valve. This was the opposite of the system used by Mercedes, which sprayed the exhaust valve with cool fuel.

A mechanical metering system used a disc-type cam to apportion the fuel delivery according to the position of the six individual slide-type throttles. The injected engine was raced on several occasions in 1956 and did demonstrate an output advantage at a sharp speed peak, but the limiting factor at that time was the ability of the Pirelli tyres to transmit the added power to the road. The greater flexibility of the carburetted engine was superior in most conditions. In Italy, Webers had seen off the competition.

SPECIFICATIONS	
Cylinders	I6
Bore	84.0mm
Stroke	75.0mm
Stroke/bore ratio	0.89:1
Capacity	2,493cc
Compression ratio	12.5:1
Connecting rod length	143.0mm
Rod/crank radius ratio	3.8:1
Main bearing journal diameter	60.0mm
Rod journal diameter	51.0mm
Inlet valve diameter (1 valve)	46.0mm
Exhaust valve diameter (1 valve)	40.0mm
Inlet pressure	1.0Atm
Engine weight	434lb (197kg)
Peak power	290bhp @ 7,500rpm
Piston speed (corrected)	3,906ft/min (19.5m/s)
Peak torque	209lb ft (283Nm)
	@ 6,000rpm
Peak bmep	208psi
Engine bhp per litre	116.3bhp per litre
Engine weight per bhp	1.50lb (0.68kg) per bhp

Opposite left: A 250F cylinder block in the course of manufacture in 1954 shows the mountings for the two magnetos and the inserted wet cylinder liners. Opposite right: Machined *from the solid, the crankshaft had seven main bearings and full counterweighting. Material was removed from the faces of the counterweights to achieve optimum balance.*

1957

VANWALL V254 2.5-LITRE FOUR

The link with Norton went back some years. In addition to being a maker of high-quality thin-wall copper-lead bearings, Guy Anthony 'Tony' Vandervell was a director of the famed British motorcycle maker and his father was Norton's chairman. Norton's 500cc single-cylinder racing engine was a force to be reckoned with in both motorcycle and Formula 3 racing. It provided the foundation for the success of Vandervell's Vanwall racing car, the Formula 1 manufacturers' world champion of 1958 and the car with which Stirling Moss missed the driver's championship by a single point that year.

At the end of the 1940s BRM had obtained a contract to build a water-cooled version of the air-cooled Norton. By virtue of the higher compression ratio allowed by liquid cooling it produced 47bhp, 6 per cent more than the air-cooled original. Tony Vandervell remembered this when, fed up with the problems of the V16 BRM (qv), he decided to start work on a racing engine of his own.

In 1952 at his Park Royal toolrooms in the London borough of Acton Vandervell began making a 2-litre engine that quadrupled the liquid-cooled Norton cylinder. As a basis for the engine's bottom end a Rolls-Royce military engine, the B40, was selected. Former BRM engineer Eric Richter, who had worked on the water-cooled single, integrated these disparate components into a robust four-cylinder racing engine.

Vandervell works director Fred Fox oversaw the building of the 2-litre engine, which ran in December 1953 and raced only once in May 1954. A 2½-litre version for the new GP Formula 1 was already in hand, with five main bearings instead of the four of the original B40, which lacked a centre main. This first raced in September with an Amal-carburetted engine. Fuel injection was added in 1955 and in '56 the four was installed in a new Vanwall with chassis by Colin Chapman and aerodynamics by Frank Costin. By 1957 this was a winning combination.

In all Vandervell built seven 2½-litre engines, designated V254. The unit's cylinder dimensions were 96 x 86mm (3.78 x 3.39in) for 2,490cc. It was composed of a high-topped, deep-walled crankcase of RR53B aluminium alloy into which the individual cast-iron cylinders were very deeply spigoted, a water jacket and a shallow cylinder head of RR50 alloy with separate camboxes and exposed valve springs. The whole was held together by 10 long high-tensile-steel tie bolts from the head to the main bearing caps.

Nestling inside the tie bolts and topped and bottomed by rubber sealing rings, the cast RR50 aluminium water jacket steadied and sealed the whole assembly. A structural role was played by the cylinders, which fitted into a radiused countersink in the head. Fire sealing at this crucial joint was problematic until 1956, when corrugated stainless-steel Cooper rings were adopted.

Skirts of the smooth-sided crankcase extended well below the crankshaft centreline. A deep bottom-finned sump capped the bottom of the V254, keeping the BP oil well out of the crankshaft's way. Ample support was provided for the five 70mm (2.75in) main bearings and the forged EN19 steel crank, with its four integral counterweights. Rod journals were 51mm (2.0in) in diameter and gudgeon pins – retained by circlips – were 25mm (1.0in). Although the bearings were of generous width the engine's length was such that the crank webs could be a reassuring 20mm thick.

Forged of EN24 nickel steel, the connecting rods had I-section shanks that blended tangentially with the gudgeon-pin end. They were machined all over to a web thickness of ⅒in and then polished to eliminate stress raisers. Forged by Hepworth and Grandage, the RR59 aluminium-alloy pistons had full skirts and carried two Dykes compression rings and one oil control ring. Their crowns were high and sharply peaked, with deep contoured cut-outs for valve clearance. Set at 12.5:1 on methanol-based fuel, the compression ratio was reduced to 11.5:1 for 1958, when the engine was converted to run on aviation petrol. At that time an oil jet was added to cool the underside of the piston crown.

The cylinder head was a compact and spiky-looking casting. Hot water was extracted from it by a manifold between the cams. Mounted low at the front of the crankcase, the water pump was driven by an extension of the oil pressure-pump input

Opposite above: In an era when aerodynamics were implemented to enhance a car's sheer speed, the Vanwall reigned supreme. A NASA inlet in its bonnet admitted induction air to the engine.
Opposite below: Although constructed and assembled with the greatest care and quality, the Vanwall V254 engine always looked like what it was: an amalgamation of different design concepts that added up to a remarkably successful unit.

valves were symmetrically inclined at an included angle of 60°, with the intersection of their axes slightly offset toward the exhaust side of the engine to make room for the 53mm inlet valve and ports that were 48–49mm on various engines. The 43mm exhaust ports were covered by 45mm valves. The valves seated on bronze-alloy inserts.

These large valves were challenging to fabricate, especially as by 1958 both were hollow to contain sodium salts to transfer heat away from the head to the guides; the exhaust guides were finned and in direct contact with the cooling water. Vandervell ultimately set up his own imported machinery to make valves that met his exacting standards. Valve timing was as follows:

Inlet opens 70°BTDC Exhaust opens 75°BBDC
Inlet closes 90°ABDC Exhaust closes 49°ATDC

This provided a handsome 119° of overlap.

All the gear for opening the valves was housed in magnesium castings which were bolted to the block and head. A train of ball-bearinged spur gears rose at the front, with one idler twirling the single BTH magneto which supplied sparks to two KLG plugs per cylinder. The gear train also drove the triple-pinioned scavenge pump in the sump, thus configured so that it could draw from two screened pickups.

Each of the two overhead cams rotated in its own case under the cover of a flat plate and a multiplicity of cap screws. Eight studs with supporting flanges held each case a short distance above the head, with the valve stems also extending up to be capped by short cylindrical hollow tappets sliding in bronze guides set into the cam cases. This followed the Norton original exactly, as did the use of twin hairpin-type springs for each valve, placed out in the open in a manner that recalled pre-World War I practice. It worked for the V254 because it gave access to the tie-rods and cleared space for the dual spark plugs. The cam lobes had an unusually small base and considerable lobes as a consequence, working on the small-diameter radiused tappets.

The hairpin springs turned out to be a weighty cross for the team to bear, afflicted as they were by random failures. 'Before any springs were used on an engine,' wrote Denis Jenkinson, 'they were run on a test-rig for one hour at 2,000rpm, then ten

pinion. It supplied cool water to the engine low on the left of the water jacket. A gauge only slightly smaller than the tachometer allowed the driver to monitor the crucial water temperature.

A prime Norton feature retained by the Vanwall was angling of the inlet ports in plan view to give more turbulence to the incoming mixture. As installed in the car they 'trailed' to the rear. The

VANWALL V254 2.5-LITRE FOUR

minutes at 7,000rpm and 50 minutes at 4,000rpm. A total of 15 hours was done on this test-rig, involving something like 1½ million "pinches".' Even after all this, rogue springs failed when the engine was tested.

The Bosch fuel-injection pump was installed just above the magneto and driven directly by the camshaft gear train. Its outer end was supported by a drilled strut from the left-hand camgear tower. Each injection nozzle was anchored by two studs to a head passage which opened on the bottom of the inlet port just upstream from the valve seat. Injected at 650psi, the spray glanced off and past the back of the head and the stem of the inlet valve. Initially fuel piping to the nozzles was by metal tubing, and as the big four had marked vibration periods at 4,500 and 7,000rpm this resulted in resonance-induced cracks and failures at unwelcome moments. Finally an aircraft-type flexible hose was found that did the job.

Amal carburettor bodies and their control system served as slide throttles. A lever arm, pullrod and shaft system regulated the Bosch pump output in proportion to throttle opening. The speed-density fuel metering used by the Mercedes-Benz M196 and Borgward (qv) was tried by Vanwall but rejected as giving poor throttle response. Ex-Norton engineer Leo Kuzmicki, who joined Vandervell to help develop the engine, finally perfected this unique system. (Drivers still had to apply the throttle with care to avoid the over-rich condition on sharp acceleration that would cause engine power to fade, creating a 'flat spot'.)

With its clutch the V254 weighed 360lb (163kg). In response to Tony Vandervell's passion for peak power it was developed on methanol/benzol-based fuels to 285bhp at 7,200rpm and, with a tip of the

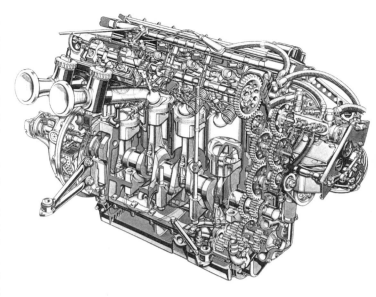

nitromethane tin, 295bhp. A special tune for Monaco to give a wider torque band reduced the power to 275bhp. In 1958 on 108/135 octane BP petrol the four produced 265bhp at 7,400rpm – a tribute to the effectiveness of Park Royal's development of this big-bore engine. It stood as such forever for the feisty Tony Vandervell who, on the advice of his physician, ceased full-season competition in 1959 and racing entries altogether after 1961.

Opposite top: Two pickups fed oil from the dry sump to the scavenge pump located low at the front of the Vanwall engine. The sides of the crankcase extended well down past the centreline of the crankshaft.

Opposite bottom: Tracing its origins to a Rolls-Royce military engine, the Vanwall's crankcase carried its individual cast-iron cylinders.

These made an important structural contribution to the Type V254.

Above: A fine Vic Berris drawing shows the motorcycle-type units that provided the Vanwall's throttle slides, the hairpin valve springs, the spur-gear drive to the camshafts and, at right, the Bosch pump that injected fuel into the inlet port close to the valves.

SPECIFICATIONS	
Cylinders	I4
Bore	96.0mm
Stroke	86.0mm
Stroke/bore ratio	0.90:1
Capacity	2,490cc
Compression ratio	12.5:1
Connecting rod length	163.5mm
Rod/crank radius ratio	3.8:1
Main bearing journal diameter	70.0mm
Rod journal diameter	51.0mm
Inlet valve diameter (1 valve)	53.0mm
Exhaust valve diameter (1 valve)	45.0mm
Inlet pressure	1.0:1
Engine weight	360lb (163kg)
Peak power	285bhp @ 7,200rpm
Piston speed (corrected)	4,293ft/min (21.5m/s)
Engine bhp per litre	114.5bhp per litre
Engine weight per bhp	1.26lb (0.57kg) per bhp

1958

BORGWARD RS 1.5-LITRE FOUR

One of the most surprising sports-racing cars of the 1950s, the Borgward RS, was built in northern Germany. Porsche, which felt it 'owned' the 1½-litre sports-car category, found itself harassed in races and hillclimbs from 1956 through to the 1958 season by the silver roadsters built by Carl Borgward's Bremen-based company. Jo Bonnier and Hans Herrmann were among the members of the Borgward team.

As well, the potent fuel-injected Borgward 16-valve fours were loaned to Stirling Moss Ltd and the British Racing Partnership for use in Cooper chassis for the 1959 Formula 2 season. Chris Bristow raced one successfully for BRP and Moss took his Cooper-Borgward to the British F2 championship. In fact only the financial collapse of Borgward at the end of 1960 kept the company from being a serious supplier to competitors in the 1961 1½-litre Formula 1. German privateer Kurt Kuhnke rescued some of the engines and sought but failed to qualify one for the 1963 German GP in his Lotus-Borgward.

The RS four was the work of Borgward's chief engine designer, Karl Ludwig Brandt. A pre-war veteran of BMW's experimental department, Brandt first tested there in 1938 the fuel injection that he applied so successfully at Borgward. After warming up on some modified Isabella engines for sports-racing Borgwards, Brandt sat down in 1955 to design an all-new competition engine. In so doing, he also kept in mind its possible suitability for production to power a small high-performance sports car. Thus although the RS was a pure racing engine, it was designed with an eye toward practicality.

Instead of the costly rollers and Hirth shaft so beloved of German designers, Brandt specified a forged crankshaft running in trimetal Glyco bearing shells. He used the main bearing shells then fitted to the six-cylinder Borgward Hansa 2400; main journal size was 60mm. Between the five mains and the 50mm rod journals were amply-dimensioned cheeks, each carrying a counterweight. The forged connecting rods with I-section shanks were close kin to production parts, expensive oilway drilling to the small end being avoided. They were polished to a chrome-like finish that smoothed out stress raisers and rendered the big-end split nearly invisible.

The heart of the RS engine was its finely-detailed Silumin block/crankcase casting. Additional bracing of the main bearings was supplied by extending the crankcase skirts well below the crank centreline, a design which also effected a strong union with the gearbox bellhousing. However, the main caps were located laterally by pins instead of by the nearby crankcase walls. The cylinder head studs penetrated the block to do double duty as the main bearing cap studs.

The pressurised oil input to the full-flow filter and the supply gallery for the main bearings stood out like arteries on the left side of the block just below a magnesium access plate to a breathing chamber. Except for the connection to the injection pump, every oil line in the RS engine was designed and drilled in place for maximum simplicity and security. Initially the RS had a wet-sump lubrication system. However consistent failures experienced with the front main bearing were traced to the oil leaving the pump pickup on turns and getting excessively foamy. To prevent this a 10-litre dry-sump system was installed.

The shallow cast oil pan sloped to a central screened pickup which was connected by cast-in piping to a scavenge pump housed in the lowest part of the deep cam-drive cover. Scavenge and pressure pumps were placed at the right and left respectively, the extra length of the gears of the former being accommodated by a deeper exterior pump cover. Both pumps were turned at 0.6 engine speed by a straight spur gear at the crank nose.

Centrifugally cast iron liners were sunk wet into the block, biting very tightly at the bottom and embraced by twin O-ring seals. About an inch below a flange at the top of the liner, eight 'feet' radiated out to rest on a ledge within the block, like the Jano construction of the Lancia D50 and Dino Ferrari. All locating stresses were accepted by the heavy liner section between the flange and the feet. Steel inserts around the chamber openings in the graphite-coated Diring head gasket completed the head sealing.

Cooling water flowed from a duct in the chain

Opposite above: Highly competitive in the 1500cc class against the Porsches in the late 1950s, the Borgward RS was a worthy effort by the Bremen-based firm. This is the author's car in action at Watkins Glen.
Opposite below: A duct from a nose inlet fed fresh air to the engine's single throttle valve and plenum chamber. A cylindrical reservoir for the dry-sump oiling system was placed between the radiator and the engine.

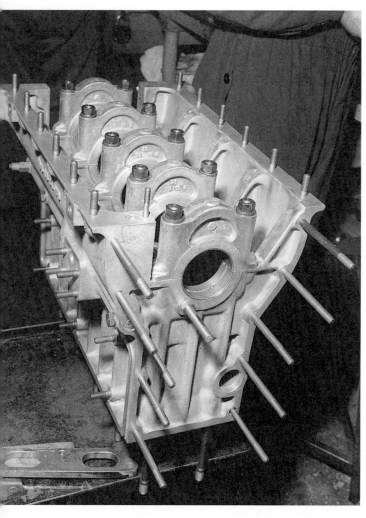

slack taken up by two externally adjustable idler sprockets.

Camshafts and sprockets were joined by a coupling comprised of two conically-tapered rings which, when pressed together by a central clamping bolt, expanded to lock the end of the cam to the sprocket. Infinite variation of valve timing was thus possible. Exhaust closing and inlet opening points were equally disposed 42° from TDC, giving 84° of overlap. The steel camshafts ran directly in straight bores through the detachable cam cases. A special Bosch racing distributor was driven from the rear of the inlet camshaft. A tiny generator was mounted at the left front of the block and driven by a fan belt which also turned the water pump.

Wide cam lobes contacted small-diameter cast-iron cup-type tappets whose sides were diagonally slotted for lightness and lubrication. The bottom of each tappet was closed except for a central puncture by a thick-thumbtack-like insert whose head contacted the valve and whose shank carried clearance-adjusting washers which were interposed between the follower and the insert head. Washer changes could be made quickly through access holes in the cam carriers. Individual upward drillings brought oil to the cam journals, whence it flowed out and around the tappets.

Symmetrically inclined at 32° from the cylinder centreline, the valves were finely finished. The tuliped inlets were 33mm in diameter (1.30in), while the 30mm exhausts were sodium-cooled. The gas velocity through each inlet valve aperture at 7,500rpm was 208 feet per second, a value close to the practical working maximum for that era of 200 feet per second. The polished oval inlet ports split into paired valve openings just as late as the designer dared without prejudicing the strength of the dividing pillar and, thus, the valve seating. With twin coil valve springs rated at about 220lb (100kg) per set, the valves stayed comfortably under control at 8,500rpm.

When Brandt conceived the RS engine its four-valve chamber, with its pent-roof form, was distinctly out of fashion. Yet, as its designer said, 'It didn't turn out too badly.' Its peak and corners were smoothly radiused, as were the edges of the holes for the two recessed spark plugs at the corners of the chamber. Also set back from the

cover into a gallery cast along the exhaust side of the block, from which it entered the interior through drillings. Water rose between the liner feet into the Silumin cylinder head. Hot water exited through two holes in the front of the head, jumping the gap of the chain case through two rubber-ringed tubes. Brandt's initial qualms about the water-tightness of this arrangement were happily unjustified.

Brandt wanted direct fuel injection for his new engine, and as well his aim was to place the nozzle in the centre of the combustion chamber. By adopting a four-valve layout he was able to achieve this. Although doubling the number of valves added complexity, Brandt countered this by ingenious simplification of the valve gear and cam drive. The latter was by means of a two-stage double-roller drive at the front of the block, with chamber surface, the injector nozzle sprayed through a 10mm hole. Scarcity of space required the valve-seat inserts to be unusually thin-walled. Valve guides of Cuprodur bronze alloy were pressed into place.

The angular piston crown was a good match for the pent-roof chamber, its central ridge being slightly rounded to deflect the injector spray in the desired manner. To hinder erosion, the surface of the crown was specially anodised to a deep graphite-grey hue. Mahle forged the pistons of aluminium alloy. Two Dykes pressure-backed rings were set above a single oil ring. Conventional gudgeon pins were retained by circlips.

At the time of its conception the Borgward RS engine must have been the only racing engine, indeed the only automotive engine, that had never run on carburettors. Even the M196 Mercedes-Benz engine was tested on Webers. Differing from that used in the Vanwall in that it retained the Bosch vacuum-controlled metering system with a plenum chamber and ram tubes, the four-plunger Bosch pump dosed the cylinders through conventional copper piping at pressures of from 1,000 to 1,100psi. Injection was initiated at 62° after TDC. A rear-mounted electric fuel pump backed up the integral mechanical pump and was used for starting.

From its initial output of 130bhp, refinements in inlet and exhaust tuning brought the power of the RS four to 165bhp at 7,500rpm. Weighing 282lb (128kg), the engine could be held at full throttle on the dyno at 8,000 revs for as long as ten minutes. Thus compared to its contemporary rival, the 1½-litre Coventry Climax FPF, the Bremen-built engine scaled 25lb (11kg) more and delivered a bonus of some 20 horsepower. Those extra horses would have come in handy in the Formula 1 racing of 1961.

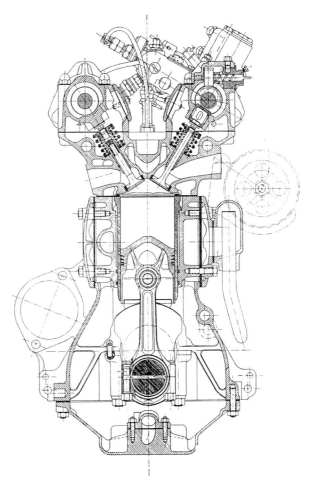

Opposite: The sides of the Borgward's aluminium cylinder block extended well down past the crank centreline. Massive main-bearing caps, also of aluminium, were retained by two studs apiece.

Above: Each of the Borgward's two camshafts was inserted longitudinally into its aluminium carrier, which in turn was bolted to the cylinder head. Cylindrical tappets were hollow with side slots for lightening and lubrication.

SPECIFICATIONS	
Cylinders	I4
Bore	80.0mm
Stroke	74.0mm
Stroke/bore ratio	0.93:1
Capacity	1,488cc
Compression ratio	10.2:1
Connecting rod length	140.0mm
Rod/crank radius ratio	3.8:1
Main bearing journal diameter	60.0mm
Rod journal diameter	50.0mm
Inlet valve diameter (2 valves)	33.0mm
Exhaust valve diameter (2 valves)	30.0mm
Inlet pressure	1.0Atm
Engine weight	282lb (128kg)
Peak power	165bhp @ 7,500rpm
Piston speed (corrected)	3,786ft/min (18.9 m/s)
Engine bhp per litre	110.9bhp per litre
Engine weight per bhp	1.71lb (0.78kg) per bhp

1958

FERRARI DINO 246 2.4-LITRE V6

Following the death in 1957 of Enzo Ferrari's son Alfredino, a young engineer of great promise, an exciting new series of Ferrari V6 engines was named 'Dino' in his memory. Their designation system was revised as well. Previously Ferrari's numbers – 166, 340, etc. – stood for the displacement in cc of each cylinder, but with the new system the first two numerals referred roughly to the total displacement in 100cc units and the last designated the number of cylinders.

After Aurelio Lampredi's departure from Ferrari a fresh start was made with the guidance of veteran Vittorio Jano, who served as a consultant. The V6 concept arrived at Ferrari from Lancia, where it had been developed for sports-racing use by Jano and Francesco De Virgilio. Its implementation at Ferrari was by engine design chief Franco Rocchi under the direction of a brilliant young engineer, Andrea Fraschetti, who was fated to be killed while testing a Dino-powered single-seater at the Modena Autodromo in 1957. Some final touches to the design of the V6 in 1½-litre form, for the new Formula 2 that was initiated in 1957, were credited to 'Dino' Ferrari before his tragic death in 1956 at the age of only 24.

Apart from its use in production and racing cars by Lancia, a six in vee form was a virtually unknown engine type in the 1950s. Thus its adoption was a surprising and exciting step for Ferrari – although of course it could be seen as half of one of his famous V12s. No less surprising was the adoption of a vee angle of 65° between the cylinder banks, as opposed to the 60° angle that would give equal firing impulses with connecting rods sharing a common crankpin. In fact engines of both configurations were built and tested. The wider angle was chosen to allow more room for inlet ducting and carburettors.

Development progressed in two stages. The initial 1½-litre Formula 2 engine had a bore and stroke of 70 x 64.5mm for 1,489cc. It was first tested by Martino Severi on the roads around Maranello on 24 April 1957. Before that year's Modena GP the V6's block and head castings were altered around the cylinder head joint and between the banks to make room for a much bigger bore – 85mm. This was only approached in stages, however. The bore was enlarged to 78.6mm

(1,860cc) for a race at Modena late in 1957. The next step embraced two engines with a new longer 71mm stroke: one with a bore of 81mm (2,195cc) and the other with a bore of 85mm for 2,417cc. Both types were raced in the Morocco GP in October 1957.

Enzo Ferrari's strong belief in the merit of the development of a big engine from a smaller one was well borne out by the result of this process, which produced the 246 Dino V6 of 2,417cc (85 x 71mm; 3.35 x 2.80in) with which Mike Hawthorn became the 1958 world champion driver. It produced 270bhp at 8,300rpm, a very respectable figure for the first Formula 1 season in which aviation petrol was mandated and exotic methanol-based brews were banned. Its smaller sister, the 156, was raced only sporadically in the Formula 2 events in which the Climax-powered Coopers were proving surprisingly competitive.

Having taken the decision to adopt the 65° vee angle, Franco Rocchi was obliged to provide a special crankshaft if he still wished the firing impulses to be evenly spaced – an inescapable requirement if the available ignition equipment were to be utilised. The GP engine crankshaft had individual 43.6mm big-end journals for each connecting rod, requiring slender cheeks between the journals and the four 68mm main bearings. By spacing the rod journals appropriately (at angles of 55° and 185°) even firing was achieved.

Another point of similarity with Lancia practice was the wet liner's location, in which all the liner clamping was contained between the cylinder head and a counterbore about 1½in down in the block. Gasketing for the detachable cylinder heads, previously avoided by Ferrari through the use of screwed-in liners, was handled by a copper-nickel insert in the first V6 and later eliminated in favour of a metal-to-metal joint.

Although an angled split of the connecting-rod big ends was a feature of the 1½-litre engine, the GP V6 had a conventional I-section rod, measuring 98mm from centre to centre and weighing 525 grams. A high-domed fully-skirted piston was

Opposite above: Front-line racing Ferraris were powered by the Dino 246 V6 engine from 1958 to 1960. Olivier Gendebien piloted this car to fourth in the 1959 French Grand Prix.

Opposite below: A single large Marelli magneto provided all the sparks needed by the twelve 14mm plugs. The drive end of the engine needed no bell housing because the clutch was integral with the car's rear-mounted transaxle.

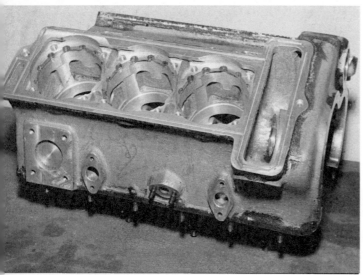

idler. This brought many more chain rollers in contact with the cam sprockets to improve load distribution and minimise wear. That chains were used at all instead of the customary gears followed the Lancia D50's example and remained an exceptional feature for a Formula 1 engine of the first rank.

New to Ferrari was the method of machining the camshaft box and carrier surfaces. For each head these were on the same plane and parallel to the head/block joint face. This technique made the head machining faster and easier and in no way compromised the valve gear. It did, however, lack aesthetic appeal. An inherited feature of the heads was the large number and close spacing of the hold-down studs, important with the detachable head and wet liners.

Valve diameters were 52mm for the inlets and 46mm for the exhausts. Their stems were symmetrically splayed at an included angle of 60°. The twin 14mm spark plugs for dual ignition were placed symmetrically in the hemispherical chambers and in a common vertical plane. Sparks were supplied by a new double-circuit Marelli magneto, with dual rotors and contacts. The first 1½-litre Dino engine was already fitted with a mounting plate for this magneto on the back of the left-hand inlet cam, indicating that it was developed specifically for this engine.

The carburettors specified were 42 DCN Webers, three double-bodied downdraught units placed in a row down the centre of the vee and mounted on a single aluminium casting incorporating paths to the ports. With these conventional carbs it was impossible to obtain a straight flow path to each inlet port. That this was not regarded as an absolute priority was indicated by the carburation experiments that had been conducted on the D50 V8 (qv) by Ferrari.

Tested on the V6s but not raced by Ferrari was a remarkable twin-throat carburettor built by Solex. Its two bores were orientated X-fashion with a common float chamber. Fitting entirely within the height of the inlet cam-boxes, this design placed the venturi and jets very close to the inlet valves – perhaps too close for full vaporisation of the charge to be achieved before it reached the combustion chamber.

The driving position in the GP Dino was so low that when Mike Hawthorn and Peter Collins found

fitted, with two compression rings and one oil ring above the gudgeon pin. Its weight with rings was 537 grams. Compression ratio of this avgas-fuelled engine was 9.8:1.

Wide cam lobes attacked Jano-type mushroom tappets which screwed onto the valve stems for adjustment. Each head was provided with its own duplex roller chain driving its camshafts. Because the chains were respectively driven by a pair of meshing gears turned by the crank nose, the cams of each cylinder bank rotated in opposite directions. Instead of running straight across between the two cam sprockets, the chain for each bank was pulled down around an intermediate themselves looking through the bulge over the carburettors they insisted that it be made transparent. This cover subsequently evolved from a simple windscreen to an enveloping shroud with a rear air opening. Because this bubble was sealed off from the engine room proper, no upward warm-air draughts would interfere with induction. As well, the carburettors could draw from cool and relatively still air.

Mike Hawthorn won his 1958 championship driving a car with an engine 3.3 per cent smaller than the regulations allowed. After he joined Ferrari as chief engineer in November 1957, Carlo Chiti set about creating a larger-bore version of the V6 measuring 86 x 71mm (3.39 x 2.80in) for 2,475cc, designated the 256. Producing 290bhp at 8,800rpm, this power unit was used by Ferrari through the last years of the 2½-litre Formula 1 until 1960.

Other variants of the four-cam V6 were spawned for special purposes. One was the 296MI, built to power a single-seater for the 1958 500 Miles of Monza on the circuit's banked track. It developed 316bhp at 7,500rpm from 2,962cc (85 x 87mm; 3.35 x 3.43in). This engine also made a brief appearance at Silverstone that year in a front-engined sports car. Another Dino-powered front-engined sports-racer was the 206 of 1958 with measurements of 77 x 71mm (3.03 x 2.80in) for 1,984cc and 225bhp. It competed at Goodwood and Naples.

As raced in Formula 1 in 1958 the 246 V6 surfaced again in 1961 as the power unit of Ferrari's first mid-engined sports-racer, the 246SP. For this application it was fitted with smaller valves – 48mm inlets and 43mm exhausts – and rated at 275bhp at 7,500rpm. Ultimately – albeit belatedly – the compactness of the V6 was an important asset to Ferrari's conversion to mid-engined racing cars.

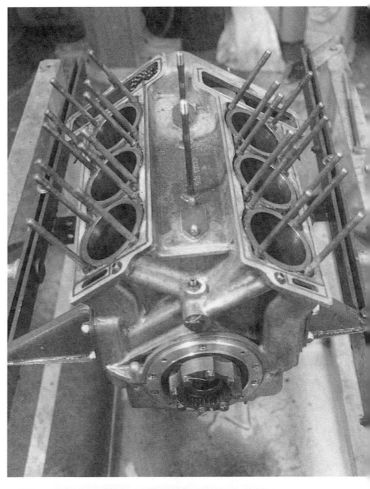

Opposite top: The compact V6 fitted neatly into the Ferrari's tubular frame, in which it was angled to allow the propeller shaft to bypass the driver.
Opposite below: A view of the cylinder block before the liners were inserted shows the ledge on which the liner flanges rested, and the bore at the bottom which was sealed by an O ring. Large apertures at the front were for the chain drive to the overhead camshafts.
Above: With its liners inserted and the multiple studs in place the cylinder block was ready to receive its heads. The vee angle was a then-unusual 65°.

SPECIFICATIONS	
Cylinders	V6
Bore	85.0mm
Stroke	71.0mm
Stroke/bore ratio	0.84:1
Capacity	2,417cc
Compression ratio	9.8:1
Connecting rod length	98.0mm
Rod/crank radius ratio	2.8:1
Main bearing journal diameter	68.0mm
Rod journal diameter	43.6mm
Inlet valve diameter (1 valve)	52.0mm
Exhaust valve diameter (1 valve)	46.0mm
Inlet pressure	1.0:1
Engine weight	298lb (135kg)
Peak power	270bhp @ 8,300rpm
Piston speed (corrected)	4,231ft/min (21.2m/s)
Engine bhp per litre	111.7bhp per litre
Engine weight per bhp	1.10lb (0.50kg) per bhp

1959

ASTON MARTIN RB6 2.9-LITRE SIX

In the year 1948 the David Brown Companies (builders of Cropmaster and Trackmaster tractors, transmissions, axles, industrial gears and gearboxes, gear cutters, steel castings, and once the Lucas Valveless and Dodgson Cars) acquired the goods and chattels of two car makers: Aston Martin and Lagonda. Among the latter's assets was a promising engine designed in 1945 by Willie Watson under W. O. Bentley, famed for his Bentley automobiles. Eleven years later this same twin-cam six – like the famous hammer that was the same except for two new heads and three new handles – powered Aston's DBR1/300 sports-racers to victory at Le Mans, the Nürburgring, Goodwood and in the Manufacturers' World Championship for sports cars.

To compete in the 3-litre class, the engine's dimensions for racing were set at 83 x 90mm (3.27 x 3.54in) for 2,922cc. Early racing versions had cast-iron heads with one plug per cylinder. Valves were equally inclined at 30° to the cylinder centreline and opened by cup-type tappets shrouding the coil springs. In time for use in the DB3S Aston for Le Mans 1954 a new aluminium head was designed by Watson. It kept the basic layout of the iron head but added twin plugs and slightly larger valves with improved porting that brought power up from 190bhp at 5,500rpm to 225 at 6,000. To fire its 12 plugs it carried two Lucas distributors driven from the back ends of its cams. Three 45mm double-bodied Weber carburettors were carried a short distance from the head by fabricated piping.

In 1955 attention was given to the cast-iron cylinder block, which was both too heavy and too weak for racing. The block had a barrel-type crankcase, a favourite scheme of Willie Watson. Three of its four main bearings were supported by split carriers, nicknamed 'cheeses', that were bolted together around the main journals before the whole assembly was threaded in from the clutch end of the crankcase. The machined exterior of each cheese mated perfectly with a corresponding interior bore. Set screws were used only to locate the carriers.

When aluminium cheeses were used in an iron block, as in the contemporary production Astons, high temperatures caused the fit to tighten. Nevertheless the structure of the block itself was inadequate for more than 200 horsepower, so much so that the cheeses were having to be made of heavy blocks of duralumin and shrink-fitted to extra-thick block castings for the racing engines. Changing the block to aluminium would have been out of the question with this construction. Accordingly, in 1955 Aston chief John Wyer instructed chief racing-car engineer Ted Cutting to design a new block from scratch. The only condition was that it should still accommodate the existing cylinder heads.

Cutting consigned the cheeses to oblivion and designed a new aluminium block with two-stud caps to carry the main bearings. The crankcase sides came down four inches past the crank centreline – as far as did the older block – so the deep main caps could also be braced by cap screws inserted from the sides. A deeply ribbed, indeed 'waffled' exterior was incorporated to enhance the block's stiffness. The old style of wet cylinder liner, which was compressed into place against a bottom flange and sealed by the cylinder head alone, was replaced by a flange at the top that was firmly clamped between head and block. The bottom end of the centrifugally-cast liner was a snug fit in an appropriate bore and sealed by O-rings.

In spite of the block's length limitations – dictated by retention of the existing cylinder head – Cutting ultimately managed to fit in seven main bearings. (The engine was initially built with four main bearings to allow retention of the existing crankshaft. It was redesigned to accommodate seven mains to gain reliability for Le Mans in 1959.) Crankshafts were machined from steel billets and selectively counterweighted. Main bearings were 2½in (63.5mm) in diameter while rod journals were 2in (50.8mm). Thin-wall lead-bronze bearings were supplied by the Glacier Metal Co. A large-diameter vibration damper at the crank nose was fitted. The new block was designed for dry-sump lubrication with a single pressure pump on the left and double scavenging unit on the right for the BP lubricant. Both had magnesium housings.

Accompanying the new crank were connecting

Opposite above: The efforts of Aston Martin to develop its RB6 racing engine led to success at Le Mans in 1959 (Carroll Shelby driving here) and to the World Sports-Car Championship.
Opposite below: Designed to accept the existing Aston Martin cylinder head, the RB6 aluminium block was designed purely for racing. Visible along its bottom are the cross bolts holding the main-bearing caps firmly in place.

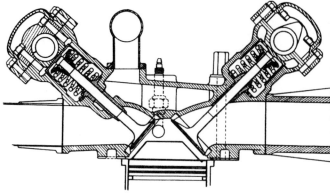

rods of a new, deeply-webbed pattern. Fully machined from rough forged blanks, they effected a 200 per cent increase in strength at the sacrifice of one additional ounce of weight. Fully skirted Hepworth and Grandage pistons initially carried one oil ring each and two narrow Dykes compression rings a respectful distance below their very peaked crowns. Later the lower Dykes ring was replaced by a plain compression ring.

When fitted with the 60° cylinder head the RB6 retained a roller chain at the top of the front accessory case to drive the camshafts. A sprocket located just below the top of the block was driven by a gear train from the crank nose. The sprocket's shaft served also to drive the water pump, which was carried in the cast magnesium timing chain cover. The pump fed a duct cast along the top of the exhaust side of the block. This directed the coolest water where it was most needed while the coolant around the liners circulated by convection only.

Underpinned by the new block, the search for more power continued. One avenue was fuel injection. Aston Martin adapted a CAV

diesel injection system to one DB3S engine. A huge Mercedes-style plenum chamber was riveted up, with an air valve at the front end and ram tubes to the ports. Injection nozzles were placed in the plenum and aimed down the ram tubes, a technique which in fact would come to the fore several decades later. The engine gave reasonable performance in a DB3S but was not adopted for racing.

In parallel a new cylinder head was designed with greater airflow potential. This task was accepted by Willie Watson just before he left the company in 1955. Watson took a classical approach with extremely steep valve inclinations of 45° from the vertical for the inlets and 50° for the exhausts. The inlet valve head was 52mm in diameter and exhaust diameter was 40mm.

'It had a combustion chamber just like a short, fat sausage,' Ted Cutting recalled, 'cut in half horizontally. At each end was a valve and the two spark plugs were in the very short cylindrical bit at the middle.' This attempt to induce some squish and swirl into the mixture failed, Cutting said, 'so we modified it by machining a cone into the chamber and making it into a close approximation of a straightforward hemispherical head.'

Of aluminium, the 95° head was fitted with cast iron and bronze guides for the inlet and exhaust valves respectively, and carried the camshafts direct without bearing shells. The guides for the sodium-filled exhaust valve stems were directly exposed to the flow of the cooling water, which left the head through manifolding just above the exhaust valves. Cup-type tappets slid in bores directly in the aluminium and surrounded two coil springs per valve.

The new head was first raced at Spa in August 1957, giving a useful power increase over the 60° head, and by 1958 the Aston team sports cars were regularly using it. The engine that powered the Nürburgring winner in 1959 was equipped with 50DCO Weber carburettors with 40mm venturis and had a 9.8:1 compression ratio. It delivered 255bhp at 6,000rpm and produced 235lb ft of torque at 5,400rpm.

In that same year the RB6 engine with its wide-angle head appeared in the Grand Prix Aston Martin, the DBR4/250. Its bore remained at 83mm and its stroke was shortened to 76.8mm (3.02in) to bring its capacity down to 2,493cc for the 2½-litre Formula 1. It was fitted with twin Lucas magnetos, instead of distributors, to fire its two 10mm plugs per cylinder. A mechanical fuel pump, driven from the front of the inlet cam, blocked off the mounting of a vertical breather pipe as used on the sports car. To suit the higher revs required, the GP engine had slightly shorter ram tubes for the 50mm Webers within its big intake airbox.

Aston revved this short-stroke RB6 much faster. It developed its peak output of 250bhp at between 7,500 and 7,800rpm. As was discovered in its first major race in 1959, however, sustained running of the engine above 7,000rpm – as was necessary to compete – caused bearing failure. The Glacier boffins said it was because the rods were flexing, so new rods with heavier big ends were designed and made but these effected no improvement.

Finally it was discovered that the oil flow in the drillings to the bearings in the crankshaft, which emerged at the top centre of the rod journal, was simply being stalled by the dynamic forces at revs the engine had never reached as a sports-car unit. Moving the location of the drillings away from top centre solved the problem. But even with another new cylinder head for 1960, the last year of the 2½-litre Formula 1, it was too late for the RB6 to shine as a Grand Prix engine. Its very considerable sports-racing successes would have to suffice.

Opposite left: As prepared for Formula 1 competition the RB6 block was given more generous ribbing through its crankcase area. The ignition distributors driven by the rear ends of the camshafts provided sparks for two plugs per cylinder.

Opposite right: Harking back to an earlier era of engine design, the RB6 cylinder head placed its two valves at a wide 95° included angle. Cup-type tappets enclosed the coil valve springs

and the exhaust-valve guide was directly exposed to cooling water.

Above: Aston Martin conducted tests of fuel injection using one of its standard six-cylinder engines as tuned for racing. The injection pump, a modified CAV unit, squirted fuel straight into the inlet ports through the side of the plenum chamber. Although not used in racing at that time, this foreshadowed a technique that would be common much later.

SPECIFICATIONS	
Cylinders	I6
Bore	83.0mm
Stroke	90.0mm
Stroke/bore ratio	1.08:1
Capacity	2,922cc
Compression ratio	9.8:1
Connecting rod length	166.0mm
Rod/crank radius ratio	3.7:1
Main bearing journal diameter	63.5mm
Rod journal diameter	50.8mm
Inlet valve diameter (1 valve)	50.0mm
Exhaust valve diameter (1 valve)	40.0mm
Inlet pressure	1.0:1
Engine weight	445lb (202kg)
Peak power	255bhp @ 6,000rpm
Piston speed (corrected)	3,403ft/min (17.0m/s)
Peak torque	235lb ft (319Nm) @ 5,400rpm
Peak bmep	199psi
Engine bhp per litre	87.3bhp per litre
Engine weight per bhp	1.75lb (0.79kg) per bhp

1960
COVENTRY CLIMAX FPF 2.5-LITRE FOUR

Apart from BRM, in the 1950s only one British company had both high-performance engine ideas and the ability to execute them. This was Coventry Climax Engines Ltd, which could trace its origins to 1903. Climax made fork-lift trucks, fire pumps and the engines that powered them. Producing its own ultra-light four-cylinder engines for its portable fire pumps, it gave them the designation 'FW' for 'featherweight'.

Climax's chairman and managing director, the urbane Leonard P. Lee, turned out to be a closet racing enthusiast who also hired engineers with racing pedigrees, among them Wally Hassan and Harry Mundy. Thus when Kieft, Lotus and Cooper came along and said that they wanted 1,100cc engines for their sports-racing cars, Lee gave his approval and from the single-overhead-cam fire-pump engine the FWA was produced, first racing in 1954.

Considerably to the surprise of Hassan and Mundy, at a Shell party at the Earl's Court Motor Show of 1952 Leonard Lee gave them the green light to design a completely new engine for the coming 2½-litre Formula 1. Harry Mundy designed this, the FPE V8, in the evenings after finishing his Climax day job. By 1954 it was producing 264bhp at 7,900rpm on 60 per cent methanol-based fuel. This was a very respectable output, as comparisons with other engines in this book will reveal. But Coventry-Climax decided not to produce and sell it for two reasons. One was that it believed that the FPE's power did not compare well with outputs claimed for other Grand Prix engines in 1954. The other reason was that its potential customers were turning their attention instead to the new 1957 1½-litre Formula 2.

To make a four-cylinder engine for Lister, Cooper and Lotus, wrote Harry Mundy, 'the cylinder head assembly, connecting rods and other components of the V8 were utilised.' The 'other components' included much of the cam gear train. From the V8 with cylinder dimensions of 76 x 68mm a 1½-litre four of 81.2 x 71.1mm was evolved, the FPF Climax.

In 1958 Lotus and Cooper, at the urging of their drivers, began entering their Formula 2 cars in Formula 1 as well. For this Climax initially produced a two-litre FPF. So powered, with a paltry 176 horsepower, Coopers astonished the Grand Prix world by winning the first two races of 1958. A transitional 2.2-litre FPF was made and then, for the 1959 season, extensive redesign took the engine to a full 2.5 litres. Work began on 1 December 1958 and the engine first raced and won in March 1959. With the FPF Jack Brabham and the Cooper-Climax won the world championships of 1959 and 1960.

In the redesign, Wally Hassan told the SAE, Climax faced 'the necessity of retaining the ability to machine the major components on existing jigging. We were, therefore, tied to the existing cylinder centres, main-bearing stud centres and only a very small variation in cylinder-head stud centres.' The cylinder-centre distance was still that of the V8, 106mm, within which Climax contrived to provide a bore of 94mm. Clearance bulges in the crankcase made room for a stroke of 89.9mm and a swept volume of 2,496cc (3.70 x 3.54in). Thus as in the cases of the Ferrari 246 Dino and Maserati Type 61 (qv) we have an example of a successful expansion to a winning engine from an original about half its size.

An important asset of the FPF in easing this transition was the robust design of its cylinder block. Like the cylinder head it was cast by Birmal of RR50 aluminium alloy. Carrying over the concept of the V8, the barrel-shaped crankcase extended down 3½in (89mm) below the crank centreline and was finned along its sides for stiffness and cooling. A shallow light-alloy finned sump closed the bottom end.

The cylinder liners were pinched at the top of the block and scaled by the laminated Cooper rings that had been developed for the Vanwall (qv). Liners were a close fit at the bottom of the jacket, where O-rings provided a seal. Ten main studs attached the head, supplemented by four additional studs on the exhaust side where the water flowed from the block to the head.

Climax used steel for the 2½-litre's main-bearing caps, which were also stabilised by cross-bolts. Bottom-end stiffness was added by bolting the oil-pump carriers as bridges across the three centre

Opposite above: Ineffectual though they may have looked, the Climax-powered Coopers showed that they had the speed to take on the big boys during the 1959 season. Maurice Trintignant drove a car from the Walker stable at Reims.

Opposite below: The compactness of the FPF engine allowed Cooper (as here) and Lotus to build very compact and efficient cars around it. A header tank accepted rising warm water and piped it to the forward-mounted radiator.

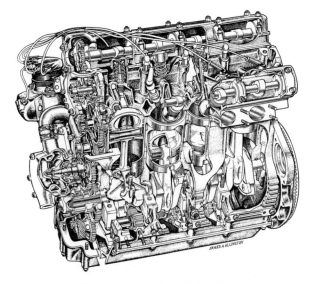

form masses made of a sintered tungsten with a specific weight 1.6 times that of lead. This achieved 100 per cent counterbalancing.

Lubrication was dry-sump, effected by the two scavenge pumps and single pressure pump mounted under the main bearings in the sump, where they were always flooded by the SAE 40 or 50 oil and thus less likely to pick up air. Oil passages were drilled into the block and crank and connections to the outside were neatly labelled 'IN' and 'OUT' for the customer's convenience. Two scavenge outlets were on the right side of the block and the inlet to the pressure pump was on the left.

Driven from the ball-bearinged spur-gear train at the front of the engine, the centrifugal water pump was mounted low at the front. It fed cooled water to the exhaust side of the block. Hot water was withdrawn through a manifold from a high point on the inlet side of the head. Phosphor bronze valve guides were used, the exhaust guides being finned and in direct contact with the coolant. Valve-seat inserts were shrunk into the heat-treated head.

Taking advice from Harry Weslake, the Climax designers curved the inlet ports in plan view to give a turbulence-inducing swirl to the incoming charge. They also positioned the single 14mm spark plug at an angle of 25° so that its face could be close to the chamber surface and positioned to suit the swirl pattern. When a new Mark II cylinder head was made in mid-1959 it had reversed swirl into the front and rear cylinders, the better to suit the carburettors, and repositioned plugs for those cylinders. This was easy to do because the head had always provided for dual ignition, which was never needed. A skew-gear pair at the crankshaft nose turned the big Lucas magneto.

The FPF's valves were vee-inclined at an included angle of 66°, 32 for the inlets and 34 for the exhausts, which allowed a shallow machined hemispherical recess in the head that encouraged a sensible combustion chamber shape. Only a gently domed piston was needed to achieve an 11.9:1 compression ratio. Brico made the cast aluminium pistons, which had full skirts and carried two Dykes-type compression rings and one oil ring, all above the gudgeon pin.

Made of high-nickel Nimonic 80 steels, the valves were solid and devoid of internal cooling.

mains. Main bearings were 2.5in (63.5mm) in diameter and the rod journals were 2.125in (54.0mm). Connecting rod length was 5.1in (129.5mm) and the gudgeon pin diameter was 1in (25.4mm). Forged of EN24 steel, the I-section rods had slender shanks and massive big ends retained by half-inch bolts. All bearings were thin-wall indium-plated lead-bronze.

Experience with his 2.2-litre FPF engines convinced Climax technical director Wally Hassan that he would have to take steps in the bigger unit to suppress what he called the 'skipping rope effect' of the inadequately-counterbalanced crankshaft that otherwise could punch out the heavily-stressed centre main bearing. The masses of the big-end journals were reduced by big internal borings, which were part of an end-to-end network of drillings inside the forged steel crank that assured an uninterrupted oil supply. Into the four counterweights were recessed and bolted arcuate-

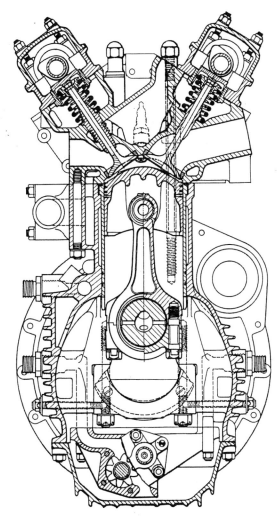

Opposite left: *Revealed by Jim Allington's cutaway of the FPF are its spur-gear drive to the camshafts, battery of oil pumps in the sump and spiral-bevel drive to the Lucas magneto.*
Opposite right: *Oil passages from and to the pumps and cylinder block are visible adjacent to the centre main-bearing caps, which are deeply recessed into the crankcase. To the extent possible all oil piping was contained within the engine's castings.*
Left: *Cross-bolts tied the main-bearing caps firmly into the crankcase. At the top of the FPF the finned exhaust-valve guides were in direct contact with the coolant. Separate blocks carried the light and short cup-type tappets.*

(132kg), maximum power was 240bhp at 6,750rpm and peak torque was 212lb ft at 5,000rpm. Racing teams purchased these engines for £2,250 per unit and 48 in all were sold.

Remarkably, its 2½-litre Formula 1 successes were not the end of the line for the Coventry Climax FPF. Reduced again to 1½ litres it served as an interim engine for the British Grand Prix teams in 1961. Bore and stroke were both increased to produce 2.7 litres for Cooper's 1961 Indianapolis 500 entry. Engines of this type were used by Dan Gurney in his Eagle Formula 1 car in 1966 until his own V12 was ready. Gurney twice finished fifth with Climax power in the 1966 season, when the FPF was giving 255bhp.

This allowed the heads of both valves to be deeply tuliped so that they cohered with the chamber's hemispherical form. Valve diameters were 42.8mm for the exhausts and 49.2mm for the inlets. A Mark II head introduced during 1959 had 52.4mm inlet valves, which brought 8 per cent more power from their 6½ per cent greater diameter. Valve lift was 10.4mm, timing duration 290° and valve overlap 90°.

Separate tappet blocks of magnesium were used with inserted iron guides in which the short inverted-cup tappets slid. These flat-topped chilled cast-iron tappets surrounded twin coil valve springs, the inner spring being far weaker than the outer. Magnesium covers were provided for the hollow-centred camshafts.

Carburation was by two Weber 58 DCO3 twin-throat units. From an engine weighing 290lb

SPECIFICATIONS	
Cylinders	I4
Bore	94.0mm
Stroke	89.9mm
Stroke/bore ratio	0.96:1
Capacity	2,496cc
Compression ratio	11.9:1
Connecting rod length	129.5mm
Rod/crank radius ratio	2.9:1
Main bearing journal diameter	63.5mm
Rod journal diameter	54.0mm
Inlet valve diameter (1 valve)	49.2mm
Exhaust valve diameter (1 valve)	42.8mm
Inlet pressure	1.0Atm
Engine weight	290lb (132kg)
Peak power	240bhp @ 6,750rpm
Piston speed (corrected)	4,072ft/min (20.4m/s)
Peak torque	212 lb ft (287Nm) @5,000rpm
Peak bmep	210psi
Engine bhp per litre	96.2bhp per litre
Engine weight per bhp	1.21lb (0.55kg) per bhp

1960

MASERATI 61 2.9-LITRE FOUR

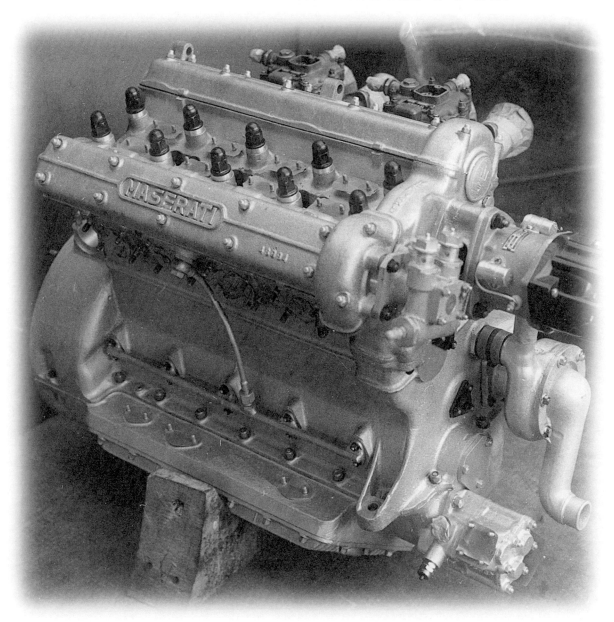

By 1958 Maserati was on its knees. 1957 had seen a costly prodigality of technical innovation and works racing entries for Juan Fangio in Formula 1 and the awesome 450S V8 sports car in endurance races. In 1958, operating under government administration to protect its financial integrity, the Modenese firm focused on its 3½-litre GT car to help restore cash flow.

If works teams had drained Maserati's coffers, the building and selling of racing cars had always been profitable – especially when their owners came back for spare parts and overhauls. In October 1958 Maserati's chief engineer Giulio Alfieri started work on a new sports-racing car that could compete in the international two-litre class, a category in which Maserati, from its 1948 A6GCS onward, had always been competitive.

To lower both its bonnet line and its centre of gravity, Alfieri canted the new car's four-cylinder in-line engine 45° to the right – thus much like one cylinder bank of the 450S V8. He offset the crankshaft centreline to the left side of the chassis to keep the engine's weight centred. Around it he fitted the uniquely intricate small-tube space-frame that inspired the car's 'Birdcage' nickname. In May 1959 the prototype of the four-cylinder 2-litre Type 60 Maserati was ready for testing in the hands of chief mechanic Guerrino Bertocchi. He found it to be very satisfactory, as did Stirling Moss.

Moss suggested that the car had the potential to be uprated to compete in endurance racing, which then was limited to 3-litre cars. Maserati took up his recommendation. They enlarged its engine to 2.9 litres, beefed up its drive train to suit and thus created the Type 61, a sports-racing car that showed in 1960 that it could take on and defeat the best that its rivals could offer.

The Type 61's engine was derived from that of the 2-litre 200SI, which in turn had been developed from the 150S. Most closely related to its forebears was the aluminium-alloy cylinder

Above: The Type 61's massive crankshaft fitted tightly within the block and was well counterweighted. Four studs retained each main-bearing cap.
Opposite above: Signs of contact with other competitors are evident as Walt Hansgen races Briggs Cunningham's Type 61 Maserati to victory at Cumberland in 1960. Wherever it raced this Maserati enjoyed great success.
Opposite below: Extending from the front case of the Type 61 engine were its oil pumps, at bottom, and the fuel pump driven by the exhaust camshaft. External oil piping that connected the main bearings also provided an oil supply to the cylinder head.

block, which housed very thin wet nitrided-iron cylinder liners and carried the crankshaft in five main bearings. No larger bore than 100mm (3.94in) could be accommodated in the block. With a stroke of 92mm (3.62in), displacement was 2,890cc. Achieving the latter required the casting of a new cylinder block 10mm taller than that of the 200SI. An attempt to lengthen the stroke to 95mm to bring the displacement to 2,985cc, nearer the 3-litre limit, failed when the test engine destroyed itself on the Maserati dynamometer.

Massive main-bearing caps were held on by four studs, two major ones close to the bearings and two minor studs outboard. The cylinder block was cut off at the crank centreline. In the design of the bottom end the experience gathered with the similarly-proportioned 450S V8 was put to good use. Main-bearing diameter was initially 60mm but this was soon enlarged to 65mm and some late engines had 67mm mains. Rod journals were 50mm and bearing shells were thin-wall lead-indium supplied by Vandervell.

Balanced both statically and dynamically, the rugged crankshaft had pairs of counterweights opposite each rod journal. The inner surfaces of the crank cheeks were undercut to give as much emphasis as possible to the mass at the periphery of each counterweight. Fully polished I-section connecting rods were handsomely shaped in the Maserati tradition with relatively slim and light two-bolt big ends. Aluminium plugs retained the gudgeon pins in the fully skirted forged Borgo pistons. Peaked with a flat top, they carried two compression rings and one oil ring.

A new deep aluminium sump was cast, liberally finned on its left side and shaped to conform to the engine's 45° slope. As on the 200SI and 150S, the pressure and scavenge pumps for the dry-sump lubrication system were exposed at the front of the sump, below the nose of the crankshaft. Nearest

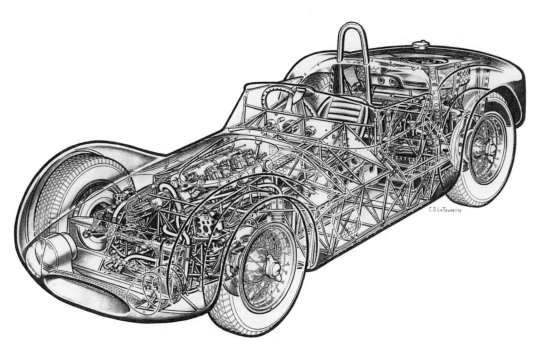

to the engine, the single pressure pump drew oil from a reservoir on the left side of the engine bay and pumped it to the engine by way of a large filter, frame-mounted next to the reservoir. SAE 50 oil was drawn from the pan by two pickups and two scavenge pumps, and returned to the tank by way of an oil cooler at the left of the water radiator.

When the cylinder head of the Maserati 200SI was adapted to the 1957 450S V8 a major change was made to the layout of its water passages. The four-cylinder 200SI engine simply let the hot water out through a pipe at the front between the cam-drive gears. For the V8 the piping of the 250F and 300S engines was adopted: hot water exited though manifolding above the inlet valve seats (on the 'high' side of this inclined engine) and cool water was pumped direct to the exhaust-valve seats and guides by another manifold on the other side of the head vee. The large water pump was driven by the gear tower at the front of the block.

With its single cylinder head placed at the precise angle of the right-hand bank of the 450S V8, the Type 61 engine kept this new water manifolding.

A major change from the V8 was the abandonment of an elaborate roller-finger cam follower that had come in with the 150S and had spread to the 200SI and 450S. For his new engine Alfieri reverted to the simple, light, space-saving finger follower that had been proven on all the Maserati twin-cam sixes including the 250F and 300S. In the latter engines it was combined with coil springs, while in the Type 61 it worked with hairpin springs for the first time. These were placed in the longitudinal plane of the engine inside the camboxes.

Twin valves for each cylinder were inclined at a 76° included angle – 37° from the vertical for the inlets and 39° for the exhaust valves. Made in-house by Maserati, their diameters were 54.0 and 42.5mm respectively. The camshafts were carried in five bearings each and lifted the valves 10.5mm

Year	Type	Bore and Stroke (mm)	Cylinder size (cc)	Maximum rpm	Corrected piston speed (ft/min)
1955	150S	81.0 x 72.0	371	7,500	3,760
1957	450S	93.8 x 81.0	560	7,000	4,000
1957	200SI	92.0 x 75.0	498	7,500	4,120
1958	2.5 litre GP	96.0 x 86.0	623	7,000	4,180
1960	60	92.0 x 75.0	498	8,200	4,480
1960	61	100.0 x 92.0	722	6,800	4,270

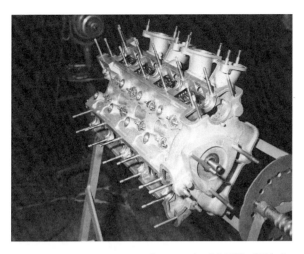

against a spring pressure that reached 175lb (79kg). Overlap was 85° with the following valve timing:

Inlet opens   45°BTDC   Exhaust opens   70°BBDC
Inlet closes   67°ABDC   Exhaust closes   40°ATDC

Drive to the camshafts was by means of a train of helical gears driven by the nose of the crankshaft.

Fully machined hemispherical combustion chambers had pressed-in bronze seats for the valves. As close as possible to the centre of the chamber were the two 14mm plugs per cylinder, inserted vertically. Lodge plugs were used – RL50 for 'mixed' circuits and the colder RL51 for fast circuits. These were sparked by dual chassis-mounted coils and a Marelli distributor driven by a gear at the top of the cam-drive tower.

Weber 48 DCO3 carburettors were fitted to aluminium stub pipes, which curved to allow them to be concealed under a modest bulge in the low bonnet line. Venturis were 40mm. Some late Type 61s had 50mm Webers. These were fed by a Fimac mechanical pump driven from the front of the exhaust camshaft. A tuned scavenging exhaust

Opposite: The engine was inclined at 45° to the right in the multi-tube chassis of the Type 61 Maserati. Chief engineer Giulio Alfieri shrewdly raided the Maserati parts bins to create this commercially successful sports-racer.
Above: A Type 61 Maserati cylinder head shows its hairpin-type valve springs and the drive to the distributor extending forward from the front of the gear train to the camshafts. Apertures were provided in the top of the head for the direct delivery of coolant to the exhaust-valve guides.

system of conventional shape was fitted on the right-hand side of the engine bay.

Just as Ferrari was able to expand his 1½-litre V6 to 2½ and even to 3 litres, so Giulio Alfieri was able to get nearly three litres from his 1½-litre four – a more difficult job with a smaller number of cylinders. The way the basic 150S cylinder was expanded and the way stresses (shown as corrected piston speed – divided by the square root of the stroke/bore ratio) increased year by year are shown in a table in relation to the maximum allowable crankshaft speeds. Also shown is another engine in this family, the four-cylinder 2½-litre engine that Maserati built and sold for use in Grand Prix Cooper-Maseratis. This turns out to have been moderately stressed for a Formula 1 engine.

With a compression ratio of 9.8:1 the Type 61 engine produced 255bhp at 6,500rpm. Its torque reached a maximum of 223lb ft at the 5,000rpm peak of a very flat curve that gave the engine great flexibility. According to 'Birdcage' expert Joel Finn some late Type 61s had more radical valve timing that brought output to 260bhp. But peak output was never the point of this powerplant. It was the right engine for a light, agile car that brought victory at the Nürburgring for Moss and Gurney in 1960 and many wins for its satisfied purchasers, especially in America where it won several SCCA championships.

SPECIFICATIONS	
Cylinders	I4
Bore	100.0mm
Stroke	92.0mm
Stroke/bore ratio	0.92:1
Capacity	2,890cc
Compression ratio	9.8:1
Connecting rod length	143.0mm
Rod/crank radius ratio	3.1:1
Main bearing journal diameter	65.0mm
Rod journal diameter	50.0mm
Inlet valve diameter (1 valve)	54.0mm
Exhaust valve diameter (1 valve)	42.5mm
Inlet pressure	1.0Atm
Engine weight	370lb (168kg)
Peak power	255bhp @ 6,500rpm
Piston speed (corrected)	4,091ft/min (20.5m/s)
Peak torque	223lb ft (302Nm) @5,000rpm
Peak bmep	191psi
Engine bhp per litre	88.2bhp per litre
Engine weight per bhp	1.45lb (0.66kg) per bhp

1961

FERRARI DINO 156 1.5-LITRE V6

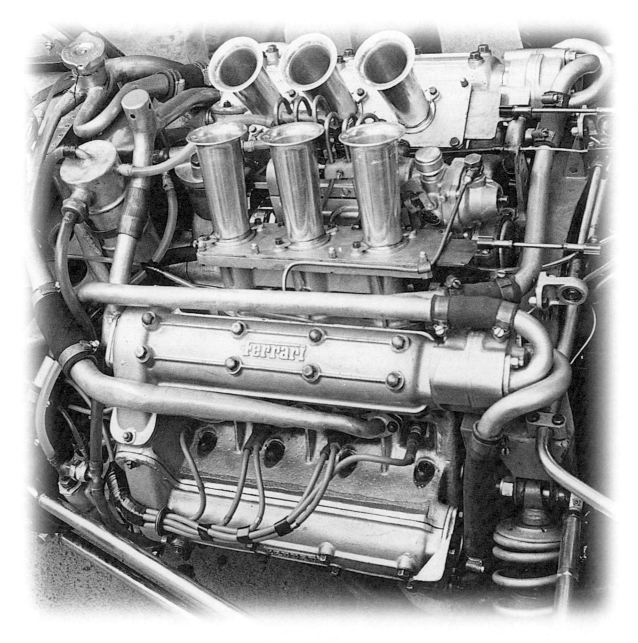

As he did so successfully so often, Enzo Ferrari prepared for the next Grand Prix Formula 1 during the previous one, taking advantage of any opportunities. The opportunity in this case was obvious: the 1½-litre Formula 2 that began in 1957 and made a smooth transition into the next Formula 1 in 1961. We read earlier of the 1½-litre Dino V6, introduced in 1957, that provided a basis for the 2½-litre Formula 1 engine of 1958–60. Ferrari remained faithful to the V6 engine for his 1961 Formula 1 engines – but in a new format.

For F2 racing in 1960 the 65° V6 was reformatted from its original 70 x 64.5mm cylinder dimensions to 73 x 58.8mm (2.87 x 2.31in), precisely those of the well-developed 250GT Ferrari V12. This gave 1,477cc. The slightly longer stroke of 59.1mm (1,484cc) had been tried but rejected by chief engineer Carlo Chiti, whose task it was to introduce Ferrari to a new era of smaller, lighter mid-engined racing cars.

In 1960 the F2 engine was raced several times in both front- and mid-engined chassis. Two engines used in October 1960 developed 172 and 177bhp. This seemed a promising enough start to the 1961 GP season, but Chiti was not satisfied. He wanted a shorter, lighter and more powerful engine that would be better suited to the new mid-engined chassis.

Chiti was friendly with a Milanese engineer, Aldo Celli, who in 1951 had designed a beautiful little 750cc V6 engine with the wide vee angle of 120°. Like the 60° angle, the 120° angle allows evenly spaced firing impulses with a simple crankshaft on which the big ends of the facing connecting rods can share a common journal. The 65° vee of the existing Ferrari V6 demanded a heavy and high-inertia crankshaft with six individual rod journals. In addition to his recollection of Celli's design, Chiti could look at the drawings of a 120° engine that been laid out, but never built, by Lampredi at Ferrari in 1950–51.

Chiti and Franco Rocchi began work on the new engine in 1959. They assigned the task of carrying out its basic calculations to a new young engineer just hired by Ferrari, Mauro Forghieri. Early in 1961 the wide-angle 156 Dino engine was ready, but getting it used in a car was another matter. Both engine types were raced at Monaco at the beginning of the 1961 season. 'At this stage,' recalled Chiti, 'there was open disagreement between Ferrari and myself, as he ultimately preferred the 65-degree. I was very determined, however, and for the next race, the Dutch GP, all the engines I set up were 120-degree. That year we won everything!'

The new unit was designed strictly as a 1½-litre engine, right to the bone for that size, so it weighed 55lb (25kg) less than its 65° sister: 265lb (120kg). Compared to the narrower-vee engine the I-section connecting rod was shorter and the big-end bearing diameter was reduced. The rods were still machined from large, very rough forging blanks, and had conventional two-bolt big ends. The pressure and scavenge oil pumps were driven from the front of the crankshaft and a disposable-type oil filter – new on racing Ferraris – was placed vertically at the front of the engine.

Possibly to bring his new engine into line with the layout used on the V12 Ferraris, Chiti offset its right cylinder bank forward. The 65° engine family had the left bank to the fore. Chain drive to the camshafts was still used, but between the cam sprockets the chain now ran straight across – as on the Lancia D50 V8 – instead of being pulled down around an additional idler sprocket. Each bank had its own double-roller chain system, driven from two half-speed gears at the nose of the crankshaft. Through spiral pinions, these gears also drove the twin Marelli ignition distributors splayed out at 120° in front of the block, sparking the twin plugs per cylinder. Magnetos had been consigned to history.

Simplification, based on experience with the Dino, was a hallmark of the new engine. Each cylinder head made do with eight hold-down studs instead of the 12 the Dino used. Wet liners continued to be fitted to a Silumin block. Though the cylinder head's structure was much simpler, its internal mechanism was a straight carryover from the Dino. Wide cam lobes still attacked broad mushroom tappets of the Jano design that screwed directly onto the valve stem for guidance and clearance adjustment, and coil valve springs were employed. The engine departed, however, from

Opposite above: The 'shark-nosed' Dino 156 Ferraris were dominant in the Grand Prix racing of 1961. Excellent testing service was provided by Richie Ginther, driving here

Opposite below: The wide-angle V6 with fuel injection was still in use by the works team at Monaco in 1964. A sub-frame adapted it to Ferrari's monocoque car structure.

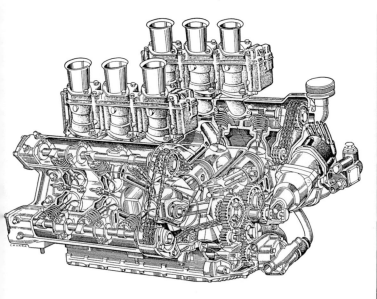

the Dino practice of machining both cam housings in the same plane, and returned to the technique of making the cut at right angles to the respective valve stems.

To suit the new engine Weber produced an elegant carburettor, an in-line three-barrel unit, the 40 IF3C, with 40mm throttle bodies. These fed inlet valves inclined at 28° from the vertical. Exhausts were angled at 32°, giving a total included angle of 60°. Only one exhaust valve size was used in this engine – 34mm – but two different inlet valve diameters were available to produce different power curves as desired: 38.5mm and 42mm. To put these in perspective, and also to show some of the changes that had been rung by that time on the popular unsupercharged 250cc cylinder size, this table provides an overview:

Engine	Bore and stroke	Valve Sizes	
		Inlet	Exhaust
NSU Special	66 x 72mm	39mm	37mm
Küchen V8	68 x 68mm	38mm	35mm
Guzzi Twin	70 x 64mm	38.5mm	33mm
BMW 253	72 x 66mm	40mm	36mm
Ferrari 120°	73 x 58.8mm	38.5mm	34mm
Ferrari 120°	73 x 58.8mm	42mm	34mm

One clear advantage of working with a six in 1½-litre size was the vast amount of experience that had been gained with the 250cc cylinder, both in cars and racing motorcycles.

It is useful to consider the gas velocities that followed from the Ferrari's two sizes of inlet valves. Applying the parameters of 195 and 260 feet per second gas speed that then most often corresponded to peak torque and peak power respectively, engine speeds of 7,200 and 9,600rpm resulted for the smaller valve, and 8,700 and 11,600rpm for the bigger 42mm valve. Since the engine's quoted power peak was at 9,500rpm, it is evident that the smaller valve was tailored to match that peak and to provide good torque, while the larger valve was intended to elevate the power curve at the top end at the expense of the rest of the speed range for use on high-speed circuits.

'The engine lived up to my expectations,' said Carlo Chiti. 'It had better pickup, it was lighter and it developed an additional 11bhp.' In round terms the output of the 65° six approached 180bhp at 9,200rpm, while the 120° version developed 190bhp at 9,500rpm. Their red lines were respectively 9,500 and 10,000rpm, showing that the new configuration allowed a significant increase in the corrected piston speed from 4,080 to 4,300 feet per minute.

Ferrari's new baby was not without her teething

troubles. By late March of 1961 the first wide-angle engine had completed 50 hours of dynamometer testing. Basic reliability was good, but she showed a tendency to suck all her oil up into the cylinder heads, leaving little in the sump. This was quickly and easily solved by the addition of scavenge pumps for the heads as well as the sump.

In the new engine's first race at Monaco the Dino was driven by Richie Ginther, who finished only 3.6 seconds behind winner Moss (Lotus-Climax). With Ginther being thought of more as a 'tester' than a 'racer', this was a brilliant result that justified Chiti's decision to go over to the new engine in spite of Enzo Ferrari's reservations. In the next event at Zandvoort the 120° engines placed one–two in a race that was unique in Grand Prix history: all the starters finished and none made a pit stop.

Ferrari achieved a stunning result in 1961's Belgian Grand Prix, won by Phil Hill. Its cars filled the first four positions, the fourth being a 65° car driven by Olivier Gendebien. Victories in Britain and Holland for Wolfgang von Trips meant that he and Phil Hill were rivals for the 1961 world title. Their duel was settled tragically at Monza where Trips was caught up in an accident and fatally injured. Phil Hill won the title in the 156 Dino with the wide-angle engine, a car with which he will always be associated.

This engine provided the basis for Ferrari's Formula 1 challenge for three more seasons until its V8 and flat-12 were ready. In 1963 it was fitted with Bosch fuel injection, which increased its output to 200bhp at 10,200rpm. With the British teams getting into their stride,

however, championship successes for the V6 were hard to come by. One came to John Surtees at the Nürburgring in 1963 and another to Lorenzo Bandini in Austria in 1964. After that the sixes were not only retired but also unceremoniously scrapped.

Opposite right: Special three-barrel carburettors were produced by Weber to suit the wide-angle Dino 156 engine of 1961. The two Marelli distributors for dual ignition were angled, like the cylinder banks, at 120 degrees.

Opposite left: Although adhering to recent Lancia and Ferrari tradition, the use by Carlo Chiti of roller chains to drive the overhead cams of his wide-angle Dino

V6 was unusual by racing standards. The drive was taken from half-speed gears turned by a spur at the nose of the crankshaft. Jano-type valve gear continued to be used.

Above: The 120° V6 was good enough to be kept in use by Ferrari for several more seasons beyond Phil Hill's championship year of 1961. A 1963 version still retained a high-placed oil filter and dual outlets from the water pump.

SPECIFICATIONS	
Cylinders	V6
Bore	73.0mm
Stroke	58.8mm
Stroke/bore ratio	0.81:1
Capacity	1,477cc
Compression ratio	9.8:1
Connecting rod length	98.0mm
Rod/crank radius ratio	3.3:1
Main bearing journal diameter	60.0mm
Rod journal diameter	43.6mm
Inlet valve diameter (1 valve)	38.5mm
Exhaust valve diameter (1 valve)	34.0mm
Inlet pressure	1.0Atm
Engine weight	265lb (120kg)
Peak power	190bhp @ 9,500rpm
Piston speed (corrected)	4,084ft/min (20.4m/s)
Engine bhp per litre	128.6bhp per litre
Engine weight per bhp	1.39lb (0.63kg) per bhp

1962

BRM P56 1.5-LITRE V8

BRM went from one extreme to the other. First it built the incredibly complex 1½-litre V16 (*qv*). Then for the 2½-litre Formula 1 its chief engineer Peter Berthon produced a four-cylinder engine. Recalled Harry Mundy, 'Berthon seemed to say, "Oh, blimey, the V16 was so complicated. Let's keep it simple."' Chronically unreliable, the four eked out a single victory with BRM under the new management of Rubery, Owen & Co., which had taken over the assets of BRM at the end of 1952. Its chief, Sir Alfred Owen, had been a strong supporter of the original BRM. He committed the resources of his Owen Organisation to this all-British racing effort.

Between these extremes BRM found the golden mean in the 1½-litre V8 it built to race in the new Grand Prix Formula 1 starting in 1961. The British teams had objected strongly to this new mini-engined Formula and consequently were late off the mark in building engines for it, but by the autumn of 1960 Berthon settled on a 90° V8 as the best configuration. With Aubrey Woods as chief draughtsman on the project the drawings were complete by the end of the year.

Berthon and Woods relied more on their experience than on abstruse calculations and tests in laying out the V8. Berthon selected the well-oversquare cylinder dimensions of 2.69 x 2.00in (68.3 x 50.8mm) for 1,490cc; the stroke was only 2½mm longer than that of the V16 so the 104.8mm connecting rods of the latter could be used. Also carried over from the sixteen were the roller bearings that carried the camshafts and the three-shaft spur-gear trains that provided the half-speed drive from the crank nose to the camshafts of each cylinder bank.

In mid-1961 when the first engine was assembled the initial 'snagging' list of problems had 26 items, many of them serious. The camshafts could not be assembled in their bearings and the compression ratio was only 8.2:1 instead of the specified 12:1. Nor was provision made for the starter motor which was mandatory under the new rules. Finally on 12 July an engine could be run and on 20 July, recalled development engineer Tony Rudd, 'it ran all day, a first for any BRM engine.' From this difficult beginning a fine engine was destined to emerge.

In its first racing season, 1962, the P56 V8 powered BRM in general and Graham Hill in particular to both Formula 1 world championships.

This had been a make-or-break season, because Sir Alfred had warned the BRM men working at Bourne in Lincolnshire that failure to achieve real success could result in the unit being shut down. That it was not a one-off result was underpinned by second-place rankings for Graham Hill and BRM in 1963, '64 and '65 – all propelled by the same basic V8 engine. In 1962 it produced as much as 193bhp at 10,250rpm.

The power was generated in a two-valve hemispherical combustion chamber with a single offset 10mm spark plug positioned to ignite the charge in line with the swirl induced by the angled inlet passages. Berthon settled on an included angle for the valves of 76°, shared 34° to the inlets and 42° to the exhausts. Inlet valve size was 39.7mm while the exhaust head measured 30.5mm – a striking differential. Respective valve lifts were 7.9 and 6.4mm. Titanium was used for the spring retainers and the clearance-adjusting caps between the stem and the tappet.

All the valve stems and heads were hollow to allow the use of internal cooling salts and to lighten them significantly. For the first time in a BRM engine Berthon specified inverted cup-type tappets. These were too small, at 28mm, to contain the twin coil valve springs (also a BRM first, replacing hairpins) which were placed below them. The tappets slid in iron guides inserted into a light-alloy tappet block that was affixed to the bottom of each cam chamber. Running in crowded roller bearings, the camshafts gave 150° of top-end overlap.

Some disagreement reigned at the V8's conception over the possible value of 'squish' surfaces in the combustion chamber, which mated surfaces on the chamber and piston that came almost into contact at top dead centre. The aim of squish is both to induce more turbulence in the charge and to provide cooler surfaces in the chamber that will help suppress detonation during combustion. Ultimately all traces of squish were eradicated, and the piston crown was rounded to improve both gas flow and the chamber shape at a reduced compression ratio of 10.5:1.

Opposite above: Graham Hill's championship year of 1962 was powered by BRM's P56 V8 engine. With its crank throws spaced at 90° it used individual exhaust pipes for much of the season.

Opposite below: A drive just below the BRM's right-hand inlet camshaft turned the alternator, below it, and the Lucas injection distributor through a cogged rubber belt.

Die-cast aluminium pistons were slipper-type, with skirting only on the leading and trailing faces. Rings numbered two: a single compression ring of pressure-backed Dykes type and a two-piece oil control ring, both above the gudgeon pin. Although the basic design of the I-section connecting rod remained unchanged from the V16, several iterations of the big-end cap attachment were needed before the use of bolts from the bottom proved to be a reliable solution. The big-end journals measured 1.60in (40.6mm) and the main bearings 2.25in (57.2mm).

Bottom-end bearings were conventional thin-wall lead-bronze type, although experiments were conducted with reticular tin bearings. 'These gave much more power,' said Tony Rudd, 'but there was a risk that with a temporary interruption of oil flow (surge in a corner) they would seize, and the seizure was pretty horrible.' Lead-bronze bearings, which were much more tolerant of oil shortages, were retained.

Machined from EN40u steel and nitrided, the five-bearing crankshaft had double counter-weights opposite each rod journal. The crank throws were spaced at 90°, as was then customary V8 practice, to gain the best balance. This did not lend itself to extractor tuning of the exhaust, however, and BRM went through 1962 with several different exhaust-pipe layouts, including individual upswept stacks for each cylinder. Two studs retained each main-bearing cap, which was closely slotted into its crankcase web to provide lateral support.

Heads and block were cast of LM8 aluminium alloy, while magnesium was used for the cam covers and the finned oil pan. The latter was extremely shallow because the block extended down virtually to the bottom of the engine. At its top a double-walled structure around the cylinders ensured adequate support and stiffness for the critical head joint. Here Berthon and Woods eschewed radical solutions (BRM's four had Ferrari-style screwed-in liners) in favour of a flange at the top of the iron liner pinched against the top of the block and sealed with a Cooper Nimonic gasket ring. The wet liner's bottom end was sealed by two rubber rings in grooves in the block.

A spur gear at the nose of the crank drove the two ex-V16 gear packs that carried the camshaft drive to each cylinder bank. Below the crank nose another gear drove the oil pumps at 0.55 engine speed. Bridging the front of the crankcase was the scavenge pump, with its three gear pinions drawing from separate pickup points at the front and rear of the sump. A forward extension drove the water pump with its twin outlets. Set into the engine's front cover on the right side of the crankcase was the oil pressure pump.

Having experimented on his four-cylinder engine with Lucas petrol injection, Berthon decided to make this a feature of his V8 from the outset. The Lucas system used a high-pressure pump feeding a distributor, which in the

P56 was mounted in the front of the engine's vee and driven by a cogged belt from a sprocket driven by an idler in the gear train. Slide-type throttles were adopted, the first time that these were used on a Grand Prix engine. Above them were smoothly tapered and flared air-inlet ram pipes.

Initially the injection was downstream in the inlet ports, but Lucas recommended a trial of injection upstream against the flow, as had been used by Jaguar. This was adopted after tests showed that it made the engine less sensitive to variations in its air/fuel ratio. From the outset of this programme it had been the policy of BRM and Owen to make these V8s available for sale to private teams; Owen was keen to commercialise its racing venture. These engines, however, were fitted with four downdraught Weber 35 IDM carburettors instead of the costly injection. They brought with them a power penalty of about ten horsepower.

In the V8's early running both the injection and the Lucas ignition were suspected of causing a severe misfire above 9,750rpm. This was still afflicting the engine when BRM took its first V8 to Monza for the Italian GP in September 1961, so the team practised with it but did not race it.

Later, still frustrated by this problem, Tony Rudd took one of the V16's magnetos off the shelf and tried it; the V8 ran to 10,500 (their dynamometer's limit) without a misfire. Thus edified, Lucas produced a powerful transistorised ignition system triggered by magnetic pole pieces on the back of the flywheel rotating past a pickup on the rear of the engine. Revving misfire-free to 11,000 was now no problem, as BRM's drivers were to discover to their considerable pleasure and reward.

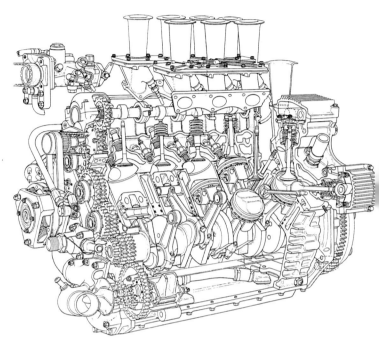

Opposite above: Viewed from the front, the P56 showed its aluminium cylinder block and heads. The distributor drive was taken from the gear train below the left inlet camshaft.
Opposite below: Taking the drive from the crank nose to the cylinder heads of the P56 were two gear packs adapted directly from those of the Type 15 1½-litre V16. The two flanges served to affix them to the top surface of the cylinder block.
Above: A cutaway by Vic Berris reveals the slipper-type pistons of the P56 with their narrow thrust faces. Inlet and exhaust valves were both hollow for lightness and cooling.

SPECIFICATIONS	
Cylinders	V8
Bore	68.3mm
Stroke	50.8mm
Stroke/bore ratio	0.74:1
Capacity	1,490cc
Compression ratio	10.5:1
Connecting rod length	104.8mm
Rod/crank radius ratio	4.1:1
Main bearing journal diameter	57.2mm
Rod journal diameter	40.6mm
Inlet valve diameter (1 valve)	39.7mm
Exhaust valve diameter (1 valve)	30.5mm
Inlet pressure	1.0Atm
Engine weight	255lb (115kg)
Peak power	193bhp @ 10,250rpm
Piston speed (corrected)	3,962ft/min (19.8m/s)
Engine bhp per litre	129.5bhp per litre
Engine weight per bhp	1.32lb (0.60kg) per bhp

1962

PORSCHE 753 1.5-LITRE FLAT-8

Rightly enough, Porsche was chuffed with the success in Formula 2 of its Type 547 flat four (qv) in a single-seater chassis. This encouraged it to build a completely new engine and car for the 1961 1½-litre Formula 1. Work on it began early in 1960. But Porsche compromised its engine in two ways: it designed it to be expandable to 2 litres for sports-car racing and it also kept in mind its possible suitability for series production. Neither move was calculated to produce an optimum Formula 1 engine.

The engine's creation was also troubled by a turbulent phase among Porsche's engineering hierarchy. Primary technical authority rested as usual with Ferry Porsche. After the retirement in October 1960 of veteran technical director Karl Rabe that post was held by Klaus von Rücker, but another senior design manager, Leopold Schmid, had good reason to covet it. Behind the scenes intrigued racing manager Huschke von Hanstein, who had the ear and the confidence of Ferry Porsche.

Thus Porsche, von Rücker and Schmid, with the advice and counsel of Rabe and von Hanstein, made the key decisions that determined the shape of the new engine. Execution after the departure of Type 547 designer Ernst Fuhrmann was by Hans Hönick and a relative newcomer to Porsche, Hans Mezger. One decision was easy, Mezger said: 'Air cooling had given a good account of itself in Porsche engines, even in racing, so there was no cause to give up this form of cooling.' Also the engine had to be as compact as possible so it would stand a chance of fitting into the engine rooms of the kinds of cars that Porsche made.

'It was estimated that the output of 1.5-litre engines, over the duration of the new Formula, would rise to about 210 to 220bhp,' added Mezger. This meant that speeds of more than 10,000rpm would be needed, which in turn led to the decision to provide eight cylinders. A flat-opposed con-figuration was adopted after consideration of a wide-angle vee. Also selected were the strongly oversquare cylinder dimensions of 66 x 54.6mm (2.60 x 2.15in) for a displacement of 1,494cc.

The 753 had an individual crank throw and journal for each of its connecting rods. The grand total of main bearings came to nine, plus a tenth ball bearing overhung at the rear. The main bearing journals were 20mm wide, which left 22mm for the width of the connecting-rod journals. A terribly intricate steel forging, the crankshaft had balancing masses integral with each of its 16 cheeks. Journal diameters of both the main and rod bearings were set at 57mm. After testing both roller and plain bearings Porsche plumped for the latter. The length of the I-section connecting rod, measured from centre to centre, was 126mm.

One of Hans Hönick's least happy decisions was his placing of the valves at the wide and symmetrical included angle of 90°. This allowed large valves to be fitted (37mm inlets and 34mm exhausts), but it also made the combustion chamber very deep. A high-domed and heavy piston with deeply-gouged cut-outs for valve head clearance was required to maintain the compression ratio of 10.0:1 or better that was needed.

On the Auto Union, Cisitalia and Type 547 four, Porsche had used shafts to drive overhead cams and the same technique was continued here. To achieve high revs, their calculations showed, the shaft runs had to be shortened in order to make them more torsionally rigid. Thus even at the eight's higher speeds they would not encounter vibration periods that would cause excessive variations in valve timing – a fault of the Type 547 four.

The 753 had two half-speed shafts, one above the crank and one below it, driven from gears at the flywheel end of the crankshaft. The upper one took care of the inlet camshafts and the lower one the exhaust cams. From each of these shafts pairs of spiral bevel gears drove (at a little less than engine speed) hollow shafts to the left and right, above and below the centre pair of cylinders. Each shaft turned another set of bevels at the centre of each camshaft.

Both the top and bottom shaft systems had extra jobs to do. From the bevel gear on the top shaft that drove the right-hand inlet cam, another gear and a short shaft rose vertically to spin an axial-flow cooling fan at 0.92 crankshaft speed. Measuring 250mm in diameter, the 17-blade fan (the same one tried on the four in late 1961 and early 1962) was made of fibreglass-reinforced plastic. Its normal

Opposite above: In the second of two victories he scored in 1962 for Porsche in Formula 1, Dan Gurney was a popular winner at the Solitude circuit near Stuttgart. He was powered by Porsche's Type 753 flat-eight. Opposite below: Lightweight glass-fibre shrouding was used to enclose the airflow passages of the Type 753. The vee-belt from the left-hand inlet camshaft drove the alternator.

power demand was only nine horsepower to pump 2,970 cubic feet of air per minute, a slightly better performance than the blower of the Type 547. Below the fan were guides and cowlings that directed an air supply to each cylinder.

Individual cylinders forged of aluminium were given chrome-plated bores. Each cylinder was capped by a finned aluminium head casting, which was held down by four studs and was symmetrical – including its twin spark plugs – about the vertical plane along the cylinder centreline. Uniting all the cylinder heads on each side was a single large aluminium casting that carried the camshafts and valve gear. Individual cam covers were of magnesium. Magnesium was also used for the eight's main castings.

The crankcase halves were split vertically down the middle. At the top they carried two Bosch distributors driven from the upper half-speed shaft. The oil pumps were placed transversely just below and on both sides of the lower half-speed shaft, and driven from the shaft to the left-hand exhaust camshaft by a pair of gears in a separate housing on the outside of the left flank of the crankcase.

Of the two oil scavenge pumps, which were in the left side of the crankcase, one was devoted solely to drawing oil out of the lower cam boxes. The other larger scavenge pump sucked oil out of the sump and pushed it, through a full-flow filter and one of the frame tubes, to the oil tank at the front of the car. Located in the right-hand half of the crankcase, the pressure pump drew the oil back through the other frame tube and delivered it to the various parts of the engine. After leaving the pump the oil passed through another full-flow filter, this one on the right side of the crankcase.

Main bearings were fed oil from a very large gallery along the right side of the crankcase. The oil to the rod bearings was fed into the nose of the crank, through an orifice that was spring-loaded against it, and from there into drillings that ran the whole length of the crankshaft. Through external flexible oil lines at the back of the engine, similar pressure-oil deliveries were made to the hollow centres of all four camshafts. From there, radial drillings fed lubricant to the surfaces of the cam lobes and thence to the valve gear.

After rig testing of an experimental desmodromic valve gear Porsche chose a conventional gear, using finger followers pivoted from hinges instead of the spherical pivots used by the 547. Valve timing for the 753 was as follows:

Inlet opens 81°BTDC   Exhaust opens 81°BBDC
Inlet closed 71°ABDC   Exhaust closes 51°ATDC

Lift was 10.55mm for the inlets and 9.3mm for the exhausts. Both valves were hollow-stemmed, the inlets for lightness and the exhausts to enclose sodium salts for internal cooling. Twin coil springs closed each valve.

With two 38mm Weber twin-throat down-draught carburettors along each side, this complex engine was a remarkably compact cube that was smaller in every dimension except length than the Type 547. It weighed, with its exhaust system and diaphragm-spring clutch, 341lb (155kg).

When the eight was first tested in December 1960 it developed a disappointing 120 horsepower. By the early spring of 1961 it had been tweaked to 160bhp with a torque curve that was not as good as that of the four-cam four. Further effort brought the power to 178bhp at 9,200rpm by early 1962, when the engine was first raced.

The improvements came from Hans Mezger's two new cylinder head designs, one with valves narrowed symmetrically to 84°, and the other with the exhaust valve at 41.5° and the inlet nearer vertical (31.5°) for a total included angle of 73.0°. In the new heads the inlet ports were smaller, to raise gas flow speeds to improve the torque, and they were sloped so that they spilled less abruptly into the chamber. Refinements to the lubrication system reduced the loss of power from internal churning of the oil.

The best performance recorded for the GP eight during the 1962 season was 185bhp at 9,300rpm with a compression ratio of 10.0:1. Its maximum torque was 113lb ft at 7,450rpm. This was enough to keep Porsche in the running but not quite enough, even with the inspired driving of Dan Gurney, to fight toe-to-toe in every race with the best British works cars. Nevertheless at Rouen in

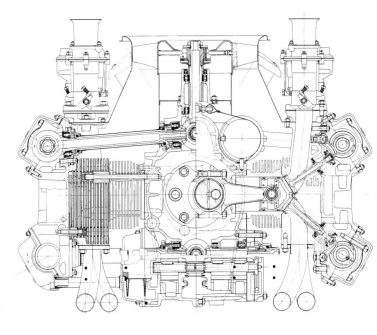

France in 1962 Dan scored Porsche's only championship Grand Prix victory with the Type 753 eight behind him. He also won an F1 race in the Stuttgart suburb of Solitude, which made both him and Porsche home-town heroes.

Opposite left: Denuded of its shrouds a 1961 test engine shows the baffling used beneath the cooling fan to distribute air equally to its eight cylinders. A transparent section in the front cover allowed study of the oiling conditions in the crankcase.
Opposite right: Space was scarce beneath the flat-eight engine for the pipework from *its exhaust ports. Oil pumps and the oil filter flanked the flywheel end of the crankcase.*
Above: With its reduced valve angle the 72° head planned for 1963 had a more compact combustion chamber that promised greater efficiency and a close approach to 200 horsepower. Heads continued to be individual castings for each cylinder.

SPECIFICATIONS	
Cylinders	F8
Bore	66.0mm
Stroke	54.6mm
Stroke/bore ratio	0.83:1
Capacity	1,494cc
Compression ratio	10.0:1
Connecting rod length	126.0mm
Rod/crank radius ratio	4.6:1
Main bearing journal diameter	57.0mm
Rod journal diameter	57.0mm
Inlet valve diameter (1 valve)	37.0mm
Exhaust valve diameter (1 valve)	34.0mm
Inlet pressure	1.0Atm
Engine weight	341lb (155kg)
Peak power	185bhp @ 9,300rpm
Piston speed (corrected)	3,663ft/min (18.3m/s)
Peak torque	113lb ft (153Nm) @ 7,450rpm
Peak bmep	187psi
Engine bhp per litre	123.8bhp per litre
Engine weight per bhp	1.84lb (0.83kg) per bhp

1965

COVENTRY CLIMAX FWMV 1.5-LITRE V8

It wasn't difficult to decide who should be the first to drive the new Coventry Climax 1½-litre V8 in a motor race. At the wheel of Coopers, Australian Jack Brabham had rendered vital service in nurturing the growth of the FPF Climax into a fully-fledged Grand Prix engine. As soon as it was judged ready for the track the new FWMV V8 was delivered to Cooper Cars on 28 July 1961. It was installed in a car and tested at Silverstone on 1 August. Cooper entered it for the German GP at the Nürburgring on 6 August, where Brabham drove it to a front-row grid position.

This laughably short development period for a new car/engine combination gives a sense of the hand-to-mouth economics of the British Grand Prix teams of the early 1960s. Seasonal budgets – especially those of Cooper and Lotus – did not run to lengthy gestation periods for innovations. When it was ready it was raced – in this case prematurely, because overheating and water loss plagued the new engine both at the 'Ring and in later entries at Monza and Watkins Glen.

By 1962 the Climax V8 was ready – but so was BRM with a more ambitious V8. In 1963 the Jim Clark/Lotus 25/Climax combination started winning. From then until 1965 the Climax engine won 18 Formula 1 races, of which all but two were to Clark's credit. His world championships in 1963 and 1965 were interrupted only by John Surtees (Ferrari) in 1964. In all 33 Climax V8s were made, plus several development engines kept at the Widdrington Road, Coventry factory.

The ambitions of Climax for its new V8 for the 1961 1½-litre Formula 1 were modest. In contrast to the five-figure rev targets of BRM and Honda, Climax envisioned running its V8 only to 8,500rpm with its nearly square cylinder dimensions of 63 x 60mm (1,496cc). Yet even this unassuming ambition seemed out of reach when the FWMV was first tested in May 1961.

Running initially with two-valve cylinder heads, output was 'much lower than was estimated,' said a dismayed Wally Hassan, Climax technical director. Checking its specification, they found that the inlet port's cross-section had been expanded close to the valve at the last minute, as a result of a suggestion from a gas flow consultant. Restoring the original port profile brought the power back.

Hassan theorised that the widened port acted as a 'pneumatic spring which dissipated the dynamic energy of the column of intake gas' and vitiated the resonant ram effect that was so vital to the power production of an unsupercharged engine.

Power was also absorbed in early tests by excessive churning of oil in the sump, fitted as a magnesium cover at the bottom of a deep-sided crankcase. Initially the sump was lowered two inches to restore this power loss. Climax found that fitting a copper gauze screen under the crankshaft had a beneficial effect, shielding the oil from the whirling crank. Thereafter the sump was lifted back to within ⅜in of its designed position.

Retirements in races in 1961 were traced to the form of block and liner construction used. Desiring to cast the interior of the new engine's block in a simpler manner than it had used for the FPF four, Hassan and his chief designer Peter Windsor-Smith gave up the four's proven liner location, clamped tightly at the top of the block. Instead the iron liner was clamped by the head against a ledge three inches down in the block, with the top of the block being of 'open-deck' design. The seal provided at the cylinder head deteriorated as a result of the differential expansion rates of the iron liner and the aluminium block. The result was fatigue failure for the Cooper sealing ring, and the cooling water was blown right out of the engine.

Over the 1961–62 winter Climax made major changes to solve this problem. An aluminium sleeve was placed in each bore and clamped against the ledge in the block; it expanded at the same rate as the block. Inside the sleeve was a thin iron dry liner with a flange at the top that contacted the sealing ring. The top of each bank of the block was made 'closed-deck' so that the top flange of the liner was precisely positioned when each head was bolted down by its ten studs.

'Probably the Coventry Climax V8 is the most straightforward and simple Grand Prix engine ever

Opposite above: Scotsman Jim Clark was powered to two world championships in 1963 and (as here) 1965 by the Coventry Climax FWMV V8 engine. It was a remarkably simple yet effective power unit.
Opposite below: For the 1965 season Climax made two engines equipped with 4-valve cylinder heads. Jim Clark used one of them to win five races that year while the other was deployed less successfully by the Brabham team. The centre spark-plug location identified the 4-valve head.

produced,' wrote former BRM and Climax engineer Harry Mundy. (Its main rival for this title would be the 1966 Repco-Brabham Type 620.) It was indeed a 'no-frills' engine and none the worse for that. Its designers could and did take advantage of their experience with the twin-cam version of a smaller fire-pump engine, the FWMC, which raced at Le Mans in a Lotus in 1961. This was a 742cc four, essentially half the V8, whose chambers, ports, valves and cam timing made contributions to the GP engine's design.

Notably carried over from the FWMC was the idea of using chains to drive its camshafts. Although chains had been used by Lancia for the D50 and by Ferrari for its Dino engines, this remained an unusual solution for a racing engine. In the FWMV a spur gear pair at the nose of the crank reduced engine speed by half. Driven by it was a jackshaft from which two sprockets drove separate Renold ⅜in single-row chains to each cylinder head. The front of the half-speed gear drove the water pump with its twin outlets. When Lucas fuel injection was fitted for the 1963 season the water

pump was moved forward to make room for an external sprocket to drive a cogged rubber belt to the fuel distributor, placed in the front of the engine's vee.

During 1964 Climax, anticipating hotter competition from BRM and Ferrari, began developing a four-valve version of the engine. To make room for the valves it had already introduced a much more oversquare version of the V8 at 72.4 x 45.5mm (2.85 x 1.79in) for 1,497cc. (An interim version of 67.9 x 51.6mm had been raced in 1963.) With the lighter valves of the four-valve, Climax felt higher speeds could be reached with the same valve-spring stiffness it used with the two-valve. However, it discovered dramatically increased cam-drive loads that even a wider chain couldn't handle. Finally a change was made to a gear cam drive. The narrow spur gears were held by carriers which were adapted to the existing cylinder head castings.

Climax made only two four-valve engines and gave each different valve sizes. One, the Mark VI, had inlet/exhaust valves of 26.4/23.7mm and produced 212bhp at 10,300rpm. This was used by Jim Clark to win five races for Lotus in 1965. The other's valves were 28.1/26.5mm, giving peak power of 213bhp at 10,500rpm but degrading output in the 7,500–8,500rpm band. This Mark VII unit was raced only occasionally by Jack Brabham. The Mark VI gave the best torque of 119lb ft at 8,000rpm. Both engines were safe to 11,000rpm and adequately sparked by the transistorised Lucas ignition system.

In the 4-valve engines the valves had the same inclination as in the 2-valve's, symmetrical at 60°. Wally Hassan concluded that this was too wide for such an engine, requiring as it did a peaked piston to get the needed 12:1 compression ratio. This

peak suppressed swirl and slowed combustion. Considerable effort was needed to get to the outputs mentioned above, which were an advance of only 10bhp on the best 1964 2-valve engine. On the plus side, said Hassan, was the much better airflow of the 4-valve head.

Valve timing was as follows:

Inlet opens 46°BTDC Exhaust opens 57°BBDC
Inlet closes 64°ABDC Exhaust closes 43°ATDC

Inlet and exhaust lifts were 8.4 and 7.9mm respectively. The chill-hardened cast-iron camshafts were carried in five steel-backed babbit bearings, in a detachable aluminium carrier in which the inverted cup-type tappets slid directly. Twin coil springs closed each valve. A 10mm Champion spark plug was at the centre of each combustion chamber surrounded by the valves of

21-4NS steel, which Climax found better than the Nimonic 80 used in the FPF fours.

Carried in Vandervell lead-bronze thin-wall bearings retained by cross-bolted steel main caps, the crankshaft had been of flat or 180° pattern since 1963 to simplify the fitting of scavenging exhaust pipes along each side of the chassis. Its journals measured 50.8mm (2.0in) for the mains and 41.3mm (1.625in) for the rods. The latter were 106.7mm in length and forged; the slim I-section shank was left in the as-forged condition. Internally tapered gudgeon pins (⅝in) were held by circlips in the fully-skirted Mahle forged aluminium pistons. Each piston held two compression rings, the top one a Dykes-type, and one oil ring.

Driven at 0.7 engine speed, the two oil scavenge pumps each had the same capacity as the pressure pump and drew from front and rear sump pickups. All were mounted at the front of the engine. The main castings were of LM8WP aluminium alloy, which contributed to the 4-valve V8's light weight of 298lb (135kg) complete with starter and alternator. It was a happy package which powered both Jim Clark and Lotus to unprecedented success.

Opposite left: A plate covering the front of the Climax V8's crankcase carried its dual-outlet water pump and the oil pumps. Fresh water was supplied directly to manifolds cast integrally with the sides of the cylinder block.
Opposite right: Although the 4-valve engine's combustion chambers were compact, Coventry Climax engineers judged later that a *narrower valve angle would have been more beneficial to turbulence in the fresh charge. While the inlet ports were siamesed, the exhaust ports continued individually to the head face.*
Above: With one head removed the Lucas injection distributor is visible in the centre of the engine's vee. The FWMV's wet cylinder liners and special pistons for the 4-valve head are also on view.

SPECIFICATIONS	
Cylinders	V8
Bore	72.4mm
Stroke	45.5mm
Stroke/bore ratio	0.63:1
Capacity	1,497cc
Compression ratio	12.0:1
Connecting rod length	106.7mm
Rod/crank radius ratio	4.7:1
Main bearing journal diameter	50.8mm
Rod journal diameter	41.3mm
Inlet valve diameter (2 valves)	26.4mm
Exhaust valve diameter (2 valves)	23.7mm
Inlet pressure	1.0Atm
Engine weight	298lb (135kg)
Peak power	212bhp @ 10,300rpm
Piston speed (corrected)	3,879ft/min (19.4m/s)
Peak torque	119lb ft (161Nm) @ 8,000rpm
Peak bmep	197psi
Engine bhp per litre	141.6bhp per litre
Engine weight per bhp	1.41lb (0.64kg) per bhp

1965

HONDA RA272E 1.5-LITRE V12

When it decided to enter Grand Prix racing in the new 1½-litre Formula 1 that took effect in 1961, Japan's Honda typically went very much its own way. Driven by the enthusiasm for motor sports of its founder, Soichiro Honda, the company had rapidly become a major force in the smaller classes of motorcycle racing. In the 1961 Isle of Man TT races its motorcycles swept the top five positions in both 125cc and 250cc classes on their way to world championships. Ready to reach out into the world of automobiles with its S600 and S800 sports cars, Honda found it natural enough to signal the seriousness of its intentions with a Grand Prix car.

Strikingly, the Honda had 12 cylinders. Only Ferrari would also race a 12 during that Formula. Even more strikingly, it was a V12 with its cylinders placed transversely. In this, of course, Honda followed the layout it used for all its motorcycles, including a 250cc in-line six. It was conventional enough in having a vee angle of 60°, giving even firing.

The east-west layout was only feasible because Honda was able to design and build the complete power train as an integrated package. In fact the engine's cam-drive gearing was completely merged with the gearing to the transverse transmission. The drive was taken from a spur gear at the centre of the crankshaft, which effectively made it two short, stiff vee-sixes as far as the crankshaft was concerned. At a reduction of 1.85:1 it drove a short transverse shaft, from which two skew gears drove shafts going downward to the gear-type oil scavenge pumps mounted in the sump.

From the transverse shaft another gear pair drove yet another east-west shaft, this one quite long. It was driven at a further reduction of 1.21:1, so this shaft turned at 44.7 per cent of engine speed. On the right end of this shaft was the multiple-disc clutch that drove the gearbox – two more transverse shafts – at another speed reduction of 1.14:1 through a pair of gears that could easily be changed to adjust the overall ratio.

On the long shaft's left end was the engine's single water pump. The pump had twin outlets, which delivered directly to coolant passages cast into the block and heads. Coolant-outlet nostrils emerged into manifolds which were integral with the magnesium inlet camshaft covers of both cylinder banks. When new covers were cast to alter the supports for the fuel-injection system on the 1965 engine, the opportunity was taken to enlarge and alter the shape of this manifolding. Cooling had presented many problems in 1964.

Near the centre of the long shaft was a spur gear from which a drive progressed up the V12's centre to all four camshafts. A very large idler gear at the centre of each cylinder head drove its two cam gears; the gearing from the long shaft to these idlers established the necessary half-speed ratio for the cams. From the top of the gear at the centre of the rearmost exhaust camshaft another gear drove the fuel-injection distributor that was used for the developed version of the engine, as installed in the 1965 RA272E Honda. It first raced in 1964 as the RA271 with six twin-throat downdraught Keihin carburettors.

Remarkably, the RA272E's cylinder size of 125cc was larger than any that Honda had used in its racing motorcycles. Its dimensions were oversquare but not excessively so, 58.1 x 47.0mm (2.29 x 1.85in) for 1,495cc. The bore was large enough to accommodate a single central 10mm NGK spark plug, two 24mm inlet valves and two 22mm exhaust valves. Valve inclinations from the vertical were 30° for the inlets and 35° for the exhausts. The Honda's was, and has remained, the smallest auto-racing engine cylinder to make use of a four-valve head.

The valves were closed by conventional paired coil springs, shrouded in long-skirted cup-type tappets which slid in bolted-in carriers in the head. The hollow camshaft was made in two pieces and joined together inside its central drive gear. Four narrow needle bearings supported each three-cylinder camshaft. Valve timing at 1mm lift was as follows:

Inlet opens 30°BTDC   Exhaust opens   30°ATDC
Inlet close   40°ABDC   Exhaust closes 30°BBDC

Lift for the inlets and exhausts was respectively 7mm and 6mm.

A single aluminium-alloy casting constituted the

Opposite above: American driver Richie Ginther put his considerable car-development skills at the disposal of Honda in the perfection of its RA272 Formula 1 car. He and Honda were rewarded by victory at the end of 1965 in the final race of the 1½-litre era.
Opposite below: Honda developed its own low-pressure fuel-injection system for the RA272E V12 engine. Transparent plastic hoses delivered fuel to each inlet port just below the slide throttle.

Matching the chamber shape, the pistons had distinct roof peaks which were flattened at the top to provide a compression ratio of 10.5:1. The pistons were fully-skirted, apart from crescent cut-outs for crank counterweight clearance. Deeply ribbed under its crown, each piston carried two thin compression rings and one oil ring. A plain bushing joined the piston to the I-section connecting rod, which was steel and 119mm long.

One single complex aluminium casting, adroitly ribbed for stiffness, constituted both the RA272E's cylinder block and its gearbox and final-drive housing. After the insertion of all the gears and reciprocating parts, its bottom was closed by another large aluminium casting that provided a common sump for the entire unit. This unification meant that no weight could be quoted save for the complete assembly, which was 474lb (215kg).

Each cylinder was an individual wet liner, ribbed around its circumference and sealed at its bottom end by O-rings in grooves in the block. Each liner had a square top which was clamped directly by the head and the 16 studs along each cylinder bank. The three adjoining square tops were machined to fit snugly together. With the insertion of sealing rings in grooves in the square tops, this gave strong and no-nonsense top-end gasketing.

The crankcase casting extended down well past the centreline of the crank, which was carried in seven main bearings. An earlier version of the V12 had an extra bearing flanking the central drive take-off gear, but this was found to be unnecessary. All the bearings were rollers because, as Yoshio Nakamura said, Honda 'found that ball and needle type bearings are always superior in performance to plain-type bearings in high-speed operations – especially when the power required for bearing lubrication is taken into account.' The RA272E bottom end required only low-pressure lubrication to the mains, which then distributed overflow oil to the roller big-ends through slinger rings.

Desiring to keep all bottom-end bearings as small as possible to reduce both friction and mass, Honda varied their diameter. The central main bearing next to the drive gear had a 40mm journal. The next two moving outward were 36mm, the next two 33mm and the outermost mains only 30mm. Uniquely, the connecting-rod journals were dealt with similarly. While the outer four rod

head for each six-cylinder bank. In a unique Honda process the head was cast around chamber 'roofs' made of an aluminium-bronze alloy which bonded to the head material. These formed the complete surface of the pent-roof combustion chamber and provided durable valve seating and spark-plug threading. As in Miller and Meyer-Drake engines, the spark-plug recesses were cast open, then closed later by inserted cups, a construction which allowed maximum control of the casting cores.

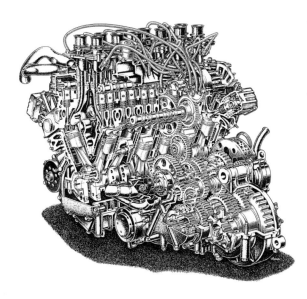

volume required would not exceed that of the head of a safety match. The small low-pressure injection pump delivered fuel to an adjacent distributor block with 12 taps for tiny hoses to jets in the inlet pipes, just below the sliding throttle plates.

Another challenge, that of high-speed ignition, was met by combining a six-coil breaker-type system with a high-tension magneto which came into effect at speeds above 7,000rpm. Nevertheless the Honda offered very little performance below 8,000rpm and was a poor starter both from cold and from the fall of the flag. But its Smiths tachometer, which read from 5,000 to 18,000rpm, was not solely decorative. The engine was fully reliable at 13,000rpm and was red-lined at 14,000. One of its drivers (Ronnie Bucknum) once saw an engine survive being revved to 16,000rpm.

That the engine was peaky was indicated by the 11,000rpm at which it generated its maximum torque of 116lb ft. Output reached 230bhp at 12,000rpm, which just outpowered the flat-12 Ferrari's 220bhp to make the Honda the 1½-litre Formula 1's most potent power unit. It brought Honda and Richie Ginther victory in the Formula's final race at Mexico City at the end of 1965.

journals were 27mm in diameter, the inner pair were 32mm in order to add strength to the crankshaft adjacent to its output gear.

All the bottom-end anti-friction bearings had one-piece outer races, thanks to the use of a built-up crankshaft. The outer races of the main bearings were steel rings fitted with ears via which they were bolted into the crankcase. Twin stiffening ribs ran around the big ends of the one-piece connecting rods. The crank's full counterweights were given additional mass by the insertion, in holes in their faces, of plugs of tungsten alloy. Simple flat cast-magnesium covers enclosed the mechanism at the two ends of the crankcase, which were cast open.

In the RA272E Honda successfully met the challenge of metering petrol into a 125cc cylinder which required, in round figures, a delivery range of from 1 to 8 cubic millimetres per cycle. The largest

Above: A masterful cutaway by Yoshihiro Inomoto discloses the ambitious complexity of the RA273E Honda V12. No smaller racing-car engine cylinder has ever been built using a 4-valve cylinder head.
Opposite top: A V12 Honda engine assembly seen from the underside showed the way in which the power unit was integrated with the

transaxle and final drive. Straight spur gears were used throughout the engine and the transmission.
Opposite below: A narrow gear train reached the centre of each cylinder head to turn the four overhead camshafts of the RA273E Honda engine. Narrow cam lobes attacked individual cup-type tappets for each valve.

SPECIFICATIONS	
Cylinders	V12
Bore	58.1mm
Stroke	47.0mm
Stroke/bore ratio	0.81:1
Capacity	1,495cc
Compression ratio	10.5:1
Connecting rod length	119.0mm
Rod/crank radius ratio	5.1:1
Main bearing journal diameter	36.0mm
Rod journal diameter	27.0mm
Inlet valve diameter (2 valves)	24.0mm
Exhaust valve diameter (2 valves)	22.0mm
Inlet pressure	1.0:1
Engine weight	474lb (215kg)*
Peak power	230bhp @ 12,000rpm
Piston speed (corrected)	4,115ft/min (20.6m/s)
Peak torque	116lb ft (157Nm) @ 11,000rpm
Peak bmep	192psi
Engine bhp per litre	153.8bhp per litre
Engine weight per bhp	2.06lb (0.94kg) per bhp
*Engine and transaxle combined.	

1966

REPCO-BRABHAM 620 3-LITRE V8

All the British racing-car builders except BRM were given furiously to think about possible engine sources for the new 1966 3-litre Formula 1. Coventry Climax, on whom they all relied, had decided not to continue. For a solution Jack Brabham turned to his home country, Australia.

Australia's Repco was one of the nation's major manufacturers of automotive parts and workshop equipment. One of its units, the Engine Parts Group under Bob Brown, had made redesigned and improved replacement parts for the 2.5-litre Climax FPF fours (qv) that were being raced in Australia and New Zealand under the Tasman Formula. Key players in this project were Engine Parts' chief engineer Frank Hallam and laboratory manager Stan Johnson.

Impressed by the work that Repco had done on the Climax engines that he had used to win Tasman races, Jack Brabham conceived a plan. If he could provide a basis – a cylinder block, say – he might persuade Repco to design and build an engine around it. 'I had been up to Japan and had a look at aluminium blocks,' he said. 'And then I went to America and decided that the best block to use was the F85 Oldsmobile.' In a fit of brave innovation, GM had introduced aluminium engines in 1961 for its Buick Special and Olds F85. Though the engines were no longer in production, the blocks were readily available.

Having first conferred with Hallam to confirm feasibility, Jack Brabham sold the project to Bob Brown on the grounds that it would bring global publicity to Repco at a time when it was seeking to expand outside Australia. Brown in turn successfully presented the idea to the Repco board. They authorised Engine Parts and its parent in the group, Russell Manufacturing, to spend £10,000 on building Jack's engine.

A talented engineer, Ross Kirkham, joined the team as project manager. Much of the machining in Australia was done by the skilled Peter Hollinger. And to assist in the V8's design they engaged as a consultant and draftsman Phil Irving, who had contributed to the successful Vincent motorcycles and was well-connected in the UK, where he went early in 1964 to draw the engine in close consultation with Brabham.

Jack's suggestion of the GM block as a basis was accepted. They opted for the Oldsmobile F85 block of the 1961–63 era with a six-stud pattern around each cylinder. This was the core of the Repco-Brabham Type 620 V8 – RB 620 for short. In the Repco numbering system '600' stood for the block and '20' for the cylinder head; their aim was to have interchangeability as their designs progressed.

Like the Oldsmobile engine on which it was based, the RB 620 required only one LM23WP aluminium cylinder head casting which was machined differently to suit both banks. Hidural 5, a copper alloy, was used for the valve guides. The centre portion of the exhaust-valve guide was finned and exposed to the flow of water after the Climax FPF model. Coolant entered from manifolds along the sides, which directed the water to the heads and left the cylinders to seek their own coolant through a few ports in the block/head interface.

Repco's search for a straight-forward engine concept was encouraged by the excellent performance of Cosworth's single-cam SCA four in Formula 2 racing. Although the SCA had two vertical valves set into a flat cylinder head, Irving and Brabham placed the valves in a plane inclined inward at 10° from the vertical, in order to make the engine narrower to reduce frontal area. The inclination required the head to have a shallow wedge-type combustion chamber into which austenitic cast-iron valve-seat inserts were shrunk.

Opposite above: Jack Brabham took the world of Formula 1 by storm in 1966 with his new V8 engine, built with the help of Repco in Australia. He took a practical approach to the new 3-litre Formula 1 and was rewarded with yet another world championship.

Opposite below: Atop the Type 620 engine as installed in the neat tube-framed Brabham chassis were the inlet ram pipes fed by Lucas fuel injection above the slide-type throttles. Ignition was by Lucas coil and distributor.

Valve sizes were 1.625in (41.3mm) for the inlets and 1.375in (34.9mm) for the exhausts. Valve gear was conventional, using chilled cast-iron cup-type tappets the same diameter as the exhaust valves and sliding directly in the head material. Dual coil valve springs exerted 220lb (100kg) pressure at the maximum lift of 0.40in (10.2mm).

No separate tappet block or cam carrier was needed for Irving's compact design. Each camshaft rested in five bearings in the head, which had bearing inserts only in the removable caps. Oil entered the hollow camshaft through its frontmost bearing and was distributed internally to its sisters. Cam timing was based on that of the SCA

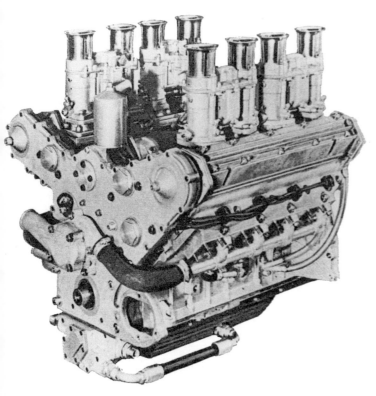

Cosworth which had inspired the cylinder head. Finned magnesium covers enclosed the cams.

Attached to the front of the Olds block was a two-piece magnesium timing case containing a two-stage Renold roller-chain camshaft drive of ⅜in pitch. The first stage was a double-roller chain from the nose of the crank to a half-speed sprocket, which drove a jackshaft positioned where the central camshaft for the pushrods used to be. From the nose of this jackshaft the water pump, just outside the timing case, was positively driven. The half-speed jackshaft drove the second stage of the chain system, a single-roller chain passing around a camshaft sprocket on the left bank, then below a centrally-mounted adjuster sprocket and back to the jackshaft. The longest unsupported length of chain was only eight inches.

The Olds cylinder block was suitably modified to undertake its new duties. In its central vee unneeded metal was machined away and the vee sealed by an aluminium plate which was Araldited in place. The 3-litre GP engine used the standard Olds F85 bore of 3.50in (88.9mm) with a stroke of 2.375in (60.3mm) for 2,996cc. It thus relied on the standard dry cast-iron cylinder liner, which was

cast in place in the aluminium block and retained by external corrugations.

The block was re-machined to take more appropriate crankshaft oil seals, and two studs replaced bolts for each of the main bearing caps. The studs were long enough to allow the corresponding nuts to secure a 5mm ladder-shaped plate of Duralumin that was affixed to the bottom of the block, which extended down well past the crank centreline. This plate, a design contribution by Jack Brabham that mirrored a similar modification he had made to the 2.2-litre Climax FPF, stabilised and stiffened the bottom end, as did the addition of a finned cast-magnesium sump.

An initial attempt to use an inertia-sensitive oil scavenge pickup misfired and a more conventional racing oil-pump array was installed. Bolted to the underside of the stiffener plate, the pumps were gear-driven from the crank nose. Pressure was maintained at a regulated 75psi and oil was delivered to the main bearings by a gallery in the cylinder block. Protective devices included a full-flow oil filter, a gauze screen covering the dry sump and large magnetic plugs in both the scavenge and pressure circuits.

A single-plane or 180° crankshaft facilitated the easiest (and most effective) exhaust manifolding because each bank could be treated like a four-cylinder engine. Jack Brabham was also amply familiar with its satisfactory performance in the post-1963 Climax FWMV V8 (qv). The fully counterweighted cranks were machined from a solid billet of EN40 steel in the classic manner by Laystall in England.

Die-cast aluminium pistons were slipper-type and had flat tops except for two shallow valve-clearance pockets; the compression ratio was 11:1. Three rings were fitted: a torsional plain iron compression ring, a multi-seal ring and a chrome-plated segmental oil ring. Gudgeon pins of 0.875in (22.2mm) were retained by circlips and the complete piston/pin assembly weighed 18 ounces (510 grams).

For connecting rods Brabham and Repco hit on the forged-steel I-section rods from the 4.5-litre British Daimler V8. This had the same big-end journal diameter as the Olds at 2.0in (50.8mm) but had a wider bearing, at 0.875 against 0.737in (22.2 vs 18.7mm). The Daimler rods were also longer, at 160mm centre-to-centre versus 144mm (6.3 vs 5.7in) for the original Buick-Olds V8.

Main-bearing diameter was 2.3in (58.4mm). For the inserts the builders could call on the Repco Bearing Co., which supplied its R77 copper-lead matrix overlaid by babbit on a steel backing. Following Climax practice, the crankshaft was drilled end-to-end with oil passages to ensure uninterrupted delivery to the rod journals.

Ancillary systems included Lucas electronic ignition and – thanks to Jack Brabham's persuasive powers – Lucas fuel injection, with its nozzles placed above the slide-type throttles. These added weight to the core engine, which scaled 300lb (136kg) without its flywheel. The first RB 620 roared into life on the dynamometer at the Repco plant at Richmond in Victoria, Australia on 21 March 1965. Quite soon it was developing 285bhp at 7,500rpm. The highest power used for racing in 1966 was 298bhp, although a development V8 showed 311bhp.

It is a matter of history that for the Grand Prix of South Africa on 1 January 1966 Brabham chief engineer Ron Tauranac installed an RB 620 engine in an existing BT19 chassis and that Jack led the race from pole position before the fuel-injection unit broke. It is further irrefutable that with this audacious engine Brabham won the French GP on 3 July to score the first-ever victory for a driver in a car bearing his own name, and that he went on to win the 1966 world championship, his third. Truth, as they say, is stranger than fiction.

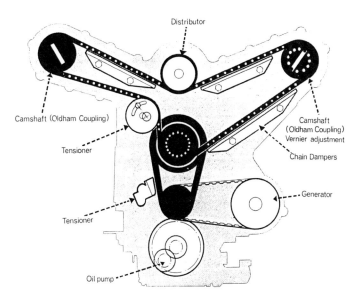

Above: With only a single overhead cam for each cylinder bank draughtsman Phil Irving had little difficulty in arranging a two-stage roller chain camshaft drive. With an efficient adjustable tensioner and chain dampers, this performed well.

Opposite left: A compact and effective unit, the Repco-Brabham 620 was also offered with Weber carburettors for sports-car racing. The front-mounted water pump fed manifolds to the block along each side.

Opposite right: The cylinder block on the left shows the way in which the valley passages of the original Oldsmobile aluminium block, on the right, were machined away and covered by a plate glued in position. A magnesium casting provided the dry sump.

SPECIFICATIONS	
Cylinders	V8
Bore	88.9mm
Stroke	60.3mm
Stroke/bore ratio	0.68:1
Capacity	2,996cc
Compression ratio	11.0:1
Connecting rod length	160.0mm
Rod/crank radius ratio	5.3:1
Main bearing journal diameter	58.4mm
Rod journal diameter	50.8mm
Inlet valve diameter (1 valve)	41.3mm
Exhaust valve diameter (1 valve)	34.9mm
Inlet pressure	1.0:1
Engine weight	300lb (136kg)
Peak power	298bhp @ 7,500rpm
Piston speed (corrected)	3,603ft/min (18.0m/s)
Engine bhp per litre	99.5bhp per litre
Engine weight per bhp	1.01lb (0.46kg) per bhp

1966

BRM P75 3-LITRE H16

After its world-championship year of 1962 and good performances in the subsequent years, BRM was once again in the good books of Sir Alfred Owen and his Owen Organisation. BRM's staff at Bourne in Lincolnshire were given the green light to plan new cars for the 1966 3-litre Formula 1. In charge of the effort was Tony Rudd, who had succeeded Peter Berthon as BRM's technical director. Chief engine designer was Geoff Johnson.

Although a 12-cylinder engine was considered, Rudd's choice fell on a radical 16-cylinder engine composed of two horizontally-opposed eights placed one atop the other and geared together. Estimates were that it would weigh 380lb (173kg) and produce 500bhp – figures which, in the event, were destined to be interchanged.

Rudd's reasoning was that the H16 could use the proven and effective porting, valve gear, combustion chamber, piston, connecting rod and cylinder liner from the successful 1½-litre V8. In the last V8s the inlet ports had been resited between the camshafts to flow down from the top of the cylinder head, so they were at the sides of the H16. The exhaust ports were at the top and bottom of the engine.

The initial plan was to place one flat-eight atop the other in such a way that they would share a single inlet camshaft along each side. However, a need for increased clearance between the crankshafts blocked this scheme. If a single inlet camshaft had performed double duty it would have forced an angle between the valve stems that was excessively large.

In fact, Rudd and Johnson then chose narrower valve angles than those of the V8, 23° for the inlets and 29° for the exhausts, which required a slightly larger bore to accommodate the valve heads. The H16's cylinder dimensions were 69.85 x 48.89mm (2.75 x 1.92in), compared to 68.5 x 50.8mm for the V8. With this move the interchangeability of pistons and liners with the V8 was forfeited, and weight rose with eight instead of six camshafts. Each side of the engine was capped by a single aluminium-alloy head – a fantastically intricate casting.

Weight rose further with the inclusion of some features in the bottom-end design that made the 16 easier to assemble. Akin to a nearly square box cast of LM8 aluminium alloy, the crankcase was split vertically 2½in (63.5mm) to the left side of its centreline to permit both crankshafts to be installed in the right-hand or primary half with separate caps for the five 2.25in (57.2mm) main bearings. Then the smaller secondary half of the crankcase was attached with separate through-bolts.

The two cranks were geared together by a separate pack of three 19mm-wide spur gears at the rear of the engine, mounted in ball and roller bearings. The roller bearings were inset into the rear panel of the crankcase and the ball bearings were carried by a separate bolted-on magnesium housing. Each crankshaft was connected to its gear by a short splined torsion shaft. Made of EN40 steel, the cranks were initially of simple flat four-cylinder design with side-by-side 115.6mm connecting rods on a common journal, located at 90° to each other by the output gearing. Two cylinders fired together in the upper eight cylinders, then two in the bottom eight 90° later.

All eight camshafts were driven from the nose of the lower crankshaft only. The two-stage gear packs originally created for the V16 drove the lower camshafts from their crank. The gear on the lower inlet camshaft drove the upper inlet cam and, through an idler gear, the upper exhaust camshaft. This introduced a long gear train between the lower crank and the topmost camshaft and an even longer train from the upper crankshaft, which was linked to the lower shaft by the output gear pack.

The Lucas transistor ignition trigger and its distributors for the whole engine were driven directly from the front of the upper crankshaft at half engine speed. Two water pumps, each powering a completely independent circulation and radiator system for its head, and two fuel-injection metering units were driven from intermediate valve-train gears at the front of the H16. The oil pressure and scavenge pumps were gear-driven

Opposite above: Although Jackie Stewart enjoyed some good races with his H16-powered BRM he was never able to better his second place at Spa in 1967 when problems with his car dropped him behind Dan Gurney at the finish. The engine was an ambitious effort that seldom threatened to deliver on its great promise.

Opposite below: Each side of the P75 engine had its own Lucas fuel-injection distributor, placed between the pairs of inlet pipes and driven by a cogged rubber belt. Asbestos lagging sought to protect the engine's warm-water exit from the heat of the adjacent exhaust pipes.

from the lower crank. Small pumps driven by the lower exhaust camshafts scavenged the lower camboxes.

'Please do not expect too much too soon,' cautioned Sir Alfred Owen at the unveiling of the new BRM engine and car at Bourne on 22 April 1966. The new H16 was also to be supplied to Team Lotus for its Grand Prix cars and, in a special 4.2-litre version, for a 1966 Indianapolis effort.

In its initial tests the engine displayed an awe-inspiring repertoire of failure modes. The cogged rubber drive belts to the Lucas fuel-metering units broke, as did the lower inlet camshaft where its drive gear was attached. Outrigger bearings were made for these, and flywheels were put on the drives to the metering units to damp their torsional vibrations. Gear and centre bearing failures in the output train between the crankshafts inevitably had expensive results, with the upper crankshaft's valves being timed from the lower crank nose.

Severe torsional vibrations affected the output gear train's centre gear and bearings, which received twisting impacts from both crankshafts at alternating intervals and in opposite directions. As a palliative the mass of four of the crank counterweights was increased by 2lb (0.9kg) apiece by bolting and welding a steel inertia ring to each one. 'This modification, crude though it was, proved effective,' recalled Tony Rudd, 'and it was then possible to install the engine in a car.'

It was also possible to obtain meaningful power figures for the first time. The highest output ever measured by BRM from its H16 was recorded in June 1966 from engine No 7504, a unit destined for delivery to Lotus. It returned 400bhp at 10,500rpm. In the first year of the 3-litre Formula 1, that was a lot of horsepower.

Taken along by BRM as a spare to Watkins Glen late in 1966 was engine No 7502, a heavily salvaged unit with metal plates and patches of Araldite holding its crankcase together. Giving 375bhp, this was rushed into service at the last minute in Jim Clark's Lotus and survived to win the United States Grand Prix – the only victory ever credited to the H16.

Over the 1966–67 winter intense development attention was given to the H16's many problems. A new steel/steel materials combination stopped excessive wear of the camshafts and tappets. Overheating was tackled by fitting a circulation system that prevented vapour locks in the complex heads from stalling the water pumps. Connecting-rod cracks were intercepted and cylinder-head stud failures were overcome, as was piston-ring breakage.

A major change allowed the H16 to run as a sequential 16, with one cylinder firing every 45° of output shaft rotation. This required new crankshafts with eight individual throws to give a firing order that allowed tuned scavenging exhaust pipes to be used. For these 'eight-pin' Mark 2 engines the diameter of the big-end journal was increased from 1.50in (38.1mm) to 1.875in (47.6mm) to enlarge the area of overlap between the main and rod journals. New crankcase castings were also needed because the offset between facing banks of cylinders had to be increased from 0.65 to 1.05in to accommodate the required counterbalances, and new connecting rods were required. The weight of the Mark 2 engine rose to no less than 520lb (236kg), but its output showed no advance on the typical level of 380bhp.

In spite of all these improvements the Mark 2 Type 75 was still prone to occasional catastrophic failure. Valve breakage was identified as the culprit. The torsional flexibility allowed by the camshafts and their drive gears permitted the valve timing to drift enough to allow the valves to touch during overlap. Eventually a head broke off, usually the inlet valve. The piston hammered the loose valve head against the cylinder head, buckling the connecting rod and shattering the cast-iron cylinder liner. Steel liners were fitted; they were better able to contain the damage. A slight reduction in valve sizes and closer attention to valve timing cured this fault that had wrecked so many engines.

The last race entry by the BRM H16 was in the first event of 1968, the South African GP, in which Mike Spence retired after eight laps. As part of a complete BRM car, the engine had done no better during its career than a second place at Spa in the Belgian GP in 1967, with Jackie Stewart at the wheel. After its initial tests the 4.2-litre Indy H16 engine posed so many problems that it had to be abandoned.

It is an incredible but documented fact of motor racing history that a single organisation, BRM, suffered two total debacles in its flirtation with the undeniably-attractive 16-cylinder racing engine. The first 16 (*qv*) was built and run against all the financial odds; the second 16 was possible only because there were few constraints on finance. Both carried flaws of design and execution that kept them from developing their projected power and endowed them with a formidable capacity for self-destruction.

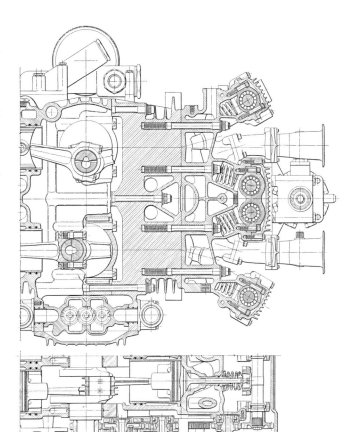

Opposite left: Viewed from the front the BRM P75 H16 was a formidable mass of machinery. Each side of the engine was supplied by its own water pump. At top centre is the disc triggering the Lucas electronic ignition.
Opposite right: For the 1967 season the H16 was converted to run as a sequential sixteen by giving it new eight-pin crankshafts. Each rod had its own individual crank journal.

This proved, in the event, to offer no improvement in performance or reliability over the previous configuration.
Above: Sections of elements of the H16 show the roller camshaft bearings carried over from the V8, the triple-gear scavenge pump within the sump and the slipper-type pistons, also reflecting successful V8 practice. In this configuration the connecting rods of facing cylinders shared a crankshaft journal.

SPECIFICATIONS

Cylinders	H16
Bore	69.85mm
Stroke	48.89mm
Stroke/bore ratio	0.70:1
Capacity	2,998cc
Compression ratio	10.5:1
Connecting rod length	115.6mm
Rod/crank radius ratio	4.7:1
Main bearing journal diameter	57.2mm
Rod journal diameter	47.6mm
Inlet valve diameter (1 valve)	39.7mm
Exhaust valve diameter (1 valve)	30.5mm
Inlet pressure	1.0Atm
Engine weight	520lb (236kg)
Peak power	380bhp @ 10,500rpm
Piston speed (corrected)	4,026ft/min (20.1m/s)
Engine bhp per litre	126.8bhp per litre
Engine weight per bhp	1.37lb (0.62kg) per bhp

1967

BMW M10 2-LITRE FOUR

In 1966 BMW astonished the racing world with its disclosure of a completely new engine concept that promised exceptional performance. The Austrian engineer who developed the new engine, Ludwig Apfelbeck, had been quietly but effectively beavering away in BMW's engine labs since he joined the Munich firm in 1957 at the age of 54. Gradually he had gained acceptance for a pet idea.

His notion was that a pure hemispherical combustion chamber with radial valves could offer an optimum in both breathing and combustion. A conventional hemispherical chamber with two inclined valves comes close to the optimum shape. But Apfelbeck's idea was to add two more inclined valves in a plane rotated 90° to the first two valves, so that in plan view the valve stems pointed to all four points of the compass.

This was not wholly new. Among motorcycle makers the layout had been tried by several, including Rudge. Ludwig Apfelbeck added a new twist. Instead of pairing like valves side-by-side he placed them diametrically opposite each other in what he thus named his 'diametral' combustion chamber. The inlet valves faced each other and the exhausts likewise. Among the advantages he saw for this were the cooling afforded to the exhaust valve seats by the adjacent inlets, and the very effective scavenging of exhaust gas from the chamber by the incoming fresh gases.

With a plan for such a head on a four-cylinder block and excellent gas-flow results from bench testing, Apfelbeck convinced BMW's technical chief, Klaus von Rücker, of the merits of his idea. Von Rücker gave the green light to the creation of a head to be tested on a single-cylinder lab engine. This gave such good results – 64½ horsepower from a 500cc cylinder – that BMW commissioned the building of a diametral head to fit on the iron cylinder block of its standard 2-litre four-cylinder passenger-car engine. Within cylinder centre distances of 100mm (3.94in) this provided 89mm (3.50in) bores. Combined with an 80mm (3.15in) stroke its swept volume was 1,991cc.

The work was done with the support of BMW's outstanding and experienced engine team: Alex von Falkenhausen in overall charge, Paul Rosche dealing with the engine's bottom end and Otto Stulle coping with development. By 1966 the M10 engine, as it was designated, was ready for testing. 'Right from the start, in a manner of speaking,' related Apfelbeck, 'the engine reached 264bhp on gasoline and indeed 310bhp on racing fuel' – methanol with a dash of nitromethane. The output on gasoline was equivalent to 133bhp per litre – even better than the test engine.

What to do with such an engine? BMW used it with racing fuel in a Brabham single-seater chassis in December 1966 to break some international 2-litre-class standing-start records. It was also fielded by the works in a Lola sports-racing chassis in the European hillclimb championship, for which this was the maximum displacement allowed. The BMW-Lola placed fourth in the championship in 1967 and second in '68.

All this was achieved with an engine that used the cast-iron cylinder block of the standard BMW 2000ti touring car. The block extended well down past the crankshaft centreline, enhancing the stiffness of the bottom end. The caps for the five main bearings were specially prepared but were retained, as standard, by two cap screws. The required bottom-end strength was provided by the fully counterweighted crankshaft, which resembled the standard part but was forged of a special steel and machined to suit this application.

I-section connecting rods were 135mm long, centre to centre, and made of titanium.

Opposite above: Using Lola chassis, BMW entered single-seater Formula racing for the first time in 1967, powered by its unique radial-valve M10 engine. From a difficult beginning BMW would eventually become supreme in Formula 2 racing.

Opposite below: As revised for the 1967 Formula 2 season in 1.6-litre form the M10 had shorter inlet ram pipes with slide throttles and fuel injection. The left-hand camshaft drove the injection pump while the cam on the right turned the ignition distributor. A large hose returned engine oil from the head to the sump.

Their weight of 440 grams usefully undercut the 550 grams of steel rods. Each rod small end and gudgeon pin engaged a piston forged by Mahle. This was of slipper-type design and carried two rings – a pressure-backed Dykes-type ring and an oil control ring. Although basically crowned, the top of the piston was pockmarked by four craters corresponding to the positions of the radially-positioned valves, providing the required clearance at and near top dead centre.

The standard BMW engine had a single overhead camshaft that was driven by a chain from the nose of the crankshaft. Under a special aluminium front cover the racing version varied this format. A

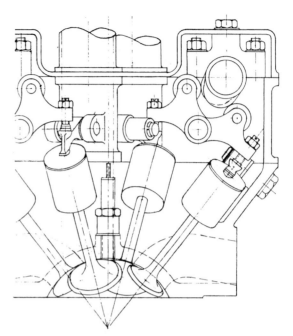

small spur gear on the crank nose turned a half-speed gear that was above and slightly to the left of it. A sprocket coaxial with this gear drove a double-roller chain that extended up to the engine's twin overhead camshafts. This was in tension on the right side of the engine, where it was paralleled by an anti-flutter guide. The chain was tensioned by an adjustable idler sprocket on its slack left side.

The half-speed gear mated with another spur gear, to the left and downward, which turned a gang of two gear-type oil scavenge pumps. These drew from the shallow dry sump, which on the 2-litre engines was formed of light-alloy sheet. A pressure pump delivered Castrol lubricant through the block's integral passages and, through an external hose on the left, to oilways inside the camshafts that released it onto the cam lobe surfaces. A pulley on the crank nose drove a vee belt to a water pump mounted on the right side of the timing chest. This delivered coolant to the left rear of the cylinder block's water jacket. Warm water was withdrawn from the rear of the cylinder head.

Ludwig Apfelbeck worked miracles, in the pre-computer-aided-design era, in devising a way for two overhead cams to operate his radially-disposed valves. Broadly speaking the exhaust valves were at the sides of the chambers and the inlets disposed between them. In their respective planes, the inlet valves were at an included angle of 54° and the exhaust valves at a 62° included angle; these angles were compatible with the hemispherical combustion chamber and with the associated valve ports as well.

The inlet valves could not simply be in the longitudinal plane of the head; their stems would clash. So the complete chamber was rotated by 21° clockwise in plan view so that the inlet stems would parallel each other instead of conflicting. The exhaust ports still made quick exits from both sides of the head; each side had its own tuned exhaust manifold.

The only solution for the inlet ports was to bring them down from the top of the head. This was a happy echo of BMW's 328 six, which also had downdraught inlet ports. The ports rose to the flat plane of the top of the head. Between them were the smaller apertures for the 12mm spark plugs, which were at the very centre of each chamber. Apfelbeck's design provided for very large 42mm inlet valves and 34mm exhaust valves. Inlet valve lift was 11mm and the open duration was 324°. Conventional dual coil springs closed each valve.

Then there was the matter of the valve gear. How were these 16 radial valves to be operated? Apfelbeck made it look easy. Contacting the stem of each valve was a short finger, pivoted to swing in the plane of the valve. Atop the end of the finger was a cup. Into this cup fitted the spherical end of the screw-adjustable tip of a roller-faced follower that swung from a pivot shaft below and inboard of each camshaft. The roller follower transmitted the cam's motion and the finger translated that motion into the plane of the valve.

The screw adjusters for the running clearances of the inlet valves were easily accessible from the top of the head, but those for the exhaust valves had to be reached through square ports in the sides of the head. These were covered by a rectangular plate along each side. The camshafts ran directly in the aluminium of their five bearings in the cylinder head.

The M10's head was a single complex casting right up to the centrelines of the camshafts. A cast light-alloy cover enclosed these and the valve gear and provided a base and mounting for the eight separate downdraught carburettors that were initially fitted to the 2-litre engine. Each was a Solex 40 PJTC unit with a 40mm throat. Instead of a float chamber each Solex contained a weir which was supplied by one fuel pump and was scavenged, at the proper level, by another pump. To improve throttle response one row of carburettors opened initially. At one-third throttle on that bank the other row began to open, gradually catching up with the first row.

By the time the M10 was used in hillclimb competition its carburettors had been replaced by much more wieldy Lucas fuel injection, with separate slide throttles and short ram pipes for each row of inlet ports. Running with a 10.5:1 compression ratio the 329lb (145kg) M10 was ultimately developed to produce 280bhp at 8,800rpm on gasoline. Its maximum torque of 174lb ft was reached at 8,000rpm but torque was at 160lb ft or better between 6,200 and 8,500rpm.

An attempt to reduce the M10 four to the 1.6-litre size of the new Formula 2 for 1967 was less successful and led to unfortunate schisms between Apfelbeck and his BMW colleagues. Nevertheless in Lola chassis this engine introduced BMW to single-seater racing, a field in which it continues to make strong contributions.

Opposite left: In its original 2-litre configuration the M10 engine designed by Ludwig Apfelbeck and Paul Rosche was fed by eight individual Solex carburettors. It was powerful enough to break international standing-start records in the 2-litre category.
Opposite right: A drawing by Ludwig Apfelbeck shows the principle of the valve gear used in the BMW M10 engine. Each valve was opened *by a pivoted finger which in turn was pressed down by a roller-tipped finger riding against the cam lobe. Geometrically it was sound but dynamically the valve gear had its shortcomings.*
Above: Through the top of an M10 cylinder head two individual inlet ports descended to the valves. Between them was the aperture for the spark plugs. The roller cam followers may also be seen.

SPECIFICATIONS	
Cylinders	I4
Bore	89.0mm
Stroke	80.0mm
Stroke/bore ratio	0.90:1
Capacity	1,991cc
Compression ratio	10.5:1
Connecting rod length	135.0mm
Rod/crank radius ratio	3.4:1
Main bearing journal diameter	55.0mm
Rod journal diameter	47.0mm
Inlet valve diameter (2 valves)	42.0mm
Exhaust valve diameter (2 valves)	34.0mm
Inlet pressure	1.0:1
Engine weight	320lb (145kg)
Peak power	280bhp @ 8,800rpm
Piston speed (corrected)	4,872ft/min (24.4m/s)
Peak torque	174lb ft (236Nm)
	@ 8,000rpm
Peak bmep	217psi
Engine bhp per litre	140.6bhp per litre
Engine weight per bhp	1.14lb (0.51kg) per bhp

1967

GURNEY-WESLAKE 58 3-LITRE V12

'We were a bit naughty even attempting it in the first place,' Dan Gurney said later. 'We'd got the minimum of backing in every area. I just felt it was an opportunity, as slim as the chances were, that I had to take.' Gurney was referring to the commitment of his new company, All American Racers (AAR), to a Grand Prix campaign. Founded with the backing of Goodyear to make its tyres more competitive at Indianapolis, AAR was only grudgingly allowed to mount a Formula 1 campaign as well.

Scantily resourced though it was, the AAR GP effort of 1966–68 never looked less than professional. Len Terry's Lotus-inspired chassis design proved equally suited to both Indy racing and GP road courses. When the Eagle was married with its Weslake-built V12 engine, agreement was widespread that it was one of the handsomest Formula 1 cars ever constructed.

Known more for its expertise in gas-flow management than for engine manufacture, Harry Weslake's establishment on England's south coast at Rye was not an obvious candidate to build a new Grand Prix engine. It did, however, have the services of a refugee from BRM, designer Frank Aubrey Woods, and a promising parallel-twin research engine built under a research contract with Shell. This ran initially in 355cc form and later, in the summer of 1965, as a 500cc twin – one-sixth of a 3-litre V12. 'The 500cc twin was making 76 horsepower,' Dan Gurney recalled, 'which times six is something like 450 horsepower. Nobody was making that kind of power at that time.'

The link between Weslake and Gurney was Woods, who became well acquainted with the American driver when he raced for BRM in 1960. Weslake and his team had carried out some successful work for AAR on special cylinder heads for the Ford V8, the Gurney-Weslake heads that won Le Mans in 1968 and '69 in GT40 Fords. Gurney liked the V12 engine concept and the price was right. In August, Woods started work on the final design and in October 1965 AAR contracted with Weslake for six engines. The V12 was named 'Gurney-Weslake', although as its complete sponsor Dan was not obliged to credit Weslake.

Visitors to the AAR pits at Monza during the Italian Grand Prix on 4 September 1966 were astonished by their first sight of the V12's small size and apparent simplicity. They were gaining a glimpse of the future; this was the first racing engine to embody top-end design features that would be commonplace a decade later. Its four valves per cylinder were at a narrow included angle (30°) that allowed a single cover to enclose both close-spaced camshafts on each bank. This would later be thought of as a Cosworth characteristic, but it first appeared on the track on Weslake's Type 58 engine for AAR.

Of the classical 60°-vee layout, the twelve was oversquare with cylinder dimensions of 72.8 x 60mm (2.87 x 2.36in) for 2,997cc, but the differential between bore and stroke was not so extreme as was then widely propounded. Harry Weslake's aim, validated by the 500-cc test engine results, was to maintain good power and torque over a wide speed range with a compact combustion chamber and judiciously-sized ports, not too small to be restrictive but small enough to keep gas speeds up to maintain an inertial ram effect. Similar dimensions (73.3 x 59.2mm) had worked well in a 2-litre BRM V8 engine, a later expansion of the P56 V8 (qv) with which Aubrey Woods was intimately familiar.

In its mechanical design the V12 was redolent of the techniques used successfully at BRM on the P56 and the 2-litre unit developed from it. The aluminium alloy crankcase was the same, with seven instead of five main bearings, its ribbed sides extending down well past the crank centreline and embracing close-fitting two-bolt bearing caps. As in the BRM, only the rear main cap was cross-bolted.

Also identical to the BRM was the cylinder design, with thin-wall centrifugally cast-iron wet liners held in place by a top flange nipped between the cylinder head and the closed top face of the block. A Cooper ring provided the fire seal around each combustion chamber. The fully machined titanium I-section connecting rods were the same length (124mm) and design as those used by the 2-litre BRM V8. The forged aluminium piston's mechanical design below the crown was also

Opposite above: In a wet Canadian Grand Prix in 1967 Dan Gurney finished third in his Eagle powered by the Gurney-Weslake V12. In that season he scored two victories, one of them in a world championship Grand Prix.

Opposite below: Having taken over from Weslake the manufacture of his engines, Dan Gurney renamed the unit the Eagle Mark 1A. This was made ready for installation in a new Eagle chassis for the 1969 season but finances were insufficient to allow that programme to proceed.

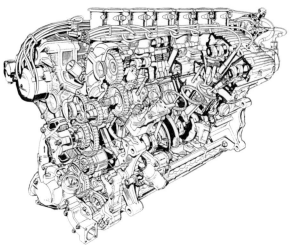

the same, with narrow slipper skirts and only two rings – a Dykes-type compression ring and an Apex oil ring.

Laystall manufactured the steel crankshaft with its nitrided bearing surfaces. It was counter-weighted but not excessively so, Woods wishing to keep its weight and inertia down. Main bearings measured 2.375in (60.3mm) and the rod journal diameter was a modest 1.625in (41.3mm) to help keep the connecting rod weight to only 320 grams, 7/10ths of a pound. Diameter of the floating gudgeon pin was 0.75in (19.1mm). Both Clevite and Vandervell were suppliers of the plain bottom-end bearings.

At the top end, the valve-gear details – apart from the use of four valves per cylinder – were pure BRM in all these respects: dual Terry coil springs, small cup-type tappets placed above the springs, a bolted-in ferrous carrier for each tappet, and camshaft support by seven crowded-roller bearings, each in a steel carrier that also formed the outer race, held down by two cap screws. Small galleries provided low-pressure oil directly to the tappets; the overflow from this was splashed by the cam lobes onto the roller bearings. A departure from BRM methods was Woods's design of the aluminium cylinder-head casting to suit both banks of the vee to make manufacturing and servicing easier.

Valve sizes were 1.20 and 0.985in (30.5 and 25.0mm) for the austenitic steel inlets and Nimonic alloy exhausts respectively. In the same order the valve lifts were 0.375 and 0.312in (9.5 and 7.9mm). Short stub manifolds down the centre of the vee joined each cylinder's separate inlet ports together to a single throat that was fed fuel by a Lucas injector nozzle located beneath the slide throttles.

The camshafts were driven by a train of gears carried by a separate split magnesium casing at the front of the engine, a design feature that Woods admitted adopting from the Ford Indianapolis V8 engine. By making this case separate, he could allow the crankcase to add more stiffness to the rear of the monocoque frame, to which it was attached by four mounting points along each side.

Gears below the crankshaft nose drove the water pump, which had twin outlets feeding galleries at the sides of the block. Metering holes delivered water to the liners and the heads, from which it was withdrawn by manifolds on the inlet sides. Next to the water pump was the oil pressure pump, which fed the engine through two remotely-mounted oil filters. Carried within the crankcase, the scavenge pump for the dry-sump system was of three-gear design to double its capacity. A shallow magnesium sump closed the bottom end.

From the timing gears other accessories were powered: the alternator and the two Lucas ignition distributors firing the Champion 10mm spark plugs. Woods originally intended to put more accessories at the front, but he moved them rearward instead to keep the twelve short enough

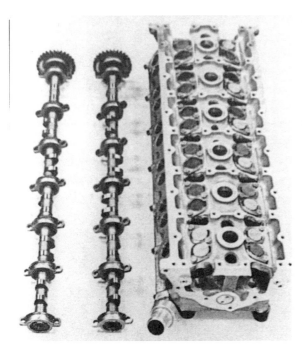

tracts of the Shell test engine had not been incorporated in his V12. Instead the inlet path was kinked where the vertical inlet pipe met the slope of the port. Astonishingly, no effort had been made to reproduce the efficient straight porting that had helped achieve such promising test results. Although higher figures were quoted from the untrustworthy Weslake dynamometer, Dan later admitted that 'I never raced it with 400 horsepower or more.'

1967 brought two high points in the career of the Gurney V12. Dan and his team-mate, fellow Californian Richie Ginther, dominated the two heats of the well-attended Race of Champions at Brands Hatch on 12 March and Gurney won the final. Then in June at the Belgian Grand Prix Dan's lone Eagle set a new lap record for Spa at 148.85mph, and outlasted Lotus and BRM challenges to win the first GP victory for an American driver and car since Jimmy Murphy and the Duesenberg (*qv*) at Le Mans in 1921.

'We won two Formula 1 races and achieved much more success than most of the pundits thought was possible,' Gurney reflected. 'We whipped the Ferrari factory and everybody else at Brands Hatch. And then at Spa we whipped them all. I look back on the whole Eagle experience as being more miraculous than it was disappointing. I thought it was very, very good.'

to fit into the space in the Eagle chassis that Len Terry had allotted to the Indy Ford V8. Driven from the rear ends of the camshafts were the mechanical fuel pump (left exhaust), the Lucas ignition trigger (right exhaust), and the fuel-injection distributor/controller (by cogged belt from the right inlet camshaft).

During August 1966 the first engine was assembled, a job requiring 1,200 man-hours; by 18 August the 390lb (177kg) V12 was ready for testing. After a week it was yielding 364bhp at 9,500rpm – vastly short of expectations. To Dan Gurney's utter dismay, the arrow-straight inlet

Opposite left: With its four magnificent exhaust megaphones the Type 58 Gurney-Weslake signalled that it meant business when it first appeared at Monza in September 1966. Its Lucas injection distributor, just above the gearbox, was driven by a cogged belt from the right-hand inlet camshaft.
Opposite right: Reaching the track well ahead of its rival, the Ford Cosworth DFV, the Gurney-Weslake V12 deserved credit for introducing to racing

the modern concept of a narrow valve included angle, in this case 30°, in combination with four valves per cylinder. This led the way toward compact, high-efficiency combustion chambers.
Above: BRM practice was evident in the way the cam-shafts were carried by roller bearings in removable outer races. The aluminium cylinder-head casting was commendably narrow and light.

SPECIFICATIONS	
Cylinders	V12
Bore	72.8mm
Stroke	60.0mm
Stroke/bore ratio	0.82:1
Capacity	2,997cc
Compression ratio	12.0:1
Connecting rod length	124.0mm
Rod/crank radius ratio	4.1:1
Main bearing journal diameter	60.3mm
Rod journal diameter	41.3mm
Inlet valve diameter (2 valves)	30.5mm
Exhaust valve diameter (2 valves)	25.0mm
Inlet pressure	1.0Atm
Engine weight	390lb (177kg)
Peak power	380bhp @ 10,000rpm
Piston speed (corrected)	4,337ft/min (21.7m/s)
Engine bhp per litre	126.8bhp per litre
Engine weight per bhp	1.03lb (0.47kg) per bhp

1967

FORD DFV 3-LITRE V8

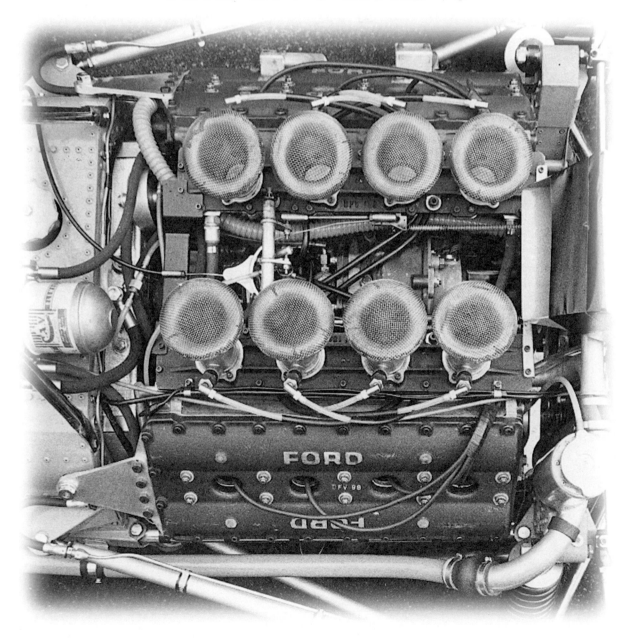

On their camshaft covers they said FORD in capital letters. It might well have read thus after Ford of Britain invested £100,000, some $300,000, in the design and development of the DFV V8 and its companion four-cylinder Formula 2 engine, the FVA. In conception and construction, however, these engines were products of Northampton's Cosworth Engineering, a company that was the joint brainchild of Keith Duckworth and Mike Costin.

Certainly they and their Ford mentors, Walter Hayes and Harley Copp, had hoped for success. But could they have anticipated the Cosworth-Ford's total domination of the Grand Prix world? In its salad days the DFV would carry drivers to a round dozen world championships, including three for Jackie Stewart, two for Emerson Fittipaldi and singletons for Jochen Rindt, Graham Hill, Nelson Piquet, James Hunt, Mario Andretti, Alan Jones and Keke Rosberg. And a developed version of the engine would power Michael Schumacher's first championship in 1994.

Keith Duckworth's DFV was a major contributor to the revival of the four-valve cylinder head as an optimum means of producing racing-engine power. The first Cosworth engine to have four valves was its Formula 2 four based on the Ford Cortina block, which had a 40° included angle between the stems. For the GP engine this was reduced to 32°. With an 11:1 compression ratio, this narrower angle allowed the top of the piston to be flat except for four machined recesses to accommodate the valve heads near top dead centre, a configuration that produced an advantageously compact combustion chamber with, at its centre, a single 10mm spark plug. Valve diameters were 34.5mm for the inlets and 29mm for the exhausts; both were closed by paired coil springs. Lift was 10.4mm and timing was initially as follows:

Inlet opens 58°BTDC   Exhaust opens 98°BBDC
Inlet closes 82°ABDC   Exhaust closes 58°ATDC

The aluminium-alloy cylinder head was so designed that one casting served for both cylinder banks. It was held down by ten main studs and, additionally, by four short studs along both sides of the head at its periphery, extending downward from the head. The seal with each cylinder was effected by a Cooper ring, set in a groove machined at the join between the flange at the top of the cylinder liner and the surface of the block. The cylinder centre distance was 4.125in (104.8mm) and the offset between cylinder banks was 0.80in (20.3mm).

Atop the head was a one-piece aluminium-alloy casting which served as a carrier for both cams and tappets. This was held down by long studs from the tops of the heads which also served to retain the cam bearing caps and, down the two centre rows, the shallow magnesium cam covers. The steel cams were carried in five plain bearings, the wider centre bearing having a groove to supply oil to a hole through which it entered the hollow camshaft to distribute oil to the other bearings. Inverted-cup tappets were made of steel and contained shims for clearance adjustment.

Keith Duckworth took care to create an inlet port that was as straight as possible to the valve. The inlet ports were oval at the head face and bifurcated internally to the two valves. Above the ports were slide throttles whose slides were supported on balls and rollers for free movement. Between the throttles and the ports were short stub 'manifolds' that contained passages through which the excess fuel returned by the injection pump could flow, and be cooled, on its way back to the fuel tank. They were refrigerated to around 30°C by the internal vaporisation of the fuel.

Opposite above: To his competitors Jim Clark was just a blur in his Lotus 49 powered by the new Cosworth-built Ford DFV engine. Clark's in 1967 was the first of a baker's dozen world championships won with this engine.

Opposite below: Although not the first to do so, Cosworth was effective in designing the DFV to serve as the rear portion of the frame structure of a Formula 1 racing car – a Matra in this instance. Designer Keith Duckworth tucked the alternator and the distributors for fuel and sparks within the engine's central vee.

Fuel was injected just above the slides by a Lucas system. Operating at 110psi, its distributor delivered the fuel starting at 30° after top dead centre. This system was suspect when, in their first four or five races, the V8s in the Lotuses were beset by erratic misfiring. Suspecting the fuel filters in the metering units, for the Canadian GP in August 1967 Colin Chapman added some large filters which bypassed the smaller built-in ones. This stopped the misfiring.

Lucas also supplied the electronic ignition which had been introduced during the 1½-litre Formula 1. An additional refinement was electronic rev-limiting. This was set with a rheostat to fade, then

Thereupon Cosworth introduced the side-mounted pumps that have since become standard wear for most racing engines.

Sprockets drove a row of pumps along each side of the crankcase. First on each side was a pump delivering coolant to the engine; the two water pumps were interconnected by a balance pipe in the sump. The pump gang driven by the right-hand cogwheel also included the oil scavenge pump and a rotary oil/air separator. The left-hand gang included a mechanical fuel pump, oil pressure pump and oil filter. The scavenge pump evolved from a Gerotor-type design to a Roots-type pump with a much greater capacity for air mixed with oil. A later DFV version, redesigned to allow car designers to fit deeper downforce-generating venturis under it, had only a single water pump mounted on the left.

At the engine's heart was its aluminium-alloy cylinder block, cut off at the crankshaft centreline. Wet cast-iron cylinder liners were clamped in the block at their top flange and grooved at the bottom to take two O-rings to secure the lower water seal. Only two of the five main bearings, the second and fourth, had conventional caps in the developed version of the engine. From 1971 the other three caps were integral with the massive aluminium casting that formed the engine's bottom cover; in the original engine all five caps were carried by the cover. The bottom of the crankcase was shaped so closely to the crank throws that it looked like a crankcase-compression two-stroke design. The objective was a reduction in losses from oil churning.

Carried in Vandervell thin-wall bearings was a crankshaft forged of EN40C steel. This was of 'flat' 180° design, resembling a four-cylinder crank and counterbalanced accordingly. Originally an oil pressure of more than 85psi was needed to ensure that oil reached the main and rod bearings, but in 1977 a breakthrough was made to a different network and angling of the internal drillings that performed better than the previous system at only 60psi and in fact was still reliable at only 45psi. The main journals measured 2.375in (60.3mm) and the rod journals 1.937in (49.2mm).

cut in again at a specific engine speed, which it held within 150rpm or so. With peak power being reached at 9,000rpm Cosworth started out in 1967 with the limiter at 9,500, then moved it up to 9,800 before the end of the season and during 1968. The fuel-injection metering unit, the ignition distributor and a small alternator were combined in a single unit mounted in the vee of the engine, and driven by a small-diameter shaft from a gearbox driven by the timing gear train at the front of the engine.

Two compound – ie back-to-back – gears were included in the train at the front that drove the camshafts. In the DFV's early years this experienced various failures that led to intensive development of every aspect of the cams and gears, including making the latter of vacuum-remelted steel. The final solution, introduced in 1971, was to introduce into the hub of the second compound gear 12 miniature torsion bars which were able to absorb the energy spikes that were troubling the gears.

A shaft through the engine's magnesium front cover turned a sprocket which powered a cogged-rubber belt to drive the engine's remaining accessories. This solution was adopted because Chapman and Duckworth had agreed that the engine would serve as the rear chassis element of the new Lotus 49 and thus should not be encumbered with pumps on its front face.

Forged connecting rods 132.8mm long connected the crank to fully-skirted pistons with gudgeon pins retained by circlips. The triple ring pack included a Dykes-type ring at the top, a conventional compression ring and an oil ring. As an

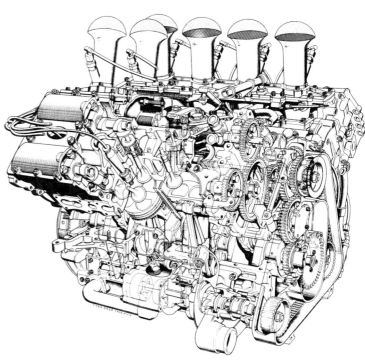

indication of Cosworth's obsession with detail, the connecting-rod forgings were checked to select and match those which were not only of similar weight but also of similar thickness, because some were 'bitten' more deeply by the forging dies than others. These then passed through machining operations together. The highly-stressed faces of the rod shank were polished to permit accurate crack detection. Then to relieve surface stresses the polished areas were shot-peened into battered roughness again.

From its first runs the 358lb (162kg) Cosworth DFV had power, 408bhp at 9,000rpm to begin with, plus or minus 3 per cent depending on the individual engine. This was produced by 2,993cc (85.7 x 64.8mm; 3.37 x 2.55in). Modifications for Monza in 1968 brought peak power to 423bhp at

9,900rpm, sacrificing some torque lower down to get it. Nearer the end of its career the DFV was producing 480bhp at 10,500rpm, while peak torque was 245lb ft at 8,500rpm. This was enough, as we have seen, to win a baker's dozen of world championships. No other engine can make that statement.

Opposite: In order to keep his V8 engine as short as possible, Duckworth put its water and oil pumps along the sides of the crankcase. In so doing he started a fashion that still continues in racing-engine design.

Above left: To cope with the high capacities required, especially when the lubricating oil contained a froth of air, Keith Duckworth replaced his original Gerotor-type oil pumps with pumps patterned

after the design of a Roots-type supercharger. These offered much-increased capacity for the same installed volume.

Above right : While trains of spur gears drove the four overhead camshafts of the DFV, a cogged rubber belt was introduced at the front of the engine to power its accessories. A triggering disk for the electronic ignition was at the nose of the crankshaft.

SPECIFICATIONS	
Cylinders	V8
Bore	85.7mm
Stroke	64.8mm
Stroke/bore ratio	0.76:1
Capacity	2,993cc
Compression ratio	11.0:1
Connecting rod length	132.8mm
Rod/crank radius ratio	4.1:1
Main bearing journal diameter	60.3mm
Rod journal diameter	49.2mm
Inlet valve diameter (2 valves)	34.5mm
Exhaust valve diameter (2 valves)	29.0mm
Inlet pressure	1.0Atm
Engine weight	358lb (162kg)
Peak power	408bhp @ 9,000rpm
Piston speed (corrected)	4,401ft/min (22.0m/s)
Engine bhp per litre	136.3bhp per litre
Engine weight per bhp	0.88lb (0.40kg) per bhp

1969

PORSCHE 912 4.5-LITRE FLAT-12

One of the boldest undertakings in the long history of Porsche was its construction of 25 sports-racing cars to meet FIA rules for 'production' Group 4 cars in 1969. The car was the Type 917 and its engine designation was Type 912. Several aspects of the engine were 'givens' from the start. One was that it would be air-cooled. As technical director Ferdinand Piëch was fond of pointing out, 'We have never lost the air.' With air cooling went the opposed horizontal layout, which deployed the cylinders receptively to the air stream.

Equally straightforward was the decision to make the new engine a twelve, composed of the same cylinder units used in the successful 908 flat-eight. Keeping the same bore and stroke of 85 x 66mm (3.35 x 2.60in) gave the 912 4,494cc. Its crank was like that of an in-line six, with each throw rotated at 120° to its neighbour and each rod journal carrying two connecting-rod big-ends. The centre distance between cylinders was 118mm except for the centre pairs of cylinders on each bank, the same spacing that had been used for both the 901/911 six and the 908 eight.

Steel-backed multi-layer bearing shells were used for both the main and rod bearings. The 912's forged titanium connecting rods were similar to those used successfully in other Porsche racing engines and were the same length, 130mm, as those of the 901/911 and 908. Rod-bearing journals measured 52mm.

This was the longest crank Porsche had yet made for a car, in its final form measuring 31.3in end to end. Analytical studies forecast large amplitudes of vibration at both ends of the shaft. But at its centre there was a node, a point that remained at rest. The Porsche men decided to power not only the camshafts but also all the drives, for the engine's output as well as for its accessories, from the centre of the crankshaft. A straight-cut drive take-off gear with 32 teeth was formed at the centre of the crankshaft. It was flanked by two larger 66mm main bearings. The remaining main bearings, three on each end, were of 57mm diameter, bringing the total main bearing count to eight.

So that its central gear could be hardened to the degree necessary, the crankshaft was forged of a chrome-nickel-molybdenum alloy steel. It was carried at the centre of a box-shaped cast magnesium crankcase that was split vertically from front to back. Studs and bolts around its periphery

were chiefly of titanium. The halves were principally bound together by 16 bolts that went all the way through from one side to the other, one above and one below each main bearing. These bolts were made of a steel alloy called Dilavar, which had a coefficient of expansion only slightly lower than that of magnesium.

Set in ball and needle bearings adjoining the centre split of the crankcase were shafts above and below the crankshaft, both driven by its central gear. The lower shaft took the drive to the clutch at the rear of the engine. Its driven gear had only 31 teeth, one less than the gear on the crankshaft because pairs of gears last longer if the same two teeth do not contact each other on each revolution.

A small step-down gear set at the front face of the output-shaft gear powered a pack of oil pumps at 0.54 times crankshaft speed. One was a pressure pump, with gears 64mm wide, and the others were separate 42mm scavenge pumps. One drew oil from the front of the crankcase while the other had a pickup about two-thirds of the way to the rear. At the front and rear ends of each exhaust camshaft more pumps were provided to scavenge spent oil from the cam boxes.

Like the 912 engine's other subassemblies, the oil pumps were mounted on the right-hand half of the crankcase, while the oil galleries were in the left-hand half. The pressure-pump output was fed to a filter at the front of the engine that also contained a relief valve set for 70psi for the oil to the main and rod bearings. Because the crankshaft had no power take-offs at either end, it was an easy matter to arrange a direct delivery of oil to the rod bearings through drillings in each end of the shaft. Each drilling supplied oil to the six rods on its side of the central drive gear.

Each of the four hardened-steel camshafts was carried in eight plain bearings 30mm in diameter. These were directly oiled, as were the cup-type tappets that slid in aluminium inserts in the magnesium cam carrier housings running the full

Opposite above: In its developed form, here racing at Watkins Glen in 1970, the Porsche Type 917 was one of the most successful sports-racing cars of all time. It was powered by the flat-twelve Type 912 air-cooled engine.

Opposite below: Nylon pipes delivered the output of the Bosch fuel-injection pump to points high on the reinforced-plastic ram pipes of the Type 912 engine. At their centre was the six-bladed cooling fan, also moulded of reinforced plastic.

length of each cylinder bank. The fact that the delivery port did not open until the tappet had been depressed two millimetres reduced the volume of flow by 60 per cent from what it would otherwise have been.

The 912 was the first Porsche overhead-cam engine to drive its camshafts by trains of gears. Four shafts carried steel gears on needle bearings between the crank and each pair of cams. All four shafts were supported by a magnesium housing that contained the gears and was principally bolted to the crankcase and also attached to the camshaft housing.

The 912's valve timing pattern was the same as the 908's, as follows:

Inlet opens 104°BTDC Exhaust opens 105°BBDC
Inlet closes 104°ABDC Exhaust closes 75°ATDC

Lift was 12.1mm for the inlet valves and 10.5mm for the exhausts. Both valves were hollow, with sodium-filled stems. Two coil valve springs around each stem were made from vacuum-melted alloy steel wire.

Valve head diameters were the same as those of the 908: 47.5mm for the inlets and 40.5mm for the exhaust valves. Cast of aluminium in a permanent mould, the individual head for each cylinder also resembled that of the 908; in fact it bore a 908 part number. Its valve angles were 30° for the inlets and 35° for the exhausts.

Individual cylinders were forged of Mahle's high-silicon aluminium alloy No 124, deeply finned by individual machining of each cylinder, and given chrome-plated walls. They bore forged fully-skirted aluminium pistons of the same alloy with two compression rings above the gudgeon pin and a single oil ring below it. Cooling-oil jets one millimetre in diameter were fitted to the main bearing webs and aimed at the undersides of the piston crowns.

Each head and cylinder was attached to the crankcase by four long cap screws. To minimise stress changes with heat, these were made of the Dilavar steel alloy that was also used for the crankcase bolts. Because these head screws were cooled by the fan, each was given an insulating jacket so it would be warm enough to maintain the proper expansion rate. Between the cylinder and the head Porsche used a flat, face-type joint that was sealed by a ring inserted in a groove machined in the top of the cylinder.

Like the 753 eight (*qv*), the 912's cooling fan was placed flat and was mechanically driven by a bevel gear from the engine-speed shaft above the crankshaft. From the front and back ends of the shaft the two ignition distributors were turned by skew gears. Each served one bank of six cylinders in the 912's dual ignition system. The Bosch system used transistorised magnetic triggering and four ignition coils. From a pulley at the front end of the accessory drive shaft a vee-belt drove an 860-watt alternator.

A double-row Bosch fuel-injection pump was mounted atop the front of the left inlet cam housing and driven by a short cogged belt from the end of that camshaft. Space-cam metering was used. Set for delivery pressures around 250psi, the injection nozzles were at the tops of the plastic inlet ram pipes and were fed by nylon tubes. Slide throttles in four separate groups of three were joined by adjustable linkages.

In confidence that the twelve would be right as designed, the company commissioned the production of the complete 25-engine run straight from the drawing board. In March 1969 the first twelve was tested. Piëch and Mezger enjoyed the enormous satisfaction of seeing it deliver a rousing 542 horsepower after only modest tuning. By the time the 912 engine was ready to be raced in mid-1969 it was producing 580 horsepower at 8,400rpm and 376lb ft of torque at 6,800rpm with a compression ratio of 10.5:1. Revs of 8,700 were allowable, but 9,000 meant a broken valve with the early engines. Weighing 530lb (241lb) complete in its original 4.5-litre 1969 guise, it was the first Porsche automobile engine to develop more than one horsepower per pound.

The flat-12 was enlarged in 1970 almost to 5 litres (86 x 70.4mm; 3.39 x 2.77in; 4,907cc), with a shortened 127.8mm connecting rod.

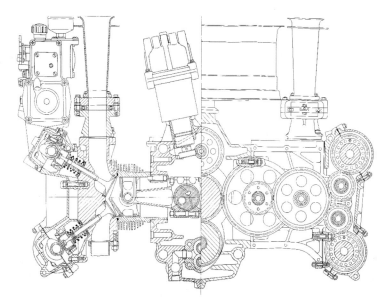

Output rose to 600bhp at 8,400rpm and torque to 405lb ft at 6,500rpm. The 912 powered Porsche's 917K to its first overall victory at Le Mans in 1970 and to its second sports-car world championship in a row. The same double was achieved in 1971, the last year the 917 was eligible to compete in that category.

Opposite left: Viewed as it was first assembled in February 1969, with its exhaust pipes positioned for dynamometer testing, the Type 912 was an awesome mechanical assembly. Separate distributors at front and rear were needed to supply its twin-plug requirements.

Opposite right: Viewed from the top, a 912 engine being assembled showed its individual cylinder heads and barrels. It was much to Porsche's credit and great experience that it was able to meet the cooling needs of such a high-performance engine with air alone. Naturally oil cooling also played a significant role.

Above: The train of spur gears shown on the right took the drive from the centre of the crankshaft to the twin cams on each side of the engine. Made as short as possible to keep engine width down, the connecting rod had a massive big-end structure.

SPECIFICATIONS	
Cylinders	F12
Bore	85.0mm
Stroke	66.0mm
Stroke/bore ratio	0.78:1
Capacity	4,494cc
Compression ratio	10.5:1
Connecting rod length	130.0mm
Rod/crank radius ratio	3.9:1
Main bearing journal diameter	57.0mm
Rod journal diameter	52.0mm
Inlet valve diameter (1 valve)	47.5mm
Exhaust valve diameter (1 valve)	40.5mm
Inlet pressure	1.0Atm
Engine weight	530lb (241kg)
Peak power	580bhp @ 8,400rpm
Piston speed (corrected)	4,128ft/min (20.6m/s)
Peak torque	376lb ft (510Nm)
	@ 6,800rpm
Peak bmep	207psi
Engine bhp per litre	129.1bhp per litre
Engine weight per bhp	0.91lb (0.41kg) per bhp

1970
DRAKE OFFENHAUSER 2.6-LITRE FOUR

The Offy might have died in 1933 with the bankruptcy of Harry Miller, the great visionary who created it. Design techniques proven in the great Miller straight-eight-cylinder racing engines of the 1920s had been used by Miller and his team to make a 2.5-litre four-cylinder unit for boat racing which also showed, by chance, excellent performance in a racing car. At first limited by racing rules to two valves per cylinder, the engine was given four valves by engineer Leo Goossen when this was allowed in 1931.

Progressively scaled up in size year by year, the engine was a 3.6-litre four in 1933 when Fred Offenhauser bought the tools, drawings and patterns to make it from a bankrupt Harry Miller. He set up his own one-man Offenhauser Engineering Company, which became two-man when Leo Goossen, the designer who had always interpreted Miller's visions, joined Offenhauser, whose engines soon became known as 'Offys'. Thus when the four first won Indianapolis in 1934 it was already officially an Offenhauser engine, of 4.2-litre size.

The 1934 win was the first of no less than 30 victories the Offy scored in the 500-mile race until 1976. In many years, especially in the 1950s, the Offy totally dominated Indianapolis. In 1954, on the first of several such occasions, all 33 of the starting cars at the Speedway were powered by the four-cylinder Offy.

The Offy used in US Championship racing had four valves per cylinder operated by gear-driven twin overhead camshafts raising the valves through inverted-cup tappets. The head and cylinders were a single casting, originally of iron and, since 1969, of aluminium with inserted dry liners. The separate crankcase was aluminium, of tunnel-type construction into which the crankshaft, with its five main bearing bulkheads, was inserted from one end.

To suit US racing rules the Offy was enlarged to 4.5 litres in 1938. In 1946 the rights to the engine were

Above: A look into the rear of an Offy crankcase showed its barrel-type construction and the circular apertures to which the diaphragms carrying the main bearings were bolted. Oval side openings gave access to the engine's interior for the mechanic.
Opposite above: One of the cars that made the best use of the Drake Turbo-Offy engine was the low-line AAR Eagle introduced in 1972. Designed to package the Drake engine efficiently, this chassis contributed significantly to Offy's success at Indy in the 1970s.
Opposite below: An integral part of the turbo-Offy package was the turbocharger supplied by AiResearch, out of view to right. With its boost controlled by an exhaust-pipe waste gate, it delivered its pressure charge to the inlet manifold without benefit of an intercooler.

bought from Offenhauser by Lou Meyer, three-time Indy winner, and Dale Drake; their Meyer & Drake Engineering continued to produce the 'Offenhauser' engine. Rule changes brought it down to 4.2 litres again in 1957, by then fed its alcohol fuel through Hilborn constant-flow port-type fuel injection. Offy customers led the way toward a new short-block configuration for the reduced-size engine.

With Lotus as its ally, Ford mounted a concerted attack on the Offy, beginning in 1963. It nearly won a controversial 1964 race and finally, in 1965, Jim Clark's Lotus-Ford beat the Offy-powered 'roadsters'. But unwilling as he was to give up on this great engine, Dale Drake built a new factory to produce the Offy in California's Costa Mesa, near the Orange County Airport. He was joined by his son John, by Leo Goossen and by Walt Sobraske, master machinist who first worked for Harry Miller in 1921. While Ford was making unsupercharged 4.2-litre eights, Drake decided to make the supercharged 2.7-litre fours that the rules also allowed.

Drake had a sound basis on which to do this, because the Offy was well-suited to supercharging with its four valves per cylinder and integrated head/block design, avoiding gasket problems. Also, supercharged predecessors had been built and raced. A 180-cubic-inch (3-litre) Offy of the 1950s was based on the 220 block and crankcase, a direct descendant of the original marine engine of 1931. In 1950, with mechanically-driven centrifugal blowers, three qualified for the Indy 500 but none finished. One qualified and failed to finish the next year, and in 1952 one blown qualifier retired during the race. A blown Offy also qualified in 1957 when the supercharged-engine displacement limit was cut to 171cu in (2.8 litres). It, too, failed to finish.

Supercharging's second wind was in large part the inspiration of Dick Jones, operator of Champion's West Coast dynamometer facility and a

man eager to see the Autolite-sparked Fords beaten. Jones carried out some tests with a Roots-type blower which yielded a much fuller torque curve than the centrifugal units. In late 1965 Leo Goossen designed a proper engine to suit the latest supercharging methods. He did so on the basis of the robust crankcase of the 4.2-litre or 255-cubic-inch Offy four and using the shorter gear tower of the 220, variants of which had served for the experimental engines built by Jones.

This new Offy had 144mm tubular-shank connecting rods and a suitably altered cylinder block. Well oversquare at 4.125 x 3.125in (104.8 x 79.4mm) for 168cu in (2,739cc), it weighed 475lb (216kg). It had its four valves equally inclined at a 72° included angle in a pent-roof combustion chamber, with a single central spark plug ignited by a Scintilla magneto prepared by Joe Hunt.

Valve diameters were 39.7mm for the inlets and 34.9mm for the exhausts. Lift by the direct-acting radiused-top tappets – held in proper alignment by a keyway – was 10.2mm, and duration was 290° for the inlets and 270° for the exhaust cams. Valve spring pressure was 160lb (73kg) static and 360lb (163kg) with the valve fully open.

Machined from a billet of SAE 4340 steel, the crankshaft was fully counterbalanced and turned in thin-wall copper-lead bearings 2.375in (60.3mm) in diameter. Diameter of the rod journals was 2.125in (54.0mm). Gudgeon pin diameter was 27mm. Pistons, carrying two compression rings and one oil ring, were configured to provide an 8.5:1 compression ratio.

Bob DeBisschop of AiResearch provided an exhaust-driven turbo-supercharger and Stuart Hilborn of the eponymous fuel-injection company helped him work out the piping and fuel delivery to adapt it to this new Offy. Mechanic Herb Porter was an important ally of the project.

On the Champion dynamometer Jones found that the turbo-blown engine produced 626bhp at 8,500rpm against 530bhp for the Roots version at the same speed. In fact, the turbo-blown engine's power curve was almost a direct extension upward of the output of the blown Offy of 1954; both produced 500bhp at 6,500rpm but that was where the old one stopped. The late-1960s version could rev safely to 9,500rpm.

The turbo-Offys staggered the first drivers to try them. 'It's the first engine I can't drive full-bore off the corners,' one said. Both versions of the engine appeared at Indy in 1966, three of each kind making the field, and all had problems, especially with cooling. The highest-placed at the finish was Bobby Unser's, eighth, a turbo-blown model. The next year seven of the eight qualifying blown Offys were turbocharged units, with two of them placing seventh and eighth at the finish.

No small amount of development was needed to get the engine to the point where it could win for Bobby Unser in 1968. At first it overheated severely. Water-passage size increases helped, and later the block was made asymmetrical for the first time to add more water capacity around its exhaust ports, which were divided into two ports with a small water passage between them. Internal pipes directed cool incoming water into this passage and onto the inner surface of the exhaust-valve seat area.

Crankcase design was changed to gain the needed strength with the higher outputs. With the high heat inputs of the turbocharged engine, block quality was also a problem. The 1966 engines had aluminium blocks, which were unpredictably porous in spite of Drake's best attempts to seal them. For the new 1967 engines a switch back to iron was made. In 1969 aluminium blocks were back, thanks to a new foundry, Turner in Bell, California.

To shrink the turbo-Offys to 159.4cu in to meet the 1969 capacity rules Drake made sets of sleeves which were pressed in, with a 0.006in interference fit, to bring the bore down to 4.030in (102.4mm) and the displacement to 2,616cc. When these were installed in an old block they created a slight combustion chamber overhang around the edges; the new 1969 blocks had a smaller combustion chamber diameter to eliminate this. New permanent-mould-cast pistons were provided. Some Offy buyers preferred impact-forged TRW pistons that seemed to give more consistent performance and reliability above 8,500rpm.

Careful development smoothed out the engine's torque curve, filling in a former low point at 6,000rpm. Joe Hunt's magnetos were replaced by flywheel-triggered Mallory ignition systems. Maximum torque was 510lb ft at 7,000rpm and peak power was 727bhp at 8,250rpm with an engine given boost of 24psi above atmospheric. The engine was further strengthened to stand up to the crew chiefs who liked to add 5–10 per cent nitromethane to the methanol fuel. These improvements underpinned the engine's subsequent success, which included five straight victories in the Indy 500 from 1972 to 1976. Not until 1981 did new engines such as the Cosworth V8 eliminate Offys from the Indy starting field.

In 1973, the year of peak supercharged development before limits on boost and fuel consumption were imposed, some engines were being boosted as high as 42psi for Indy qualifying, producing four-figure horsepower levels. On the McLaren Engines dynamometer, on 37½psi of boost the 2.6-litre Offy generated peak torque of

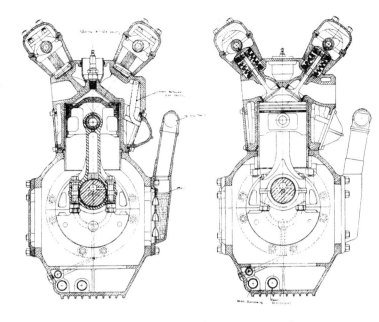

650lb ft at 7,600rpm. It produced a maximum of 959bhp at 8,000rpm and was still delivering in excess of 950bhp at 9,200rpm. This represented 369 horsepower per litre, just over six horsepower per cubic inch – the highest specific output produced up to that time by a reciprocating internal-combustion engine.

Opposite: Two Drake-built Offy fours awaiting collection at the factory in April 1972 belied any suggestion that this was a crude engine. Drake employed only the best materials and machining techniques.
Above: Leo Goossen's 1975 drawing of the developed Drake-built Offy showed, on *the left, the foam that was included in the large breather system on the left side of the crankcase. Characteristic of Miller-derived design was its use of a radiused tappet which was keyed to keep it from rotating. The inserted cup around the spark plug also followed Miller practice.*

SPECIFICATIONS	
Cylinders	I4
Bore	102.4mm
Stroke	79.4mm
Stroke/bore ratio	0.78:1
Capacity	2,616cc
Compression ratio	8.5:1
Connecting rod length	144.0mm
Rod/crank radius ratio	3.6:1
Main bearing journal diameter	60.3mm
Rod journal diameter	54.0mm
Inlet valve diameter (2 valves)	39.7mm
Exhaust valve diameter (2 valves)	34.9mm
Inlet pressure	2.66Atm
Engine weight	475lb (216kg)
Peak power	727bhp @ 8,250rpm
Piston speed (corrected)	4,881ft/min (24.4m/s)
Peak torque	510lb ft (692Nm)
	@ 7,000rpm
Peak bmep	483psi
Engine bhp per litre	277.9bhp per litre
Engine weight per bhp	0.65lb (0.30kg) per bhp

1970

FERRARI 312B 3-LITRE FLAT-12

In 1967 and 1968 the red Ferrari cars netted but a single Grand Prix victory. They were bad days for Enzo Ferrari and worse for Mauro Forghieri, his racing development engineer. The end of 1968 found Forghieri banished to a garret in Modena from which many doubted he'd ever return to the works at Maranello. His 'research office' in Modena manned by two young engineers – Ferrari (no relation) and Caliri, an aerodynamicist – was written off as a feeble attempt at saving face.

But return Forghieri did, with the design from a clean sheet of paper of an all-new Ferrari car and engine. It remained a twelve, upholding prancing-horse tradition, but a flat-opposed 12. In this Ferrari had a minor tradition. In 1965 a 1½-litre flat-12 Ferrari competed in GP racing but was denied victories. Another flat-12 Ferrari of 2 litres with 4-valve cylinder heads swept the board in the 1969 European hillclimb championship.

Early in 1969 the new 312B (for 'Boxer' – a German expression for opposed engines) took shape on Forghieri's drawing board. Its bore and stroke were 78.5 x 51.5mm (3.09 x 2.03in) for 2,991cc. The short stroke helped keep the flat engine compact and held the 312B's weight to 317lb (144kg).

Forghieri innovated boldly in the 312B's bottom end. Its six-throw crankshaft, like that of an in-line six, was conventional enough. But after tests on the 2-litre hillclimb engine proved its feasibility, the crank was carried in only four main bearings. Roller bearings were used, which required a built-up crankshaft for the assembly of the two centre main bearings. But blowups in early testing led to a switch to a one-piece crankshaft and plain bearings at the two centre mains, with rollers only at the ends. The crank was machined from a billet of steel alloyed with manganese and aluminium to obtain a suitable surface for use with the roller bearings.

After the change to a one-piece crankshaft, failures continued. A

Above: Viewed from its underside, with studs extending upwards to receive the dry-sump casting, the cylinder block of the Ferrari 312B is light, rugged and compact. Solid bulkheads hold its four main bearings.
Opposite above: In concert with his new flat-12 3-litre Formula 1 engine Mauro Forghieri and his team designed a completely new Ferrari car. This first raced in 1970, as here at Watkins Glen in the hands of Jacky Ickx. Although success for the new concept was not immediate, it did come.
Opposite below: While not completely responsible for the structure at the rear of the 312B Ferrari's frame, the engine made a major contribution to its stiffness. The frame's structure continued to the rear over and above the engine, upon which it rested and to which it was tied.

study of the crank's resonant characteristics showed that the attached mass of the flywheel brought the torsional movements of largest amplitude to a weak point on the crankshaft. Pirelli technicians helped Forghieri develop a rubber coupling between the crank and flywheel that shifted the largest amplitude to a portion of the crank that could tolerate it.

Forghieri had favoured roller bearings throughout the bottom end because they require less oil, which meant that less of it would be splashing around inside the crankcase, wasting power on oil foaming and heating. Rollers for the rods were tried but given up as too difficult and complicated and replaced by conventional bearing shells on 36mm journals. Both titanium and steel connecting rods 110mm long were used, those of the latter type being pared to the minimum along the I-section shank. Fitted with three rings, pistons were fully-skirted.

The inner surface of the crankcase was shaped closely to the radius swept by the rod big-ends. The Ferrari engine benefited from having constant crankcase volume, free from compression losses, in each group of four cylinders between the main bearing panels. Crankcase oil was collected in a deep finned magnesium sump. Outside it, along the left side of the sump, was a row of three oil scavenge pumps driven in series from a gear train at the front of the engine. Each pump sucked oil from its own section of the sump. The cylinder heads had mini-dry-sump systems of their own with a small scavenge pump at the rear driven by the exhaust camshaft.

At the rear of the battery of scavenge pumps was the oil pressure pump, whose main output was piped to the front of the engine where it entered the nose of the crankshaft. All the oil for the rod bearings flowed through a gallery drilled from one end of the crank to the other. When oil from the rod

bearings was flung off the spinning crank, some of it was captured by a gutter that ran along the upper surface of the crankcase, cast into the left-hand half. From this gutter, passages were drilled down to the two roller bearings at the ends of the crank. Originally this passage was also used to lubricate the two centre mains, but when these were changed to plain bearings a separate oil gallery was added, along the left side of the engine, to supply them with pressurised oil.

At the front of the 312B, driven by a pair of step-down spur gears, was a compact accessory box full of bevel gears. One bevel drove the water pump, placed horizontally under the box and almost hidden by it. Water entered the pump at the bottom and was spun out through two exit ports into passages cast into the sump. A gallery running the length of the block, just below each cylinder-head parting line, admitted coolant to the heads close to the seats of the exhaust valves. Inside each head the water rose and exited at the front of the head through a gallery above the inlet valve seats.

In addition to serving as the main rear structure of the 312B, the aluminium crankcase was divided into two blocks of six cylinders. A vertical split down the middle separated it into equal parts and formed the parting line for the four main bearings. The bulkheads that supported the mains were massive. From the top to the bottom of each bulkhead no less than six studs knitted the blocks together laterally – three above and three below each main bearing.

A radical departure from the Italian tradition of wet cylinder liners was made by the 312B, which had integrally cast cylinders. These made the block stronger at the price of additional labour for the foundry. The cylinder running surface was provided by an inserted cast-iron dry liner which was surrounded, at its top, by a water jacket next to a shoulder against which the liner was clamped, 28mm below the head parting. Fourteen studs retained each cylinder head, and also an aluminium casting with which the cam and tappet carriers were integral.

The twin overhead camshafts were driven by a train of ruggedly-mounted spur gears which were spread across the output (rear) end of the block. Forghieri settled on this instead of the more space-consuming cogged rubber belt he'd considered at one stage of the design. Spaced closely together, the camshafts operated four valves per cylinder through small-diameter piston-type tappets.

Experimentally, Forghieri tried included angles

between the inlet and exhaust valves that varied from 20° to 27° and found relatively little difference in output over that range. He settled on a 20° included angle. The valves were closed by single coil springs, fabricated in Germany of Swedish steel. Valve sizes were 31mm for the inlets and 27mm for the exhausts.

The shallow valve inclination facilitated a straight and thus efficient inlet port, in which the injection nozzles were downstream of the slide throttles. It also created smooth, compact and efficient combustion chambers – not easy to obtain in a large-bore high-compression engine. The valve heads were only slightly recessed into the surface of the cylinder head, and shallow cut-outs in the flat piston tops provided clearance for the valves at top dead centre. The single central spark plug was mounted within a boss that protruded slightly downward into the chamber to place the plug gap close to the centre of the chamber volume.

Considering the novelty of this engine, remarkably few changes were needed during its first full season on the track. The casting at the front that housed the accessory drive gears was redesigned to provide a more convenient connection to the crankshaft oil supply hose. New camshaft covers had handier exits for the oil scavenged from the cylinder heads. At the front,

the transverse throttle shaft was given an overhung bearing where it was linked to the Lucas fuel-injection metering unit. And a bevel drive from the right-hand inlet camshaft replaced a cogged-belt connection to the Lucas fuel pressure pump.

When the 312B was first raced in 1970 its output was quoted as 455bhp at 11,500rpm. Most engines were producing 460bhp at 11,600rpm by mid-season, though 11,000 was considered the upper limit for race reliability. By 1971 the Grand Prix engine was rated at 475bhp at 12,000rpm. Thus was laid the foundation for the engine that took Ferrari drivers to world championships in 1975, 1977 and 1979 with constructors' championships in those years and 1976 as well. By its final season in 1980 the 312B's cylinder dimensions had been amended to 80.0 x 49.6mm (3.15 x 1.95in) for 2,992cc, and its output had risen to 515bhp at 12,400rpm with peak torque of 239lb ft.

Forghieri's flat-12 also made an appearance in 1971 in the 312P roadster built to compete in the sports-car championship with its 3-litre limit. With an 11.5:1 compression ratio, its engine was rated at 450bhp at 10,800rpm. Backed by a fine driving team and first-class pit management by Peter Schetty, the 312P dominated the ten out of eleven races it entered to win the championship in 1972. Grand Prix racing was not the only successful domain for Mauro Forghieri's brainchild.

Opposite: Drive gearing to the overhead camshafts of the 312B flat-12 was positioned at the rear of the engine adjacent to the output to the transaxle. The engine's design achieved an extremely low profile.

Above: At the centre of the 312B combustion chamber the plug was carried by a boss that positioned its spark gap as close as possible to the centre of the fresh charge. Large spur gears carried the drive to each pair of camshafts.

SPECIFICATIONS	
Cylinders	F12
Bore	78.5mm
Stroke	51.5mm
Stroke/bore ratio	0.66:1
Capacity	2,991cc
Compression ratio	11.5:1
Connecting rod length	110.0mm
Rod/crank radius ratio	4.3:1
Main bearing journal diameter	50.0mm
Rod journal diameter	36.0mm
Inlet valve diameter (2 valves)	31.0mm
Exhaust valve diameter (2 valves)	27.0mm
Inlet pressure	1.0Atm
Engine weight	317lb (144kg)
Peak power	460bhp @ 11,600rpm
Piston speed (corrected)	4,840ft/min (24.2m/s)
Engine bhp per litre	153.8bhp per litre
Engine weight per bhp	0.69lb (0.31kg) per bhp

1970

MATRA MS12 3-LITRE V12

During the years of Grand Prix dominance by the Ford-Cosworth V8 no one was in a better position to challenge it than Matra, makers of the chassis of the car that won the world championship in 1969 under Jackie Stewart, powered by the four-cam Ford. Matra had a perfect yardstick for direct comparisons.

French aerospace company SA Engins Matra found itself in the automobile business in 1964 when it acquired the small sports-car company of René Bonnet. Acquiring with it a taste for automotive competition, Matra used its excellent government contacts to obtain a grant of FFr6 million toward the construction of France's own V12 Formula 1 engine. Matra's head of engine design, Georges Martin, quietly negotiated a contract with BRM to design much of the engine, but this was annulled when Sir Alfred Owen spoke indiscreetly about it to an industry gathering. Nevertheless Matra's V12 did manifest some BRM characteristics.

Launched in 1967, Matra's first V12 had four-valve combustion chambers with the valves inclined at a 56° included angle, requiring a deep chamber and a high-domed piston. Martin was already well aware that this was not ideal. The MS9's output of 390bhp at 10,500rpm was good but not – Matra knew – up to the standard of the Ford, especially in combination with the twelve's relatively high fuel consumption.

While the MS9 (MS = Matra Sport) went into action, Matra's power unit consultants, Moteur Moderne in Paris, built a single-cylinder test engine with a narrower valve angle and a flatter piston top. A single 10mm central spark plug for the chamber was kept, but the narrower angle forced the inlet ports away from the centre of the head – where they had been on the MS9 – and back to the centre of the vee of the complete engine.

Based on these tests major engine revisions were made in time for the 1970 season. Under the finned magnesium cam covers of the new MS12 V12 were inlet valves inclined at 16° and exhaust valves at 17½° for a total included angle of 33½°. The inlet valves were made of 30NCD16 nickel-chrome-molybdenum steel and had 31mm heads, while the exhaust valves were 27mm in diameter. A later development of the 1970 engine had valves 33.0 and 27.2mm in diameter. Both valves had bronze guides and nickel-bronze seats, which were inserted after being shrunk in liquid nitrogen.

To keep them small and light, the inverted-cup tappets did not extend down around the dual-coil valve springs. The latter were individually checked before assembly by cycling them at a speed equivalent to 14,000rpm for six hours in a special rig. The tappets slid directly in their bores in the removable light-alloy carrier for both tappets and cams that was affixed to the top of each head. Bimetal bearing inserts carried the seven-bearing hardened-steel camshafts.

A train of narrow case-hardened spur gears at the front of the block drove the camshafts. Running in ball and roller bearings, the gears and their shafts were supported by the block and a bolted-in aluminium plate, the whole being encased by a magnesium front engine cover. The single central 12-bladed water pump was driven by the lower-speed gear directly above the crank nose. Its output was piped to a large gallery down the centre of the 60° vee, from which coolant flowed outward around the wet cylinder liners, before rising into the head and being drawn off by a manifold that was integrated with the central casting that carried the slide throttles and vertical injection ram pipes.

Located below the crankshaft in the MS9, the oil scavenge and pressure pumps were taken out of the sump and mounted ahead of the front end of the engine, below the water pump, to help lower the installed profile of the MS12. Separate scavenging pickups were sited at the front and rear of the cast-magnesium sump. Study of the Cosworth V8 led to a tighter encasement of the crank for reduced windage losses, above a curved baffle that aimed to keep outgoing oil away from the crank webs.

Matra's 1970 plan was to use the engine as part of the chassis, Cosworth-style. The sump casting was designed to take most of the lower-level stresses, while those at the top were fed into the new cam/tappet layer bolted atop each cylinder head.

Opposite above: Followers of racing loved the high-pitched exhaust note of the Matra V-12s, which revved to and above 10,000rpm. Henri Pescarolo, shown, was one of the team's drivers in the Matra MS120, powered by the MS12 V12.

Opposite below: Robust attachments at the front end rear of each cylinder head allowed the MS12 engine to serve as an integral part of the chassis in which it was installed. A large central water pump at the front delivered coolant to an integrally cast manifold running down the engine's vee.

the engine to make, machined as it was from the solid, and because several were in the manufacturing pipeline, it was carried over generally unchanged to the MS12. It was of conventional six-throw 120° design with side-by-side rod big ends. Retained were the 52mm main bearings and their caps, which were held in the deep-sided block by two vertical studs and two side-bracing cap screws.

Also carried over were the 116mm-long titanium connecting rods with their 44mm big ends running, like the mains, on trimetal Vandervell bearings. The matching faces of their big ends were given special surface treatment to avoid the scuffing to which titanium is prone. A bushing at the small end held the 21mm gudgeon pin, which was held in the piston by circlips. Forged of aluminium and fully skirted, the flat-topped piston carried two Dykes-type compression rings and one oil ring. In some installations only a single compression ring was used.

Wrapped around the crankshaft was a new aluminium block-cum-crankcase that was based on the previous design but extensively improved. Its exterior ribbing was simplified and realigned to suit the twelve's new chassis-structural role. Cylinder liners of forged steel were clamped by the head at the top of the block and were a press fit in the block at their lower ends, where they were grooved to carry two O-rings for water sealing. Except for the very top of its travel, the full vertical movement of the piston was cooled.

Carried over from the MS9 were its markedly oversquare cylinder dimensions of 79.7 x 50mm (3.14 x 1.97in) for 2,993cc, the largest bore and shortest stroke among the then-current Grand Prix 12-cylinder engines. As on the MS9, the MS12's accessories were at the back. The ignition distributor and Lucas injection metering unit were driven from the rear of the inlet camshafts and the alternator was turned by the left-hand exhaust camshaft. Injection took place through a nozzle sited in the centre of the ram pipe above the throttle slide.

Late in 1969 Matra was ready to put the MS12 to the test on its dynamometer at Saclay, five kilometres from the handsome Matra plant at Velizy, an aerospace centre south of Paris. The results showed that the new narrower V12 equalled the Cosworth V8's power to 10,000rpm

The latter, like the block, were cast of AS9KG aluminium alloy. Combustion chambers were very shallow in the surfaces of the heads, which were retained by 14 studs. Additional sealing security on the exhaust side was provided by six cap screws from the block up into the head. The compression ratio was 11.0:1.

Because the MS9's fully-counterbalanced steel crankshaft was one of the most expensive parts of

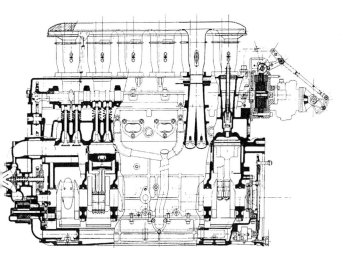

and had the potential to rev higher. In fact the Matra engines were celebrated in their day for a high-pitched wail at speed that was unmatched by any other GP competitor.

The new cylinder heads brought a substantial improvement to 450bhp at 11,000rpm. Maximum torque, at 8,000rpm, was 253lb ft. Initial tests in Matra chassis at the Bugatti Circuit at Le Mans and at Albi suggested that the MS12 would also be quicker on the road than a Cosworth-powered car. Could 1969 world champion Jackie Stewart, who had won his title with a Ford-powered Matra, be persuaded to use the all-French car in 1970? Jackie and Ken Tyrrell preferred instead to stick with the Cosworth and to build a special car to use it.

Matra built the new MS120 GP car for 1970, fabricating its chassis to aerospace standards in an enclave in its main missile and satellite shop. Its drivers were Henri Pescarolo and Jean-Pierre

Beltoise. They managed a few finishes on the bottom step of the podium. After a financially unrewarding season with March, New Zealander Chris Amon joined Matra for 1971. That year and in 1972, when Matra ran a single car for him, Amon showed tremendous pace with several lap records and a win in the non-championship 1971 Argentine GP.

The MS12 came into its own in the open MS660 sports-prototype built around it. It demonstrated its speed in 1971 and then in 1972, in developed MS670 form, achieved Matra's goal of a Le Mans victory. The team of Pescarolo with Graham Hill won, and François Cevert was second paired with Howden Ganley. This basic engine was still used in 1973 and 1974, when Matra won both the constructors' championship – defeating Ferrari in 1973 – and Le Mans. The 24-hour race was won both years by Henri Pescarolo driving with Gerard Larrousse.

When visiting Matra to research this engine in 1969 the author was told of the company's Le Mans ambitions. 'If we were to win,' a Matra official told him, 'we might consider making a small series of 2½- or 3-litre V12 road cars.' Regrettably this was one challenge that Matra did not accept.

Opposite above: Pescarolo was at the wheel again at Le Mans in 1973, a race which was won by this Matra MS670, powered by the MS12 engine. His co-driver was Gerard Larrousse.

Opposite below: To lower the profile of the MS12 its oil pumps were moved from the sump, as positioned in the previous model, to a mounting low at the front of the engine. Fuel-injection

nozzles were positioned inside the vertical ram tubes supplying each cylinder.

Above: Although not achieving the narrowest valve included angle or the straightest inlet ports, the Matra MS12 was a good example of current practice in 1970. A curved shield below the crankshaft showed an attempt to minimise windage losses in the sump.

SPECIFICATIONS	
Cylinders	V12
Bore	79.7mm
Stroke	50.0mm
Stroke/bore ratio	0.63:1
Capacity	2,993cc
Compression ratio	11.0:1
Connecting rod length	116.0mm
Rod/crank radius ratio	4.6:1
Main bearing journal diameter	52.0mm
Rod journal diameter	44.0mm
Inlet valve diameter (2 valves)	31.0mm
Exhaust valve diameter (2 valves)	27.0mm
Inlet pressure	1.0Atm
Engine weight	370lb (168kg)
Peak power	450bhp @ 11,000rpm
Piston speed (corrected)	4,556ft/min (22.8m/s)
Peak torque	253lb ft (343Nm) @ 8,000rpm
Peak bmep	209psi
Engine bhp per litre	150.4bhp per litre
Engine weight per bhp	0.82lb (0.37kg) per bhp

1975

ALFA ROMEO 115-12 3-LITRE FLAT-12

After Alfa Romeo retired from Grand Prix racing following its 1951 championship season with the Type 159 Alfetta (*qv*) it remained active in many branches of the sport, including sports-prototype racing in 1953 and GT category successes in the 1960s. In 1964 a former Alfa Romeo engineer returned to the fold: Carlo Chiti. Encouraged by Alfa's enthusiastic chief Giuseppe Luraghi, in 1964 Chiti founded a new company near Milan, Autodelta, to develop and race cars for Alfa Romeo. It was a role not unlike the one that Enzo Ferrari had had with Alfa in the 1930s.

Engineering for Autodelta's projects was carried out by Chiti's team with the blessing of Alfa engineers Orazio Satta and Giuseppe Busso. Taking the sports-car racing category seriously, Chiti decided to build a completely new car for it, the Type 33TT3. This had a tubular space frame, and its gearbox was located between the engine and the final drive. Although this first raced with a 3-litre V8 engine, a new flat-12 was being built to suit it. Thus-equipped the car became the 33TT12.

First raced in 1973, by 1974 the new car was mature enough to win the 1,000 Kilometres of Monza with the team Andretti/Merzario. In 1975 the 33TT12 won the world championship of makes for Alfa Romeo. For 1977 Autodelta built a new chassis, the 33SC12, with an aluminium monocoque frame. This was fastest qualifier and winner of all eight rounds of the makes world championship against modest opposition.

The Alfa twelve was rated at 470bhp at 11,000rpm at its launch in 1973, and at 490bhp at 11,500rpm in 1974 with 240lb ft of torque at 9,000rpm. By mid-1975, with a compression ratio of 11.0:1, its peak output was a very impressive 526bhp at 12,000rpm with a power curve giving in excess of 400bhp from 9,000rpm upward. These were heady figures in 1975, the year when another Italian flat-12 powered Niki Lauda to a Formula 1 world championship. Indeed, no one at that time was claiming a higher output from a 3-litre unsupercharged engine.

Bernie Ecclestone, then the proprietor of Brabham, negotiated successfully with Alfa Romeo to gain the exclusive use of their engine for his team in 1976. The flat-12 was raced by Brabham from 1976 to 1978 in cars designed by Gordon Murray. The first year was difficult, the second less

so and in the third a number of good placings were achieved plus two victories for Niki Lauda at Sweden's Andersdorp and Italy's Monza. (The Andersdorp victory was with the controversial 'fan car' Brabham, which used a 'cooling' blower to add downforce. The concept was banned after this race.)

In designing the Brabhams, Murray was challenged by the flat-12's size and weight. It was, first of all, massive. Its weight in endurance-racing form was a substantial 396lb (178kg), some 10 per cent more than most GP engines of the same displacement. In its GP version the twelve's weight was reduced to 385lb (175kg).

It was also wide, wider than the flat-12 engine fielded by Ferrari. One reason for this was its longer stroke. Its cylinder dimensions were 77.0 x 53.6mm (3.03 x 2.11in) for 2,995cc. The Ferrari's stroke was only 49.6mm in its final form. Another reason was that its inverted-cup-type cam followers were placed above its twin coil valve springs instead of being made large enough in diameter to shroud the springs. This effected a vital saving of mass in the follower, helping the engine reach its high speeds, but at a cost in engine weight and width.

It had four valves per cylinder, measuring 33mm on the inlet side and 28mm for the exhausts. (Dimensions in the endurance-racing engines were 30 and 25.5mm respectively.) They were inclined at the narrow included angle of 27°, 13° for the inlets and 14° for the exhausts, and had very long stems to accommodate the placing of the followers above the springs and to allow the inlet port to enter the cylinder at the shallow angle of 38° to its centreline. Previously the valves were alloy steel; in Grand Prix tune the Alfa engine used valves made of titanium.

Attached by long studs to each cylinder head was an aluminium cam-and-tappet carrier whose bottom parting line was near the tops of the coil springs. Down the centre of the head the studs were long enough to serve also to retain the magnesium cam cover. Within the carrier the seven bearings

Opposite above: Designed, built and raced for Alfa Romeo by Autodelta, the 33TT12 added considerable lustre to Alfa's sporting history. In various forms it was world makes champion in both 1975 and 1977.
Opposite below: In the configuration raced in Formula 1 by Brabham in 1977 the 115-12 had moved its injection distributor to the top of the engine, replacing the ignition distributor. Ignition was now electronically triggered. In this application the engine had four main bearings.

A lighter-duty spur gear at the nose of the crankshaft drove the engine's pumps. A single central water pump served both banks of the flat-12 through passages cast into both the block and the heads. Coolant was drawn off through a head-length passage just above the inlet ports.

All the engine's main castings were of aluminium. Individual wet cylinder liners were fitted. In a construction not unlike that of the flat-12 Ferrari, the top two-fifths of the liner was of a heavier section which, at its bottom, was clamped by the head against a ledge in the block's bore. Only to that depth was the liner surrounded by water; its lower three-fifths were pressed into the aluminium block. Although in the sports-racers the liners were iron, in the GP engine they were made of aluminium with chromed bores to reduce the engine's weight.

The Alfa engine was a typical flat-12 in that it carried side-by-side connecting rods on a six-throw crankshaft. Although the endurance-racing version had seven main bearings, the F1 edition followed the example of the Ferrari 312B in having only four. All were plain trimetal bearings except for the rear main, which was a ball bearing. This allowed the use of larger counterbalancing masses in the GP engine where the eliminated main bearings had previously been. To augment the crank's counterbalance mass in a compact crankcase, the peripheries of the counterbalances were fitted with bolted-on crescent-shaped tungsten-alloy masses.

Titanium connecting rods 112mm long from centre to centre had robust I-section shanks. The caps were retained by nuts on two studs set into the rods. Aluminium pistons were slipper-type in the GP engine. They carried two compression rings and one oil ring above the gudgeon pin.

The main-bearing supports were integral with the webs of the split two-piece aluminium block-crankcase; there were no separate main bearing caps. The slice down the middle of the crankcase separating the two halves wasn't made vertically as it was in every other such engine. It was on a plane slightly counter-clockwise from the vertical, as viewed from the front of the engine, skewed at about 7°. Studs across the top and bottom of the crankcase held its halves together.

A long opening in the underside of the crankcase was closed off by a shallow cast magnesium sump.

for each camshaft were held in place by individual caps, each with its own pair of retaining studs.

The spur-gear train to the camshafts was located at the rear of the engine, adjacent to the clutch. A gear train upward drove the distributor for the Marelli Dinoplex ignition system, which sparked one plug per cylinder. This was on the left, while the distributor for the Lucas fuel injection was on the right. The injection fed nozzles that were set into the sides of the short ram pipes, just above the slide throttle.

In its Formula 1 form the flat-12 was designated the Type 115-12. Its power output continued to be rated at 'over 520bhp' in its Grand Prix trim, for which the main effort was not to get more power but to shed more weight. Another goal was to broaden the engine's narrow power band. 'It feels a bit like a diesel,' said driver Larry Perkins in 1976. 'When you back off it all goes off and you find it takes a moment to come back when you put your foot down again.'

In reaching their deal with Brabham the Alfa Romeo men saw it as a scouting expedition to see how well their engine would perform in a new racing world. Finding it promising, they designed and built a Grand Prix car of their own. By 1977 work on this car, the Type 177, was under way and by 1978 Vittorio Brambilla was testing it at Alfa's private Balocco proving grounds west of Milan. This car made several race sorties in 1979 in the hands of Bruno Giacomelli but was superseded late that year by the Type 179.

Like the Brabham of the same year, the Type 179 and its successor of 1982 the T182 was powered by a version of the 115-12 engine with a 60° vee instead of a 180° vee. Using essentially the same heads as the flat-12, this was created to make more room for the ground-effects venturis that were just coming into use. In neither installation, however, was the narrow-angle version of the twelve successful.

Opposite above: Looking forward from the transaxle of the 33TT12, its Type 115-12 engine is all but hidden beneath the inlet airboxes at the sides and the frame members crossing above it. Its oil filter and ignition distributor can just be distinguished.

Opposite below: As raced by Autodelta in 1975 and as initially tested for Formula 1 purposes by Brabham, the 115-12 had its fuel-injection distributor at the left rear supplying injectors in the inlet *ram pipes through nylon tubing. The distributor was above the crankcase at the rear, where the gear train to the overhead camshafts was located.*

Above: As originally constructed for endurance racing the 115-12 flat-12 Alfa engine had seven main bearings. The bulkheads for these are visible through the apertures that will be covered by the light-alloy sump. Exhaust ports exited individually from each cylinder head.

In the endurance-racing engine this was scavenged by a battery of three double-sided gear-type oil pumps bolted to the side of the sump, sucking oil from six screened drains. For the Formula 1 application the pumps were moved to the front in order to lower the engine's centre of gravity. Separate scavenge pumps for each cylinder head drew from passages within each tappet carrier and cover. Chiti had not forgotten his oil-scavenging experiences with the 120° Ferrari V6 (*qv*).

SPECIFICATIONS	
Cylinders	F12
Bore	77.0mm
Stroke	53.6mm
Stroke/bore ratio	0.70:1
Capacity	2,995cc
Compression ratio	11.0:1
Connecting rod length	112.0mm
Rod/crank radius ratio	4.2:1
Inlet valve diameter (2 valves)	33.0mm
Exhaust valve diameter (2 valves)	28.0mm
Inlet pressure	1.0Atm
Engine weight	385lb (175kg)
Peak power	526bhp @ 12,000rpm
Piston speed (corrected)	5,059ft/min (25.3m/s)
Engine bhp per litre	175.6bhp per litre
Engine weight per bhp	0.73lb (0.33kg) per bhp

1984

RENAULT EF4 1.5-LITRE V6

Renault's racing engine company bore a proud name. In the 1940s and '50s Amédée Gordini had worked miracles to preserve for France a presence in Grand Prix racing. In 1957 Gordini joined forces with Renault, which closed his original workshop and established new facilities for car and race preparation at Viry-Chatillon, south of Paris. It continued to be called Usine Amédée Gordini.

Renault's Gordini works accepted a new challenge in 1972 with the design from scratch of a 2-litre V6 to power a competitor in sports-car racing to be built by a sister Renault company, Alpine, at Dieppe. Alpine's activities were strongly supported by Elf, the French national oil company, which subsidised the creation of the new engine. The choice of a V6 configuration and a 90° vee angle provided a publicity link to a new engine of the same layout that Renault was introducing for passenger cars. François Castaing directed the racing engine's design and would have much to do with its subsequent evolution.

No sooner had the resulting V6 been introduced than Gordini began turbocharging it. Scenting an attractive idea, Elf backed the building of two prototypes of a blown 1½-litre version that could compete in Formula 1 against the naturally-aspirated 3-litre engines. The first such Renault Gordini V6, dubbed EF1 in honour of the Elf contribution, ran in July 1975.

In 1977 a Renault turbo F1 engine raced for the first time and a victory was first scored in 1979. In 1983 Renault and Alain Prost were vice-champions in both the driver and manufacturer categories, using the EF3 version of the V6. For 1984 Renault laid down a new version of the V6, which had the doubly-oversquare cylinder dimensions of 86 x 42.8mm (3.39 x 1.69in) for a displacement of 1,492cc. This EF4 would be raced by Renault's own team (Derek Warwick and Patrick Tambay) and also by two other teams: Lotus, with Elio de Angelis and Nigel Mansell, and Ligier with Andrea de Cesaris and François Hesnault.

An aluminium cylinder block had been introduced the previous year for the EF3 to replace the V6's original thin-wall cast-iron block. Instead of being made outside by Messier, however, the 1984 block was cast in-house by Renault and incorporated design changes that increased its strength. These were needed in order to cope with the advances being made by turbocharging, which year on year was increasing Formula 1 horsepower by huge handfuls.

Critical on a highly-boosted engine was the joint between the block and the detachable heads. The block/head attachment was both by conventional studs and by downward-facing short studs to nuts along the periphery of each head. A composite metallic gasket provided the Renault's gas seal while Viton rubber seals took care of oil and water passages. The wet cylinder liners of nitrided steel were clamped into the block by a recessed collar at their very top. At the bottom end of each liner two O-rings provided a water-retaining seal against the bore in the block.

Divided at the crankshaft centreline, the bottom end of the EF4 was simplicity itself. The caps for the four plain Glyco main bearings were integrated into the sump casting, also of aluminium, bolted to the bottom of the block. This sump casting carried the lower mounts for the engine, which was a stressed member of the chassis. The 58mm main bearings carried a steel crankshaft machined from a solid billet. It had only three 48mm throws spaced at 120°, each carrying two connecting-rod big ends. Substantial counter-weights extended from the crank webs opposite each throw and all bearing surfaces were nitrided.

Instead of the usual I-section the shanks of the nitrided steel connecting rods were of H-section, favoured by some designers for high-speed engines because they place less mass at the periphery of the rod. The big ends of the 123mm rods were two-bolt.

Gerotor-type pumps mounted externally at the sides of the sump powered the lubrication system. Provided were a pressure pump, main scavenge pumps and smaller scavenge pumps for the two turbochargers. In all, the scavenging capacity was ten times that of the pressure pump. Driven from the back of each row of pumps was a centrifugal water pump which delivered directly to a manifold cast into the lowest level of the side of the block.

Opposite above: Britain's Derek Warwick was at the wheel of the 1984 Formula 1 Renault, powered by the new EF4 turbocharged V6. Although the pioneer of turbocharging in Formula 1, Renault had yet to reap the full reward of its initiative.
Opposite below: Within the side pods of the Renault RE50 Formula 1 car were engine-cooling radiators, toward the front, and behind them the substantial intercoolers for the compressed air entering the engine. A turbocharger was positioned on each side behind the intercooler.

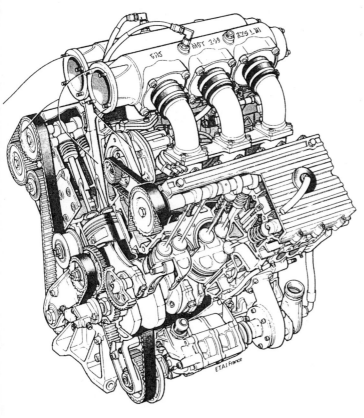

Water was drawn off from the front of the inlet side of each cylinder head.

The two pump arrays were driven by the same system of cogged rubber belts that drove the EF4's camshafts – an impressive validation of this drive medium for an engine running up to 11,000rpm. A disadvantage was the longitudinal space that the belts occupied at the front of the engine, and an important advantage was their light weight compared to gears or even chains.

A small gearcase above the crank nose contained two speed-reduced spur gears, each of which drove a sprocket for one bank's belt. One spur gear was driven by the crank nose and the other was driven by its neighbour; by this means the two belts were made to counter-rotate so that they could be laid out symmetrically. From a wrapping idler the inner tension side was the shortest, pulling the belt around the large cam sprockets. Another idler ensured a tight wrap around the exhaust cam sprocket. The pump gangs were driven by the bottoms of the slack runs of the belts.

The aluminium cylinder-head castings were

particularly deep. This served several objectives. It accommodated the very-long-stemmed valves that were needed to allow the inlet ports to run as straight as possible to the valve heads. Stem length was further increased by the decision to place the cup-type tappets above rather than around the valve springs. The tall head also provided room for water passages around the exhaust-valve guides, whose cooling is critical in a turbocharged engine. To this same end the valve stems were hollow and filled with heat-conducting sodium salts.

Atop each head was a shallow aluminium casting which carried the cup-type tappets and the four lower Glyco bearing inserts for each steel camshaft. The bearing caps were incorporated in the wide one-piece camshaft cover. Twin coil springs supplied by Schmitthelm closed each valve. Valve-stem inclinations were very slight: 10° for the 29.8mm inlets and 11½° for the 26.1mm exhausts. This facilitated a chamber with a very shallow pent-roof shape that stimulated turbulence of the fresh gases. A single spark plug was at the centre of the chamber.

The shallow chamber allowed the top of the forged Mahle piston to be flat except for slight indentations for valve clearance. Three rings were carried, two for compression and one for oil control. The piston of the EF4 was given a higher crown than its predecessor, raising the compression ratio half a point to 7.5:1 to help improve fuel consumption for 1984, in which only 220 litres were allowed for the race distance. Achieving adequate ring and piston life in the turbocharged engine was a major challenge for the Renault engineers. An oil jet initially provided to cool the underside of the piston crown evolved into a Mahle design that incorporated an internal cooling-oil gallery.

Below a carbon-fibre inlet plenum and ram-tuned magnesium downpipes, each inlet port was fed Elf's racing petrol blend by a nozzle supplied by a mechanical Kugelfischer injection system. The plunger-type pump was in the engine's central vee and was driven by a cogged belt from the rear of the right-hand inlet camshaft. Control of its fuel-metering cam was by an aerospace servomotor reacting to a Renault-developed electronic micro-processor which responded to five engine parameters. A separate processor, triggered by a pickup in the bellhousing, controlled the timing of the Marelli Raceplex capacitive-discharge ignition system.

Each bank of the V6 was equipped with its own turbocharging system, using turbo units made by Garrett AiResearch to Renault's specifications. They had specially-developed turbine wheels and compressor impellers machined from solid billets of aluminium alloy. Boost pressure was controlled by a valve in each three-branch exhaust manifold – a wastegate – that vented exhaust to the atmosphere when the desired boost was reached. In races boost of up to 32psi was used, with more readily available for qualifying.

Butterflies at the forward-facing inlets to the turbochargers provided throttle control, upstream from a Renault-developed device, the *Dispositive Prerotation Variable* or DPV. This inserted vanes into the incoming air which could be varied in incidence, either to provide a pre-swirl or to close so that the impeller would be in a semi-vacuum that would help maintain its speed. Turbo output was delivered through an air-to-air intercooler alongside the front of the V6 and was then ducted

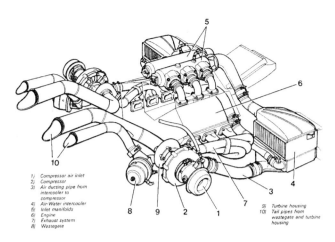

1) Compressor air inlet
2) Compressor
3) Air ducting pipe from intercooler to compressor
4) Air-Water intercooler
5) Inlet manifolds
6) Engine
7) Exhaust system
8) Wastegate
9) Turbine housing
10) Tail pipes from wastegate and turbine housing

to the bank's inlet plenum, within which water was injected – in proportion to boost pressure – further to cool the incoming air.

Complete with starter, clutch and turbos, this was a 342lb (155kg) package that was capable of producing between 660 and 750bhp at 11,000rpm, depending on boost pressure. Its torque peak, reached at 8,500rpm, was 354lb ft. The EF4's most successful 1984 user was Team Lotus, whose drivers put the 95T on pole twice and were on the podium six times. The V6 took Elio de Angelis and Lotus-Renault to third in the two respective world championships.

Opposite left: Inside the front case of the Renault V6, spur gears took the drive from the crank nose and transferred it at reduced speed to the two cogged-belt drives. Accessories driven along the left side of the engine included the oil pumps and one of the two water pumps.

Opposite right: Uniquely among front-rank racing engines the Renault Gordini EF4 and its predecessors used cogged rubber belts to drive the overhead camshafts.

Lightness and simplicity were important assets of this drive method, as was a low rotating moment of inertia.

Above: Twin turbochargers suited the engine's vee layout and, at the same time, offered better throttle response by virtue of their smaller diameter and lower inertia. Liquid-cooled intercoolers improved volumetric efficiency by reducing the temperature and thus increasing the density of the incoming compressed-air charge.

SPECIFICATIONS	
Cylinders	V6
Bore	86.0mm
Stroke	42.8mm
Stroke/bore ratio	0.50:1
Capacity	1,492cc
Compression ratio	7.5:1
Connecting rod length	123.0mm
Rod/crank radius ratio	5.7:1
Main bearing journal diameter	58.0mm
Rod journal diameter	48.0mm
Inlet valve diameter (2 valves)	29.8mm
Exhaust valve diameter (2 valves)	26.1mm
Inlet pressure	3.2Atm
Engine weight	342lb (155kg)
Peak power	700bhp @ 11,000rpm
Piston speed (corrected)	4,379ft/min (21.9m/s)
Peak torque	354lb ft (480Nm)
	@ 8,500rpm
Peak bmep	588psi
Engine bhp per litre	469.2bhp per litre
Engine weight per bhp	0.49lb (0.22kg) per bhp

1987

TAG-P01 1.5-LITRE V6

Porsche was rightly renowned for its racing-engine expertise. Since its work as consultants to Auto Union and Cisitalia (*qv*), however, Porsche had been designing and building engines on its own account. Key to its successful work in this field since the 1960s was the expertise of Hans Mezger, who made major contributions to the Type 753 of 1962 and the Type 912 engine used in the 1969 917 (*qv*). Mezger's talents were given a new challenge in the 1980s when Porsche was asked by a customer to design a Grand Prix engine.

With first Renault (1977) and then Ferrari (1980) demonstrating the advantages of 1½-litre turbocharged engines for Formula 1 racing, the McLaren team realised that it would have to leave the naturally-aspirated ranks and look for a turbo of its own. Since October 1980 McLaren – originally established by driver Bruce McLaren in the 1960s – had been virtually a new company, McLaren International, under the direction of part-owner Ron Dennis. A fellow director was engineer John Barnard.

When turbocharging was considered Porsche had to come into the frame, not least because the Stuttgart company had pioneered in the application of turbos to sports-racing cars for the Can-Am series and endurance racing. After the first contact was made by McLaren on 26 August 1981, Porsche carried out a four-month initial feasibility study for a new Formula 1 engine. Completed in May 1982, this was followed by a full contract, which was financed by a Saudi Arabian company managed by McLaren ally Mansour Ojjeh, Techniques d'Avant-Garde or TAG. The resulting engine was thus identified as a TAG unit and given the designation TAG-P01. Its cylinder dimensions were established as 82 x 47.3mm (3.23 x 1.86in) for 1,499cc.

First run on the test bench on 18 December 1982, the engine was ready to compete in four GPs in the autumn of 1983 in a provisional McLaren chassis – outings that were declared as tests, not serious entries. In its first full season, 1984, the Porsche-designed unit took Niki Lauda to the drivers' world championship ahead of Alain Prost in a sister car. It was Prost's turn to win the championship in 1985 and he did so again in 1986. He had to settle for fourth in 1987, the last season in which the TAG engine was used. From 1984 to '87 the McLaren-TAGs won more races than any other team.

The engine that made this possible was by no means a cost-no-object exercise. It was built by Porsche to TAG's strict budget and specifications. As well, it was planned by Porsche to fit snugly within a central underfloor channel at the rear of a new car which was planned to generate record high levels of downforce. Before this could be built, however, the racing authorities introduced new rules requiring GP cars to have flat bottoms. Thus some of the engine's features, such as high-placed exhaust pipes and a narrow crankcase, became redundant.

A V6 configuration was chosen in preference to the more costly and complex V8 alternative. Hans Mezger set its banks at an 80° included angle, narrow enough to allow room under its sides for the (planned) venturi tunnels yet wide enough to accommodate the central induction piping. His analysis of the first- and second-order vibration forces that the engine would generate showed that an 80° vee was a good compromise between the two. The angle also suited the expressed requirement for the engine to mount in the chassis as a stressed member, using the same attachment points as the Ford-Cosworth V8.

The P01's cylinder block was compact, its deeply-ribbed casting extending down only to the crankshaft centreline and up to the detachable cylinder heads. They and the rest of the engine's major housings were cast of aluminium alloy by Honsel Werke AG. Inserted into the block were wet cylinder liners of aluminium, their bores coated with Nicasil, a Mahle-developed hard-wearing plated surface of nickel carrying silicon carbide particles.

Long-time Porsche partner Mahle also supplied the aluminium pistons, which had an internal gallery through which oil flowed to cool the crown and ring lands. Lightly concave to provide a compression ratio initially of 7.5:1, the piston crown had cut-outs for top-dead-centre valve-head

Opposite above: Powered by the TAG-P01 V6, the McLaren MP4/2 was the dominant Formula 1 car of the 1984 season, scoring a dozen victories. Niki Lauda (shown) beat Alain Prost in a sister car for the drivers' title.

Opposite below: To control the boost pressure of the TAG-P01 engine Porsche used its own waste gates, placed just where the three exhaust pipes entered the turbo's turbine. A discreet badge on the engine's plenum chamber identified its maker.

clearance. For the 1987 season compression was upped to 8.0:1. Two compression rings and one oil ring were carried above the gudgeon pin. Connecting rods were made of titanium. Both pistons and rods were made more robust for the final 1987 season.

The large bore allowed the four valves to be inclined to the left and right at modest angles. Inlet inclination was 14° from vertical and exhaust angle was 15°. In addition the valves were angled slightly in the fore and aft direction to give the chamber a slightly spherical surface and to improve the gas flow in the chamber. To permit this, the tappets were similarly angled and the cam lobes were given a conical profile. Diameters of the Glyco-made valves were 30.5mm (inlets) and 27.5mm (exhausts).

Hollow stems in the Nimonic-steel valves contained salts that accelerated their internal transfer of heat away from the head to the stem and thence to the valve guide. Extraction of heat from the exhaust-valve seats was significantly improved by tiny drillings that allowed water to circulate through the metal around the seats. A system patented by Porsche, this had its own pipework taking 10 per cent of the water-pump output.

Two coaxial coil springs closed the valves, which were opened by inverted-cup-type tappets. Twin camshafts in each aluminium head were driven by a train of gears from the crank nose. Turned by an idler above the crank nose, the first half-speed spur gear for each cylinder bank also drove a water pump mounted on the face of the P01's front cover. Both rotating clockwise, the pumps delivered coolant to the centre of the vee to manifolds cast into the cylinder block, and to the previously-mentioned exhaust-seat cooling

Above: As originally raced in the 1984 McLaren the TAG V6 developed some 650bhp at 11,500rpm. Its turbo units were set outboard at some distance from the engine.
Middle: Development of the engine to 1987 brought a number of changes, including a more compact positioning for the turbochargers and their waste gates. On each cylinder bank the rear of the exhaust camshaft drove a simple 3-cylinder ignition distributor.
Below: A small header tank primed the two water pumps at the front of the TAG-P01 V6, each pump delivering to its own cast manifold in the cylinder block. Closed by a deep ribbed sump, the block was cut off at the centreline of the crankshaft.

TAG-P01 1.5-LITRE V6

system. Water flowed back along the cylinder liners, up past the exhaust valves and out through passages on the inlet side of the head. Magnesium was used for the pipes to the water pumps and from the heads.

Also mounted on the front cover were the scavenge and pressure oil pumps. These were placed at the front instead of in the increasingly-popular side-mounted location, as pioneered by Cosworth's Ford V8 (qv), in order to meet the objective of a narrow crankcase that would offer minimum obstruction to an underbody venturi. Tunnels along the sides of the sump casting collected oil flung from the crankshaft and fed it to the scavenge pumps. The pressure oil feed to the crankshaft was through the nose of the crank, as had been Porsche racing practice since the Type 753 flat-eight (qv).

Made by Alfing Kessler, the nitrided-steel crankshaft had the straightforward layout of four main bearings and three rod throws – with side-by-side rods – that was pioneered for the racing V6 engine by Carlo Chiti's 1961 120° vee Ferrari (qv). Fully counterbalanced, it was carried in Glyco thin-wall lead-bronze bearings, as also used for the rod big-ends. Although with the 80° vee angle this did not provide equally-spaced firing impulses, the uneven timing could easily be accommodated by the Bosch Motronic engine management system.

At Bosch, Dr Udo Zucker headed the team that progressively developed the TAG engine's control system. By 1985 all the control elements were combined in a single package, which – at a time when fuel consumption was critical – could tell the driver how many laps he could complete with his reserve of fuel at the boost pressure he was running. The final Bosch MP1:7 system used two solenoid-controlled valves, aiming at 30° down into each inlet port, to inject fuel volumes that varied according to a highly detailed map of engine speed plus such factors as humidity, altitude, torque and engine deceleration or acceleration. Throttle control was by individual butterflies above the injection nozzles.

Long-time Porsche partner KKK supplied the engine's twin turbochargers. Frustratingly for perfectionist engineer John Barnard, KKK took a year and a half to produce mirror-image units that allowed him to improve exhaust-gas flow to the right-hand turbocharger. Porsche's own wastegates, finned for cooling, provided boost pressure control in the exhaust manifolds just upstream of the turbine entries. The turbo-compressors delivered through air-cooled intercoolers to individual plenum chambers feeding each cylinder bank.

The policy of McLaren and Porsche was to run essentially the same engine in qualifying and the race. Three different turbines and two compressor types were available for the HHB model KKK turbochargers. These could be mixed and matched to tailor the set-up to the circuit, with the larger turbine giving more power but at a sacrifice in throttle response. Typical power in racing trim was 820bhp at 12,000rpm with a boost of 36psi. Maximum torque was 390lb ft at 8,800rpm. With a higher qualifying boost of 41psi the V6's horsepower exceeded 900. The engines ran on a special toluene-based petrol developed by Shell.

High reliability helped Porsche fulfil its TAG contract with remarkably few engines. Only 15 were used in the first full season and a mere 50 or so for the entire programme. In relation to the resources expended the project was a resounding success.

SPECIFICATIONS	
Cylinders	V6
Bore	82.0mm
Stroke	47.3mm
Stroke/bore ratio	0.58:1
Capacity	1,499cc
Compression ratio	8.0:1
Connecting rod length	115.0mm
Rod/crank radius ratio	4.9:1
Main bearing journal diameter	48.0mm
Rod journal diameter	45.0mm
Inlet valve diameter (2 valves)	30.5mm
Exhaust valve diameter (2 valves)	27.5mm
Inlet pressure	3.48Atm
Engine weight	331lb (150kg)
Peak power	860bhp @ 12,000rpm
Piston speed (corrected)	4,904ft/min (24.5m/s)
Peak torque	390lb ft (529Nm)
	@ 8,800 rpm
Peak bmep	645psi
Engine bhp per litre	573.7bhp per litre
Engine weight per bhp	0.38lb (0.17kg) per bhp

1992

HONDA RA122E/B 3.5-LITRE V12

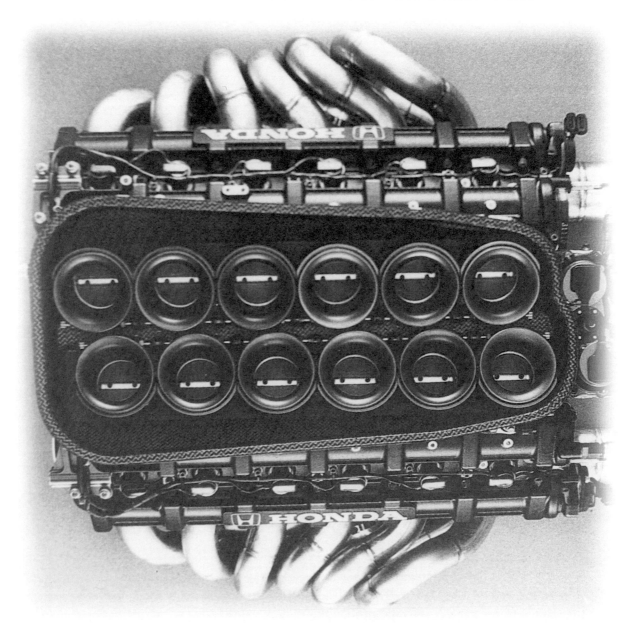

When Honda returned to Formula 1 racing in 1983 it did so with the clear objective of achieving an international reputation as one of the 'noble' automotive brands. Noting the participation in GP racing of such great firms as Mercedes-Benz and Alfa Romeo, and concluding that taking part in the highest level of motor sports had added great lustre to their names, Honda decided to go and do likewise to enhance its own reputation and that of its new upmarket US Acura brand.

Much like Renault, Honda launched this new initiative by turbocharging a V6 that had previously been used in Formula 2 racing. In partnership with Williams it won the constructors' championship in 1986 and 1987, adding a drivers' trophy for Nelson Piquet in the latter year. The last year for a Honda turbo was 1988, when McLaren moved from the TAG engine (*qv*) to become a Honda team. This saw another constructors' championship with 15 wins in 16 races and a season-long battle between Alain Prost and Ayrton Senna for the driver's championship in which the latter triumphed.

With turbos banned, after such a spectacularly successful year Honda gave serious consideration to withdrawing from F1. Soichiro Honda counselled continuation, however, pointing out that a new level playing field had just been created on which Honda could confirm its superiority. Accordingly it began the new 3½-litre Formula 1 of 1989 with a V10 engine and a continuation of its McLaren partnership, which was to last until 1992.

The V10 was raced in 1989 and '90, bringing two more constructors' cups and driving championships for Prost and Senna. To meet the intensifying competition from Ferrari and Renault a 60° V12 was introduced in 1991. Under development since 1989, this RA121E brought McLaren-Honda both championships again with Senna the lead driver. However, the pace of progress was such that Honda elected to build an all-new V12, the RA122E/B, for 1992. Begun in July 1991, work on it was delayed by the concentration late that season on the improvement of its predecessor to meet the demands of both McLaren and Ayrton Senna.

The new engine's vee angle was widened to 75° to lower its height and centre of gravity and to make more room in the vee to package the fuel pump and alternator. Compared to the previous twelve's cylinder dimensions of 86.5 x 49.6mm (3.41 x 1.95in) the new unit was more oversquare at 88.0 x 47.9mm (3.46 x 1.89in) for 3,496cc to suit the then-current 3½-litre Formula 1. High-silicon aluminium alloy was used for both the block and the heads. The block terminated at the crankshaft centreline. Bolted to its bottom surface was a large casting of Elektron WE54 magnesium alloy which incorporated the caps for the seven main bearings, the sump and the mountings for the accessory-drive gears across the front of the sump, driven from the crank nose.

Each of the six individual sump chambers, housing a crank throw with its two connecting rods, had a close-fitting circular cross-section. A slot along its lower right-hand side was fitted with guides to collect oil thrown from the crank and channel it to the scavenging pumps. For the first time, Honda placed all the Gerotor-type scavenging pumps on the right of the engine's sump – four large pumps to exhaust the crankcase, two small ones for the cam cases and a single small pump for the gear case for the drive to the camshafts, which was at the rear of the V12. The pump capacity was high enough to reduce the pressure in the crankcase to 30 per cent of atmospheric, which – compared to 64 per cent of atmospheric – increased engine power by 2 per cent at 14,000rpm.

On the left side of the engine the gear train drove the water pump and the pressure oil pump. All pumps were positioned as far forward as possible to allow the downpipes from the tuned exhaust manifolds to be tucked closely to the crankcase. This in turn improved the packaging of the adjacent cooling radiators and their ducting. Cast-in galleries for both oil and water ran down the engine's central valley. Included in the oiling system were jets to the underside of the pistons that reduced the temperature of the ring lands by 10–20°C.

Short fully-skirted pistons carried two compression rings and a single oil ring in a

Opposite above: Although Honda's last year in Formula 1 was not its most successful, it scored five victories in 1992 with the help of Ayrton Senna and Gerhard Berger.
Opposite below: Butterfly throttle valves were used for the new 75° V12 for 1992. Within each inlet tract fuel was injected through two nozzles just below these butterflies. At the rear of the engine were the servos that operated its variable-length inlet trumpets.

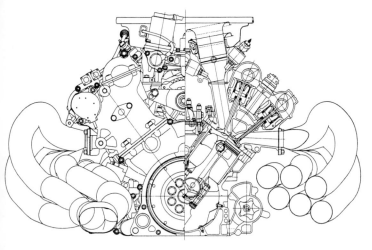

configuration optimised to reduce blow-by. Although pent-roofed, their crowns had marked indentations that exactly matched the slightly tuliped contours of the four valve heads. By this close attention to detail Honda was able to give the RA122E/B the high compression ratio of 12.9:1 in spite of its very large cylinder bore. The cam lobe forms were tailored asymmetrically to reduce the need for valve-head clearance near top dead centre. Surrounding the pistons were aluminium wet liners with a Nicasil running surface, clamped by a top flange into the block. Two O-rings in grooves in the liner completed the bottom seal.

Circlips retained the gudgeon pins in the pistons. The bushing at the small end of the 111mm connecting rod received oil through a drilling at its top. Made of titanium, the rods had a robust I-section and massive two-bolt big-ends. Each 40mm rod journal was doubly counter-weighted in a crankshaft configuration that resulted from tests by Honda of many prototype designs. Drillings in the steel crank cheeks adjacent to the journals helped lighten the throws to reduce the balance mass requirement.

Trains of spur gears up the rear of the block drove the V12's four overhead camshafts. Having relatively large 30mm base circles, the cams were hollowed for lightness. They were carried in plain bearings which were between the valve pairs, although many designers of high-speed engines were now putting the bearings between the valves in each pair to minimise any chance of unwanted cam flexing. Inverted-cup-type tappets were used.

Honda's analysis of coil valve springs showed that if a spring force of 236lb (107kg) were needed to avoid valve bounce at 13,000rpm, a force half again as great would be needed at 15,000 and twice as large at 15,700rpm. This led it to adopt pneumatic valve closing for the RA122E/B. Weighing half as much as coil springs and their retainers, the pneumatic system reduced the valve reciprocating weight by 20 per cent.

Honda chose nitrogen as the system's working gas, the McLaren carrying a reserve supply at 150 atmospheres in two small cylinders mounted on the firewall. Gas was metered at 6 to 8 atmospheres to the volume under each tappet. There the space was sealed by an inverted tulip-shaped titanium cup, called a 'piston' by Honda. It was sealed to the valve stem and had a ring seal at its bottom, sliding in the tappet bore. Careful tweaking of the system allowed an 800rpm speed increase before the onset of valve bounce, even with the unusual cam profile adopted to keep the valves away from the piston at top dead centre.

Complete with the required gas passages, bulky tappet-carrying blocks were bolted into each cylinder head. Gas seals were also provided for the inserted valve guides. Extra cooling for the exhaust-valve guide was provided by exposing a short portion of it directly to the coolant. Mutually inclined at an included angle of 28°, the 36.5mm inlet valves were made of titanium alloy and the 28.5mm exhaust valves of nickel alloy. The latter were made hollow for lightness, and sealed at the head.

A feature Honda had introduced during 1991, variable-length inlet ram pipes, was engineered from the start into the new V12. A hydraulic actuator for each bank of pipes moved the top funnels over a 25mm range. From 8,000 to 15,000rpm an electronic controller operated solenoid valves to raise and lower the funnels three times to help fill in troughs in the power curve. Below the funnels were the butterfly-type throttle valves, and below them were two nozzles for the electronically-controlled sequential fuel-injection system.

Senna and Berger had no direct control over the Honda's throttles. Each row of six butterflies was operated by a four-phase electric stepping motor, which was able to position the throttles within 0.1° and move them from closed to open in an eighth of a second. Inputs to the electronic control included engine speed and gear selected as well as throttle position, which dramatically reduced incidents of engine overspeeding – thus making another contribution to reduced valve-to-crown clearance and a high compression ratio.

Reliability of these new and complex systems was not 100 per cent; the failure of a stepping motor cost Senna victory in the Canadian GP, which Berger won. Nor was the high-revving Honda a paragon of fuel economy. McLarens had to start some of the faster races with more than 220 litres of fuel compared to 185 for cars with Cosworth V8 power, a 60lb (27kg) weight handicap. But the V12's output by the end of the

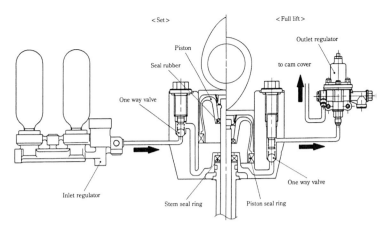

season of 774bhp at 14,400rpm offered considerable compensation, as did its torque of 297lb ft at 12,000rpm.

Although its new MP4/7A chassis was not one of McLaren's best efforts, Ayrton Senna won at Monte Carlo, Hungary and Monza and Gerhard Berger added season-ending Australia to his Canadian win. The two drivers were fourth and fifth in the world championship in Honda's penultimate official season in Formula 1 in the twentieth century, for after 1992 it decided to withdraw – until 2000.

Above: Honda first used pneumatic valve closing in the RA122E/B. Inside each cup-type tappet was a 'piston' made of titanium, sealing against the bore in which the tappet slid. Nitrogen was the system's working gas.
Opposite left: *The 3.5-litre Honda engine was extremely oversquare at a stroke/bore ratio of 0.54. Accordingly its four valves did not need to take full advantage of the available space in the*

cylinder head to have adequate area to develop the required performance. Over a small section of their circumference the exhaust-valve guides were exposed to the coolant.
Opposite right: *An integral sump carried the main-bearing caps of the Honda V12 as well as the gear train low at the front that drove the accessories. The main gear drive to the camshafts was at the rear of the engine.*

SPECIFICATIONS	
Cylinders	V12
Bore	88.0mm
Stroke	47.9mm
Stroke/bore ratio	0.54:1
Capacity	3,496cc
Compression ratio	12.9:1
Connecting rod length	111.0mm
Rod/crank radius ratio	4.6:1
Main bearing journal diameter	54.0mm
Rod journal diameter	40.0mm
Inlet valve diameter (2 valves)	36.5mm
Exhaust valve diameter (2 valves)	28.5mm
Inlet pressure	1.0Atm
Engine weight	339lb (154kg)
Peak power	774bhp @ 14,000rpm
Piston speed (corrected)	5,964ft/min (29.8m/s)
Peak torque	297lb ft (403Nm) @ 12,000rpm
Peak bmep	210psi
Engine bhp per litre	221.4bhp per litre
Engine weight per bhp	0.44lb (0.20kg) per bhp

MERCEDES-BENZ 5001 3.4-LITRE V8

A peculiarity of the rules at Indianapolis in 1994 left a loophole big enough to drive a Mercedes-Benz through – and that's just what happened. To fill up the field, turbocharged engines using stock production cylinder blocks were allowed a displacement of 3,430cc in no more than eight cylinders, 29.4 per cent more than the 2.65 litres that pure racing engines were permitted. Such engines also had to have non-overhead single camshafts and two valves per cylinder operated by pushrods. For Indy they could be supercharged at 12½psi, which was 22 per cent higher than the 2.65-litre engines were allowed.

These advantages were not convincing when such engines were built using stock blocks, but when the rules were changed to allow special blocks to be made some people smelt an opportunity. Among them were Mario Illien and Paul Morgan of Ilmor Engineering, Northamptonshire, makers of racing engines for Chevrolet and latterly Mercedes-Benz. Mercedes and Ilmor part-owner Roger Penske approved a plan to build a unique engine to these rules for the 1994 race.

Bottom-end elements of the Mercedes 500I, as it was named, resembled those of Ilmor's four-cam 2.65-litre Indy V8 with the exception that the gear drive to the single camshaft was at the front instead of the rear. Five plain main bearings were carried in bulkheads in the aluminium block and capped at the bottom by a single aluminium casting also forming the dry sump. Together they were stressed and structured to serve as an integral part of the car's frame.

Within the matching block and sump castings each rod journal rotated in a circular cavity shaped to generate as little drag as possible. Oil was drawn out of each cavity through a slot at its bottom right, each cavity having its own scavenge pump mounted outside the sump on the right side. These pumps used Roots-type rotors which have high capacity for their size and also a high tolerance of any aeration of the oil.

On the left of the sump was a single water pump. It fed the left side of the block directly and the right side by a channel under the sump and then through the housing of the forwardmost scavenge pump. Behind the water pump in the same alignment were a centrifuge to fling air out of the oil, a pressure oil pump and an oil filter. All

these pumps were carried over from Ilmor's four-cam Indy V8, although with a stepped-up ratio for the toothed rubber belt that drove them.

A gear on the crank nose drove a compound spur-gear train to the single central camshaft. A take-off from an intermediate gear drove a toothed belt to the oil and water pumps. At the nose of the camshaft, planned as an integral part of the concept, was a pendulum-type vibration damper. The rear end of the camshaft drove the scavenge pump for the turbocharger, which was mounted astern of the engine.

Within cylinder centres of 109.0mm a bore diameter of 97.0mm (3.82in) was accommodated. The stroke of 58.0mm (2.28in) provided a capacity of 3,429cc – a scant 0.9cc less than the legal limit. Cylinder banks were set at a 72° vee angle. The wet cylinder liners were steel, topped by a flange that was grooved to take a solid sealing ring. The cylinder head clamped the ring and liner flange against the closed top deck of the block. The liner's bottom end floated in the block and was sealed with O-rings. Each head was attached by 10 main studs extending deeply into the block. Rows of four cap screws along each side faced downward in the central vee and upward beneath the exhaust ports with their four attachment studs.

Short-skirted slipper-type pistons were forged of aluminium by a contractor using Ilmor's dies and then finish-machined by Ilmor. Each carried two compression rings and one oil-control ring. The periphery of the piston crown was very precisely machined to give a 'squish' effect to the mixture during the compression stroke. Compression ratio was 11.0:1.

As mandated by the Indy rules, the gudgeon pin and connecting rod were made of steel. The rod, with its two-bolt big end, was forged and had an I-section shank. It measured 116mm from centre to centre. A 180° flat-plane crankshaft, with four large counterweights, was machined from a solid

Opposite above: Working to a set of rules for the Indianapolis 500-mile race that offered an engraved invitation to ingenuity, Ilmor Engineering built a racing engine for Mercedes-Benz that dominated the 1994 running of the 500-mile race. Al Unser, Jr was the winner on behalf of the Penske team.

Opposite below: With the Indy rules giving a major advantage to an engine with only two valves per cylinder operated by pushrods from a central camshaft, Ilmor built such an engine from scratch. All the components of its valve gear, from the cam-following roller fingers to the roller-tipped rocker arms, ran on needle bearings.

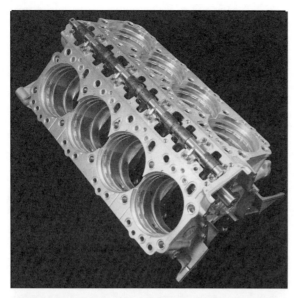

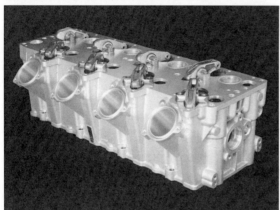

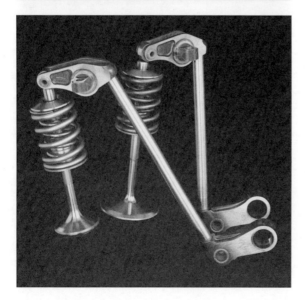

steel billet. To increase its mass, the periphery of each counterweight was drilled and tapped to accept a row of screwed-in tungsten-alloy plugs of high specific weight.

The 500I's valve layout could be likened to an inclined-two-valve chamber rotated by 20°, in plan view, from the 'conventional' transverse-valve position. In their plane, the inlet valve was inclined at 10° and the exhaust valve at 13°. A single 12mm Bosch spark plug was also positioned at compound angles and sloped toward the exhaust-port side of the head. The heads of the titanium valves differed sharply in size: 52.5mm for the inlets and 39.7mm for the exhausts. Valve-seat inserts in the aluminium head were used, those for the exhaust valves having a higher proportion of copper in the alloy for improved heat transfer.

The valves were closed by dual coil springs with titanium retainers. Opening them was a unique pushrod valve gear arrangement. Instead of the cylindrical tappets that were used in almost every other known pushrod engine (automotive and aviation) Ilmor selected a pivoted finger-type follower with a roller in contact with the cam lobe. Down the centre of the engine vee ran a shaft from which all the finger followers hinged downward. A dedicated oil supply to and along this shaft provided lubrication for the follower pivots and to the rollers and cam lobes as well.

From each follower a stainless-steel pushrod went up to its rocker arm. Each rocker pivoted on

Top: Within the vee of the cylinder block a shaft carried the suspended fingers whose roller faces were actuated by the single camshaft rotating beneath them. These in turn opened the valves through pushrods. In this view the engine's wet cylinder liners have yet to be fitted.
Middle: A 500I cylinder head shows the way in which the rocker arms, each on an individual pivot, were attached to the flat surface of the top of the head.

Clever planning was required to keep the pushrods from interfering with the large round inlet ports.
Bottom: The valve-gear components are shown in roughly their operating position in the 500I engine, with the exhaust valve on the left. Development of the roller-tipped cam followers, at lower right, was one of the most exacting aspects of the creation of a pushrod engine able to run continuously at 10,000rpm.

its own dedicated shaft, which was attached by two studs to the flat surface of the head. The rocker arm was roller-tipped where it contacted the cap atop the valve stem. Between the follower and the rocker arm a lift multiplication ratio of 2.175:1 was provided from the cam lobe. Valve lift was a generous 15.7mm for the inlets, 14.4mm for the exhausts. The 500I cam profile gave the following timing:

Inlet opens 87°BTDC Exhaust opens 84°BBDC
Inlet closes 87°ABDC Exhaust closes 84°ATDC

Every rotating element of this entire valve train ran on anti-friction bearings. The camshaft turned in four caged roller bearings on 45mm journals and, at the front, a ball bearing to retain it in place. Every other bearing in the valve gear consisted of needles, crowded without cages. Each of the finger followers pivoted on two rows of needles. The follower rollers, the rocker-arm pivots and the rocker-arm roller tips – all turned on needle bearings.

Atop the engine was an aluminium plenum chamber with internal ram pipes, patterned after the successful design used on Ilmor's smaller Indy V8s. Electronic injection nozzles mounted in the top of the plenum chamber sprayed fuel straight down into each inlet ram pipe. Delco electronic ignition fired the spark plugs. In the plenum two Rochester fuel injectors for each cylinder, 16 in all, were under the control of a Delco electronic engine management system.

Exhaust manifolding from both cylinder banks was united at the rear of the engine and fed into the exhaust scroll of its single Garrett AiResearch TA74 turbocharger. The turbocharger's dimensions were strictly controlled by the USAC rules, which made no distinction in this respect between overhead-cam and pushrod engines.

An exhaust waste gate responding to boost pressure regulated the turbocharger's compressed-air output. Its response was tailored to bring the engine to the maximum allowable boost pressure at 4,000 to 4,500rpm and then to hold it level, to generate a flat torque curve. Adjustment of the boost to suit atmospheric conditions was made by the driver with a rotating wheel that varied the bleed of boost pressure to the diaphragm controlling the waste gate.

At only 273lb (124kg) without its turbocharger the V8 was impressively light. Its peak output was an uncorrected 965 to 970bhp at 9,800rpm. Corrected for temperature and atmospheric conditions the peak power was 1,024bhp. Peak torque was 557lb ft at 8,000rpm. The engine could survive at speeds up to 10,400rpm but for the '500' a 10,000-rpm rev limit was set – still a remarkable speed for a pushrod engine.

During May's practice for the 500-mile race, driving a 500I-powered Penske PC94 Emerson Fittipaldi set the fastest lap speed of the month at a staggering 230.438mph. The fastest lap by an 'ordinary' 2.65-litre car was Michael Andretti's 227.698mph. In a sister PC94-500I Al Unser, Jr qualified for the race in the coveted pole position with a four-lap average of 228.011mph with a last lap at 229.481mph.

In the only Penske-Mercedes to reach the finish, Unser assumed the lead on lap 184 and held it to the final flag. He covered the 500 miles in 3 hours and 6½ minutes for a winning average speed of 160.872mph. Only seven laps of the race had not been led by the 500I engine. The victor's purse was a handsome $1,373,813.

SPECIFICATIONS	
Cylinders	V8
Bore	97.0mm
Stroke	58.0mm
Stroke/bore ratio	0.60:1
Capacity	3,429cc
Compression ratio	11.0:1
Connecting rod length	116.0mm
Rod/crank radius ratio	4.0:1
Main bearing journal diameter	58.0mm
Rod journal diameter	50.0mm
Inlet valve diameter (1 valve)	52.5mm
Exhaust valve diameter (1 valve)	39.7mm
Inlet pressure	1.86Atm
Engine weight	290lb (132kg)
Peak power	1,024bhp @ 9,800rpm
Piston speed (corrected)	4,823ft/min (24.1m/s)
Peak torque	557lb ft (755Nm) @ 8,000rpm
Peak bmep	402psi
Engine bhp per litre	298.6bhp per litre
Engine weight per bhp	0.28lb (0.13kg) per bhp

SPECIFICATION COMPARISON

Year	Marque	Model	Cylinders	Bore (mm)	Stroke (mm)	Stroke/ Bore Ratio	Capacity (cc)	Comp. Ratio (to 1)	Con. Rod Length (mm)	Rod/Crank Radius Ratio	Main Bearing Dia
1913	Peugeot	L3	I4	78	156	2.00	2,982	5.6	261	3.3	50.0
1914	Mercedes	18/100	I4	93	165	1.77	4,483	–	–	–	46.0
1921	Duesenberg	183	I8	63.5	117.5	1.85	2,977	5.2	222	3.8	57.2
1925	Bugatti	35	I8	60	88	1.47	1,991	6.0	185	4.2	63.5
1927	Delage	15-S-8	I8	55.8	76	1.36	1,487	6.5	152	4.0	49.0
1932	Alfa Romeo	B	I8	65	100	1.54	2,655	6.5	216	4.3	61.0
1936	Auto Union	C	V16	75	85	1.13	6,006	9.2	168	4.0	70.0
1937	Austin	Seven	I4	60.3	65.1	1.08	744	6.5	127	3.9	63.5
1937	Mercedes-Benz	W125	I8	94	102	1.09	5,560	8.9	167	3.3	63.0
1939	Auto Union	D	V12	65	75	1.15	5,577	10.0	168	4.5	70.0
1939	Mercedes-Benz	W154/163	V12	67	70	1.04	2,962	7.2	158	4.5	54.0
1949	Cisitalia	Porsche 360	F12	56	50.5	0.90	1,493	7.6	101.6	4.0	55.0
1950	Maserati	4CLT/48	I4	78	78	1.00	1,491	6.0	161	4.1	62.0
1951	Alfa Romeo	159	I8	58	70	1.21	1,480	7.5	147	4.2	52.0
1951	BRM	15	V16	49.5	48.3	0.98	1,487	7.5	104.8	4.3	58.4
1952	Küchen	V-8	V8	68	68	1.00	1,976	14.0	138	4.1	52.0
1953	Ferrari	500	I4	90	78	0.87	1,985	13.0	142	3.6	60.0
1954	Jaguar	XK	I6	83	106	1.28	3,441	9.0	196.9	3.7	69.9
1954	Ferrari	553	I4	100	79.5	0.80	2,496	12.0	138	3.5	60.0
1955	Lancia	D50	V8	73.6	73.1	0.99	2,490	11.9	135	3.7	60.0
1955	Mercedes-Benz	W196	I8	76	68.8	0.91	2,496	12.5	137.5	4.0	51.0
1955	Porsche	547	F4	85	66	0.78	1,498	9.5	132	4.0	52.0
1956	Ferrari	750 Monza	I4	103	90	0.87	3,000	9.2	142	3.2	60.0
1956	Novi	V-8	V8	81	72.1	0.89	2,972	9.0	139.7	3.9	60.3
1957	Maserati	250F	I6	84	75	0.89	2,493	12.5	143	3.8	60.0
1957	Vanwall	V254	I4	96	86	0.90	2,490	12.5	163.5	3.8	70.0
1958	Borgward	RS	I4	80	74	0.93	1,488	10.2	140	3.8	60.0
1958	Ferrari	Dino 246	V6	85	71	0.84	2,417	9.8	98	2.8	68.0
1959	Aston Martin	RB6	I6	83	90	1.08	2,922	9.8	166	3.7	63.5
1959	Maserati	61	I4	100	92	0.92	2,890	9.8	143	3.1	65.0
1960	Coventry Climax	FPF	I4	94	89.9	0.96	2,496	11.9	129.5	2.9	63.5
1961	Ferrari	Dino 156	V6	73	58.8	0.81	1,477	9.8	98.0	3.3	60.0
1962	BRM	P56	V8	68.3	50.8	0.74	1,490	10.5	104.8	4.1	57.2
1962	Porsche	753	F8	66	54.6	0.83	1,494	10.0	126	4.6	57.0
1965	Coventry Climax	FWMV	V8	72.4	45.5	0.63	1,497	12.0	106.7	4.7	50.8
1965	Honda	RA272E	V12	58.1	47	0.81	1,495	10.5	119	5.1	36.0
1966	Repco-Brabham	620	V8	88.9	60.3	0.68	2,996	11.0	160	5.3	58.4
1966	BRM	P75	H16	69.85	48.89	0.70	2,998	10.5	115.6	4.7	57.2
1967	BMW	M10	I4	89	80	0.90	1,991	10.5	135	3.4	55.0
1967	Gurney-Weslake	58	V12	72.8	60	0.82	2,997	12.0	124	4.1	60.3
1967	Ford	DFV	V8	85.7	64.8	0.76	2,993	11.0	132.8	4.1	60.3
1969	Porsche	912 (917)	F12	85	66	0.78	4,494	10.5	130	3.9	57.0
1970	Drake	Offy	I4	102.4	79.4	0.78	2,616	8.5	144	3.6	60.3
1970	Ferrari	312B	F12	78.5	51.5	0.66	2,991	11.5	110	4.3	50.0
1970	Matra	MS12	V12	79.7	50	0.63	2,993	11.0	116	4.6	52.0
1975	Alfa Romeo	115-12	F12	77	53.6	0.70	2,995	11.0	112	4.2	50.0
1984	Renault	EF4	V6	86	42.8	0.50	1,492	7.5	123	5.7	58.0
1987	TAG	P01	V6	82	47.3	0.58	1,499	8.0	115	4.9	48.0
1992	Honda	RA122E/B	V12	88	47.9	0.54	3,496	12.9	111	4.6	54.0
1994	Mercedes-Benz	500I	V8	97	58	0.60	3,429	11.0	116	4.0	58.0

† Piston speed is corrected in accordance with the Lanchester Formula. See 'Corrected piston speed' in Glossary.

* Engine & transaxle combined. See text for bearing sizes.

All data presented are derived from official sources or, in a few instances, estimated on the basis of contemporary technology.

Copyright © 2001 Karl E. Ludvigsen

Inlet Valve Dia (mm)	Exhaust Valve Dia (mm)	Inlet Pressure (Atm)	Engine Weight (pounds)	Peak Power (bhp)	@ RPM	Corrected Piston Speed (ft/min)†	Peak Torque (lb ft)	@ RPM	Peak bmep (psi)	Engine bhp/litre	Engine lb/bhp
40 (2)	40 (2)	1.00	–	92	2,900	2,099	–	–	–	30.9	–
43 (2)	43 (2)	1.00	–	106	3,100	2,520	209	2,000	116	23.6	–
39 (1)	27 (2)	1.00	–	115	4,250	2,409	–	–	–	38.6	–
23.5 (2)	35 (1)	1.00	–	100	5,000	2,384	–	–	–	50.2	–
31 (1)	29 (1)	1.50	–	170	7,500	3,205	–	–	–	114.3	–
39 (1)	39 (1)	1.76	–	215	5,600	2,963	210	3,750	196	81.0	–
35 (1)	32 (1)	1.97	–	520	5,000	2,620	630	2,500	260	86.6	–
38.1 (1)	38.1 (1)	2.50	260	116	7,600	3,124	–	–	–	155.9	2.24
39 (2)	39 (2)	1.86	491	575	5,500	3,534	683	3,000	304	103.4	0.85
34 (1)	31 (1)	2.66	–	485	7,000	3,207	405	4,000	180	87.0	–
30 (2)	30 (2)	2.31	603	480	7,500	3,370	365	5,500	305	162.1	1.26
34 (1)	29 (1)	3.07	–	340	10,500	3,664	–	–	–	227.7	–
40 (2)	40 (2)	2.72	364	260	7,500	3,839	–	–	–	174.4	1.40
36 (1)	36 (1)	3.10	363	420	9,300	3,888	–	–	–	283.9	0.86
31.8 (1)	37.8 (1)	4.85	525	430	11,000	3,529	–	–	–	289.1	1.22
38 (1)	35 (1)	1.00	216	200	8,000	3,570	116	7,000	145	101.2	1.08
48 (1)	44 (1)	1.00	348	185	7,500	4,123	152	5,700	190	93.2	1.88
47.6 (1)	41.3 (1)	1.00	530	250	6,000	3,693	242	4,000	174	72.7	2.12
50 (1)	46 (1)	1.00	352	270	7,600	4,446	–	–	–	108.2	1.30
46 (1)	44.5 (1)	1.00	–	250	7,700	3,706	–	–	–	100.4	–
50 (1)	43 (1)	1.00	451	290	8,500	4,033	183	6,300	182	116.2	1.56
48 (1)	41 (1)	1.00	225	125	6,500	3,195	95	5,500	157	83.4	1.80
50 (1)	46 (1)	1.00	353	250	6,000	3,791	–	–	–	83.3	1.41
41.3 (1)	36.6 (1)	3.40	585	550	7,500	3,761	–	–	–	185.0	1.06
46 (1)	40 (1)	1.00	434	290	7,500	3,906	209	6,000	208	116.3	1.50
53 (1)	45 (1)	1.00	360	285	7,200	4,293	–	–	–	114.5	1.26
33 (2)	30 (2)	1.00	282	165	7,500	3,786	–	–	–	110.9	1.71
52 (1)	46 (1)	1.00	298	270	8,300	4,231	–	–	–	111.7	1.10
50 (1)	40 (1)	1.00	445	255	6,000	3,403	235	5,400	199	87.3	1.75
54 (1)	42.5 (1)	1.00	370	255	6,500	4,091	223	5,000	191	88.2	1.45
49.2 (1)	42.8 (1)	1.00	290	240	6,750	4,072	212	5,000	210	96.2	1.21
38.5 (1)	34 (1)	1.00	265	190	9,500	4,084	–	–	–	128.6	1.39
39.7 (1)	30.5 (1)	1.00	255	193	10,250	3,962	–	–	–	129.5	1.32
37 (1)	34 (1)	1.00	341	185	9,300	3,663	113	7,450	187	123.8	1.84
26.4 (2)	23.7 (2)	1.00	298	212	10,300	3,879	119	8,000	197	141.6	1.41
24 (2)	22 (2)	1.00	474*	230	12,000	4,115	116	11,000	192	153.8	2.06
41.3 (1)	34.9 (1)	1.00	300	298	7,500	3,603	–	–	–	99.5	1.01
39.7 (1)	30.5 (1)	1.00	520	380	10,500	4,026	–	–	–	126.8	1.37
42 (2)	34 (2)	1.00	320	280	8,800	4,872	174	8,000	217	140.6	1.14
30.5 (2)	25 (2)	1.00	390	380	10,000	4,337	–	–	–	126.8	1.03
34.5 (2)	29 (2)	1.00	358	408	9,000	4,401	–	–	–	136.3	0.88
47.5 (1)	40.5 (1)	1.00	530	580	8,400	4,128	376	6,800	207	129.1	0.91
39.7 (2)	34.9 (2)	2.66	475	727	8,250	4,881	510	7,000	483	277.9	0.65
31 (2)	27 (2)	1.00	317	460	11,600	4,840	–	–	–	153.8	0.69
31 (2)	27 (2)	1.00	370	450	11,000	4,556	253	8,000	209	150.4	0.82
33 (2)	28 (2)	1.00	385	526	12,000	5,059	–	–	–	175.6	0.73
29.8 (2)	26.1 (2)	3.20	342	700	11,000	4,379	354	8,500	588	469.2	0.49
30.5 (2)	27.5 (2)	3.48	331	860	12,000	4,904	390	8,800	645	573.7	0.38
36.5 (2)	28.5 (2)	1.00	339	774	14,000	5,964	297	12,000	210	221.4	0.44
52.5 (1)	39.7 (1)	1.86	290	1,024	9,800	4,823	557	8,000	402	298.6	0.28

GLOSSARY

Air-cooled, air cooling: Any mechanism which gives off heat (such as an engine or generator) may be cooled by the passage of air, often helped by a fan. All engines are, of course, 'air cooled', including so-called 'water-cooled' engines (in which water is the cooling medium but is itself cooled by air passing through the radiator) but the term *air-cooled engine* is reserved for engines cooled by air which passes directly over the cylinder heads and barrels.

Air/fuel mixture: Mixture of petrol and air in the carburettor barrel (mixing-chamber) – or, in the case of a fuel-injection system, at the inlet ports or in the cylinder in the case of direct injection – which must be supplied to the engine as a very fine spray or mist (atomised), so that it will vaporise and burn.

Alusil: High-silicon alloy of aluminium, suitable for cylinder blocks, in which the final finishing of the cylinder bore may leave the silicon crystals standing proud and thus providing a wear-resistant surface.

Amal: British manufacturer of slide-throttle carburettors especially suitable for motorcycles.

Balance weights: see *Counterweights*.

Bevel gears: Gears whose shafts are at an angle to one another, as with a crown wheel and pinion.

Big end: The large, lower end of a connecting rod which is attached to the crankshaft. It is normally fitted with split bearings (called big-end bearings) in which the big-end journal rotates. Engines with roller big-end bearings may have one-piece big ends.

Big-end bearing: The shell or anti-friction bearing in the big end.

Big-end journal: Crankshaft journal on which the big-end bearings on the connecting rod rotate.

Blower cooling: Use of a fan or blower to cool the head(s) and cylinder(s) of an air-cooled engine that is not directly exposed to air flow from the motion of the vehicle.

Bore: The inner or working surface of a cylinder. Also called barrel, cylinder barrel, cylinder bore, cylinder wall or wall.

Boxer engine: A flat-opposed engine, in which the pistons in the opposing cylinders are connected to separate big-end journals so that they move in opposite directions and thus provide a counterbalancing effect.

Camshaft: The shaft in the engine which carries the cams operating the inlet and exhaust valves (via the valve gear), and which is itself driven from the crankshaft (via the timing chain, belt or gear). In many engines it also drives the fuel pump, distributor and oil pump.

Carburettor: A device controlled by the driver through the accelerator pedal, for mixing petrol and air in a finely atomised spray (the air/fuel mixture), in the correct proportions, for all engine requirements. These include cold starting, slow running, accelerating and cruising, which different carburettors achieve in different ways. A carburettor's venturi (popularly called choke) and its jet create and largely control the air/fuel mixture.

Centric: British maker of a vane-type supercharger in which the vanes are restrained by carriers mounted on ball bearings.

Centrifugal compressor: A fast-rotating bladed wheel or impeller which imparts centrifugal force to a gas or liquid and impels it outward to increase flow, pressure or both. Air is sucked into its centre and forced outwards, and compressed, by the impeller, which is mechanically driven at high speed. As used in turbochargers, the impeller is powered by the turbine rotor, which is driven by exhaust gas.

Coil ignition: The once near-universal ignition system using an ignition coil.

Combustion chamber: Space at the top of a cylinder where combustion of the fresh charge (air/fuel mixture) takes place. The inlet and exhaust valves open directly into it and the spark plug is screwed into it. For practical purposes, it exists only for the moment when the piston is at the top of the compression stroke (around TDC) and combustion takes place.

Compression ratio: The volume of a cylinder (including the combustion chamber) when the piston is at its lowest point (BDC) compared to the volume when it is at its highest (TDC). In other words, it is the ratio of total volume (clearance volume plus swept volume or displacement) to clearance volume alone.

Compressor: Pump which raises the pressure of air or gas, as for example the compressor in an air-conditioning system, supercharger or turbocharger.

Connecting rod: Bar or link connecting piston to crankshaft. It consists of a small end, shank and big end. The small end pivots on a gudgeon pin in the piston, while the big end is attached to a journal (called the big-end journal) on the crankshaft.

Constant-vacuum carburettor: This type of carburettor – best known is the SU – has a variable venturi and a variable jet. The area of the venturi is varied by the movement of a piston sliding in a cylinder which has a suction chamber at the top and is at right angles to the carburettor barrel (which is usually side-draught). The base of the piston, projecting into the barrel, carries a tapered needle which fits into the fuel inlet – called the main jet – on the opposite side of the barrel. Movement of the piston is controlled by mixing-chamber depression; for example, when this is high the piston is drawn up, enlarging the size of both the venturi and the jet and thus drawing in more air in step with more petrol.

Corrected piston speed: Mean piston speed at a given rate of revolutions per minute is first calculated by multiplying twice the stroke length, in feet, by the rpm. Then, in a method first set out by English engineer Frederick Lanchester, the mean piston speed is divided by the square root of the stroke/bore ratio. The resulting *corrected piston speed* gives a considerably more accurate representation of the actual stresses prevailing in an engine. The resulting values are higher than the uncorrected values where the engine is oversquare (as are most of the engines in this book) and lower where they are undersquare. This reflects the heavier piston mass of an oversquare engine for a given displacement.

Counterweights: Weights (in the form of extensions and thickening of the crank-webs) used on crankshafts to counterbalance the forces generated by the reciprocating and rotating masses of the pistons and connecting rods. Any rotating mass, such as a flywheel, may be balanced in the same way, always with the object of eliminating vibration.

Cozette: Producer of a mechanically-driven vane-type supercharger.

Crowded needle or roller bearing: Anti-friction bearing in which the rolling elements are not guided by cages. Rather the needles or rollers completely fill the available space and rub (roll) against each other during engine operation.

Crankcase: Lower part of the cylinder-block casting. Early engines were constructed with a separate housing for the crankshaft – the crankcase – and the cylinders, which were cast separately, were mounted on this.

Crankshaft: Main shaft in the engine connected to the pistons by the connecting rods and turned by the downward thrust of the pistons on their power-strokes. (In its shape it is 'cranked' to enable the reciprocating movement of the piston to be converted to a rotary movement.)

Cylinder bank: One in-line row of cylinders of a vee-type engine.

Cylinder block: Main engine casting, housing the cylinders. The cylinder head is attached to its top and the crankshaft is supported in main bearings below, in a short extension of the block: all that remains of the crankcase of earlier engines.

Cylinder centre distance: The distance between the centrelines of the adjoining cylinders of an in-line engine or the cylinder bank of a vee engine.

Cylinder head: One of the main parts of the engine, a casting bolted to the top of the cylinder block. Incorporates the combustion chambers, inlet and exhaust ports and valves, some or all of the valve gear which operates them, valve guides and threaded holes for the spark plugs. The casting also incorporates part of the water jacket (circulating coolant around the valves.)

Cylinder liner: Many engines – including many of

those made of aluminium alloy – have (replaceable) cylinders called liners. They are thin-walled sleeves made of alloys with superior resistance to wear.

Cylinder offset: The distance by which the cylinders of one bank of a boxer or vee-type engine are displaced from the other bank(s), when they are so displaced. Determined in a vee-type engine by the width of the connecting-rod big end and in a boxer engine by the thickness of the crankshaft cheeks.

Die-cast, -casting: Manufacturing process in which molten (liquid) metal, such as aluminium or zinc alloy, is forced under pressure into a die. Used, for example, to make carburettor bodies and cylinder blocks.

Displacement: The volume described by the movement of a piston of a given bore size through one stroke of a given length. Also known as capacity or swept volume.

Distributor: Part with three separate but related functions in the ignition system:
a) the centre section of the distributor (cam and contact-breaker assembly) makes and breaks – connects and disconnects – the low-voltage ignition-circuit to produce pulses of HT (high-voltage) in the ignition coil;
b) the bottom section (advance mechanism) controls the precise timing of the sparks to meet the requirements of the engine;
c) the top section (distributor cap and rotor arm) channels or feeds the pulses of HT from the ignition coil to each spark plug in the correct sequence: hence the name 'distributor'.
The distributor in many modern engines is used only for purpose c) – the other functions being carried out by electronic control systems.

Dry sump: System employing a separate tank for engine oil (in place of the usual sump) which is kept full by a scavenge pump. This arrangement, found in most racing engines and some high-performance cars, lowers engine height, helps solve oil surge problems and improves cooling.

Dykes-type ring: Compression piston ring designed with an L-shaped cross-section which allows gas pressure to be exerted behind the ring, making its wall pressure proportional to the pressure in the chamber and hence to the sealing requirement.

Eaton pump: See *Gerotor pump*.

Electronic ignition: System which uses transistors to do the switching that is normally done by the contacts in the distributor. Two basic types:

Capacitive-discharge ignition and inductive-discharge ignition. Contacts may still be used, but only to activate the switching. Otherwise magnetic or optical triggering devices replace contacts. Ignition timing may be conventional or electronic.

Elektron: A type of magnesium alloy; term widely used in Germany in the 1930s and employed in Italy after the war.

Engine power: The power developed by an engine, measured in brake horsepower (bhp) or watts. It is determined by the engine's torque and rpm combined and is easily remembered as: power equals force multiplied by speed, or torque multiplied by revs.

Engine speed: Rate at which the crankshaft rotates, expressed in rpm (revolutions per minute) or radians per second. Also called engine revolutions or engine revs.

Exhaust manifold: Casting or fabrication of short tubes connecting the cylinder head's exhaust ports to the rest of the exhaust system.

Exhaust valve: One of the valves in the cylinder head, operated by the camshaft, which allows combustion gases out of the combustion chambers into the exhaust port. Nearly always a poppet valve.

Finger: Part of the valve gear: an arm with a fixed pivot at one end. The other end pushes down the valve stem under pressure from a cam which operates on the upper surface of the arm. Also finger-follower.

Four-stroke cycle: Continuous sequence (cycle) of events in a single cylinder which take place as the piston moves up and down twice (four piston strokes) to produce one power stroke (the one which turns the crankshaft). The crankshaft rotates half a turn to complete each stroke, therefore it rotates two complete turns for the full four-stroke cycle. The four strokes are: induction stroke, compression stroke, power stroke and exhaust stroke.

Fuel injection: Alternative to the carburettor in which fuel, maintained under pressure by a pump called a fuel pump, is sprayed (injected) by injectors into the inlet ports where it is mixed with air. Fuel may also be injected directly into the cylinder.

Generator: A machine which converts mechanical energy into electrical energy. Operating principle is electromagnetic induction. Generators, belt-driven

by the engine to charge the battery and supply power to electrical circuits, are of two types:
a) alternator, producing alternating current;
b) dynamo, producing direct current.

Gerotor pump: Also known as Eaton pump, a gear-type pump originated by the Eaton Corporation in which an externally-toothed inner rotor with a special tooth profile drives an internally-toothed outer rotor. Widely used for oil pumps.

Grey iron: Unalloyed cast iron.

Gudgeon pin: The pin or shaft joining the small end of the connecting rod to the piston. Also known as wrist pin or piston pin.

Hairpin spring: Spring formed in a coil with its two ends extended to be attached to the system to be controlled; two are required for use as a valve spring.

Helical teeth, gear: Curved gear teeth which cross the periphery of a gear wheel at an angle to its axis. Quieter than spur gears but produce side (axial) thrust.

Inlet valve: One of the valves in the cylinder head, operated by the camshaft, which lets the air/fuel mixture into the combustion chamber from the inlet port. Nearly always a poppet valve.

In-line, in-line engine: Describes an engine in which the cylinders are placed in a line: the most common engine layout. Also called straight, straight engine.

King shaft: A shaft used to drive an overhead camshaft from the crankshaft, usually with a pair of bevel gears at each end.

Knocking: A metallic hammering sound caused by detonation in the combustion chamber. Usually follows the use of fuel with too low an octane rating, or an over-advanced ignition. Also called pinking, pre-ignition, pinging or spark-knock.

Kugelfischer injection: Mechanical fuel injection produced by the Kugelfischer company that used a three-dimensional cam to control fuel delivery by varying the stroke of the injecting pistons.

Liquid cooling: The engine cooling system used in the vast majority of vehicles. The term may be used to distinguish this system from direct air-cooling. Also known as water cooling.

Load: Power output or work demanded of an engine, as by hill climbing or acceleration. The terms full-load and part-load may be used to describe an engine working at maximum load or, as when cruising, at some portion of this.

Magneto: Device for generating sparks, using permanent magnets, driven by the engine and incorporating a distributor. Once universal, it was superseded by the battery-powered coil ignition system.

Monobloc: Casting as a single piece the cylinder head and cylinder(s) of an engine. Eliminates the possible weakness of a cylinder-head gasket.

Nicasil: Galvanically-deposited (plated) layer of nickel containing silicon crystals, suitable for use as a cylinder-wall coating in an aluminium-block engine.

Nimonic: Nickel alloyed with chromium to create a highly temperature-resistant material suitable for use as turbine blades in gas turbine and jet engines.

Octane rating: (Octane is short for iso-octane. May be shortened to octane, as in 97 octane, etc.) A measure of petrol's ability to resist detonation. Petrol with too low a rating causes knocking.

ohc: Overhead camshaft, camshaft positioned in or above the cylinder head and valves.

ohv: Overhead valves, valves placed in the cylinder head above the combustion chamber.

Overhead-valve, valves: In modern engines all inlet and exhaust valves are overhead (in the top of the combustion chambers) but until the 1950s they were commonly positioned beside the cylinders. Abbreviated as OHV or ohv.

Overlap: The period, determined by the valve timing, when the two valves in a cylinder are both open. An overlap is necessary in order to achieve an efficient flow of gases in and out of the combustion chamber.

Piston: Cylindrical part, closed at the top, which moves up and down in an engine cylinder and is connected to the crankshaft below by the connecting rod. It turns the crankshaft when combustion of the air/fuel mixture forces it down.

Piston ring: Ring which fits in a groove around the top of a piston and springs out to make a gas-tight fit with the bore (cylinder wall). Upper rings are for maintaining compression in the combustion chamber and the lower ring is for scraping off excess oil. The upper rings are called compression rings, the bottom one the oil-control ring or oil ring.

Plain bearing: Bearing in the form of a sleeve, most often main bearings and big-end bearings. To be fitted on a crankshaft this type must, in effect, be split lengthways, thus becoming a split bearing, unless the crankshaft can be dismantled. The halves are called bearing shells.

Pre-ignition: Firing of the air/fuel mixture, before the spark occurs, by a hot spot in the combustion chamber such as a spark-plug electrode and tip, incandescent carbon or an overheated exhaust valve. Causes a knocking noise, poor running and engine damage if allowed to continue. See also *Knocking*.

Pushrod: Part of the valve gear in OHV engines whose camshaft is mounted remote from the cylinder head. The rods are moved up and down by the camshaft via the tappets to operate the rocker arms, which in turn operate the inlet valves and exhaust valves.

Radial blower: See *Centrifugal compressor*.

Rocker arm, rocker: Part of the valve gear: a lever, or arm, which pivots on a shaft (rocker shaft) or stud. When one end is lifted by the camshaft (in the case of OHV engines via a pushrod), the other pushes down on the valve stem and opens the valve.

Rocker-arm ratio: The ratio between the lengths of the two arms of a rocker arm in relation to its pivot point.

Rocker shaft: Shaft on which the rocker arms pivot.

Roller bearings: Bearings using a ring, or rings, of very hard pins (rollers) to reduce friction and wear. Can carry heavier loads, and some types (tapered roller) can resist axial thrust better than ball bearings.

Roller rocker arm: Rocker arm fitted with a friction-reducing roller to accept the forces from the cam lobe.

Roller tappet, roller finger: Tappet or finger follower incorporating a shaft-mounted friction-reducing roller, riding against the cam lobe, to reduce friction.

Roots supercharger: A positive-displacement air pump through which the air is moved at low pressure by a pair of rotors, working like those of a gear-type oil pump.

Side-valve engine: Obsolete design in which the valves stand beside the cylinders (and are therefore called side valves). The combustion chambers extend over the valve heads and because of their shape these are sometimes known as L-head engines.

Squish, squish volume: see *Turbulence*.

Small end: The upper end of a connecting rod; it pivots on a gudgeon pin in the piston.

Solex: French carburettor manufacturer and licenser of production in other countries, including Germany.

Stroke: One of a continuous series of movements such as a piston being driven up or down a cylinder.

SUM: Carburettor made in Berlin by the Carl WirSUM company.

Supercharger, -charging: Means of increasing engine power by using a compressor to force (blow) more air/fuel mixture into the cylinders than will be provided by atmospheric pressure.

Tappet: Part of the valve gear. Term used interchangeably with cam follower or simply follower. Two different kinds:
a) in pushrod-operated OHV engines: a plunger – a simple inverted piston – fitted between the camshaft and a pushrod to withstand the lateral force exerted by the cam;
b) in OHC (overhead-camshaft) engines: a plunger fitted between the cam and the valve stem; popularly called bucket. Also called bucket cam-follower, bucket tappet, cup-type tappet, inverted-bucket tappet, piston-type tappet.

Tensioner: A self-adjusting device fitted to most engines to prevent fluttering movement in a timing belt, timing chain or vee-belt by taking up the slack. This prevents whipping which causes wear and noise.

Timing belt: Internally-toothed belt to drive an overhead camshaft from the crankshaft or to power timed engine accessories. Made of reinforced rubber or plastic and driven by a crankshaft sprocket. Also called cogged belt.

Timing chain: Part of the timing gear. Chain, driven by a crankshaft sprocket, which drives the camshaft(s) from the crankshaft. May be single (simplex) or double (duplex).

Torque: Twisting or turning effort; the application of a rotary force.

Tunnel crankcase: Special crankcase design formed in one piece as a tunnel, into which the crankshaft is inserted from one end. Provides high stiffness and oil-tightness.

Turbocharger, -charging: Means of increasing engine power by using a centrifugal compressor to force more air/fuel mixture (or air only in the case of fuel-injected or diesel engines) into the combustion chambers than atmospheric pressure would provide. The compressor is driven by a turbine mounted on the same shaft and driven by the energy of the exhaust gases. A special type of supercharging, 'turbocharging' is a shortening of turbo-supercharging.

Turbulence: Swirling or agitation of the air/fuel

mixture in the combustion chamber causing the flame to spread very rapidly. This effect, encouraged by the design of the inlet port, may be increased by having the piston compress part of the fuel charge much more than the rest. (The resulting violent displacement is called compression-turbulence or squish, and the area in which it takes place the squish zone or squish volume.)

Two plugs per cylinder: Adopted for aviation engines to give redundancy for safety reasons. Claimed to improve combustion and in particular to ignite a leaner air/fuel mixture (as may be caused by valve overlap), leading to reduced fuel consumption and lower exhaust pollution. Secures complete combustion in racing engines.

Two-stroke engine: Engine in which the combustion cycle takes two strokes of a piston: one turn of the crankshaft: instead of the usual four strokes.

Valve clearance, clearances: Gaps between rocker and valve stem, or between camshaft and tappet (which may be called tappet clearance or valve lash) to allow for expansion by heat. If there were no gaps, the valves would be prevented from closing fully.

Valve gear: Gear (mechanism) operating the inlet valves and exhaust valves (but excluding the valves themselves), driven from the crankshaft and incorporating the camshaft.

Valve timing: Arranging, by correct design and assembly of the valve gear, that the valves open and close at the correct time for greatest efficiency.

Vee engines: Vee engines have two banks of cylinders, often set at an angle of 60° or 90° to one another, making a vee formation with the crankshaft in the middle. Generally shorter than in-line engines of equivalent displacement.

Vibration damper: Small flywheel, set in rubber, generally fitted at the end of the crankshaft. Used in most cars to reduce vibration in the crankshaft caused by uneven firing impulses common to all engines. May also be of pendulum type.

Water jacket: Space and passages (galleries) within the cylinder head and cylinder blocks which surround the hottest parts of the engine (the cylinders, combustion chambers, valves and exhaust ports), through which coolant is circulated to absorb heat.

Water pump: Centrifugal pump, belt-driven by the engine from the crankshaft pulley, which circulates coolant round the cooling system. The radiator fan, where fitted, is usually mounted on the pump shaft.

Waste gate: Valve for releasing pressure in the exhaust system of a turbocharged engine. When engine speed rises, the boost pressure in the induction system becomes excessive. This pressure is used to open the waste gate, which allows exhaust gas to bypass the turbine, thereby reducing its power, and thus the boost pressure. In some systems boost pressure is relieved at the inlet manifold.

Weber: Italian manufacturer of carburettors and fuel-injection systems.

Zenith: English manufacturer of carburettors and licenser of production in other countries, including Germany.

Zoller: Swiss-German inventor and producer of vane-type mechanical supercharger.

INDEX

About the Author

A winner of numerous awards for his books and articles, Karl Ludvigsen has been active for 60 years as an automotive enthusiast, author and historian. As author, co-author or editor he has more than five dozen books to his credit. Three of his books have received the Nicholas-Joseph Cugnot Award from the Society of Automotive Historians, which in 2002 gave him its highest accolade, Friend of Automotive History.

Ludvigsen's career includes a dozen years in the auto industry as an executive with General Motors, Fiat and Ford and 15 years as the head of a leading London-based motor-industry management-consulting company. Born in Kalamazoo, Michigan in 1934, Ludvigsen has lived in England since 1980. In addition to his work as an author and historian he is a contributor to leading periodicals and a frequent speaker on automotive topics.

Karl has been a Member of the Society of Automotive Engineers since 1960 and is currently a member of its Historical Committee. He is a founder member of the International Motor Press Association, member of the Society of Automotive Historians, the Society For the History of Technology and the Guild of Motoring Writers.

Karl Ludvigsen has been active for 60 years as an automotive enthusiast, author and historian, and has won numerous awards for his books and articles. As author, co-author or editor he has more than five dozen books to his credit. Three of his books have received the Nicholas-Joseph Cugnot Award from the Society of Automotive Historians, which in 2002 gave him its highest accolade, *Friend of Automotive History*.

Karl has been a Member of the Society of Automotive Engineers since 1960 and is currently a member of its Historical Committee. He is a founder member of the International Motor Press Association, member of the Society of Automotive Historians, the Society For the History of Technology and the Guild of Motoring Writers.

Selected Books from Bentley Publishers by Karl Ludvigsen

 Porsche — Excellence was Expected ISBN 978-0-8376-0236-6

 Porsche — Origin of the Species ISBN 978-0-8376-1331-4

 The V12 Engine ISBN 978-0-8376-1733-6

 Ferdinand Porsche — Genesis of Genius ISBN 978-0-8376-1557-8

 Battle for the Beetle ISBN 978-0-8376-1695-7

 Classic Racing Engines ISBN 978-0-8376-1734-3

 Corvette — America's Star-Spangled Sports Car ISBN 978-0-8376-1659-9

 Classic Grand Prix Cars ISBN 978-0-8376-1735-0

Other Engineering Titles from Bentley Publishers

The Hack Mechanic Guide to European Automotive Electrical Systems *Rob Siegel* ISBN 978-0-8376-1751-0

Bosch Fuel Injection and Engine Management *Charles O. Probst, SAE* ISBN 978-0-8376-0300-1

Physics for Gearheads *Randy Beikmann* ISBN 978-0-8376-1615-5

Maximum Boost: Designing, Testing, and Installing Turbocharger Systems *Corky Bell* ISBN 978-0-8376-0160-1

Supercharged! Design, Testing and Installation of Supercharger Systems *Corky Bell* ISBN 978-0-8376-0168-7

Scientific Design of Exhaust and Intake Systems *Phillip H. Smith & John C. Morrison* ISBN 978-0-8376-0309-4

Bosch Automotive Handbook Updated 9th Edition *Robert Bosch, GmbH* ISBN 978-0-8376-1732-9

Race Car Aerodynamics *Joseph Katz, Ph.D.* ISBN 978-0-8376-0142-7

Lot# 201707R002

 Bentley Publishers® .com